Inside Moves

Press

D0515137

Microsoft®

AGE
of
EMPIRES™

Steven Kent

PUBLISHED BY
Microsoft Press
A Division of Microsoft Corporation
One Microsoft Way
Redmond, Washington 98052-6399

Copyright © 1997 by The PC Press

All rights reserved. No part of the contents of this book may be reproduced or transmitted
in any form or by any means without the written permission of the publisher.

Library of Congress Cataloging-in-Publication Data
Kent, Steve L.
    Microsoft Age of Empires : Inside Moves / Steven Kent.
        p.   cm.
    Includes index.
    ISBN 1-57231-529-6
    1. Microsoft Age of Empires.   I. Title.
    GV1469.25.M54K46   1997
    793.93'25369--dc21   97-29192
                                                          CIP

Printed and bound in the United States of America.

1 2 3 4 5 6 7 8 9   MLML   2 1 0 9 8 7

Distributed to the book trade in Canada by Macmillan of Canada, a division of Canada Publishing
Corporation.

A CIP catalogue record for this book is available from the British Library.

Microsoft Press books are available through booksellers and distributors worldwide. For further
information about international editions, contact your local Microsoft Corporation office. Or contact
Microsoft Press International directly at fax (425) 936-7329. Visit our Web site at mspress.microsoft.com.

DirectPlay, DirectX, Microsoft, Microsoft Press, and Windows are registered trademarks and
Age of Empires, Close Combat, Deadly Tide, and Hellbender are trademarks of Microsoft Corporation.
The Personal Computing Press is an imprint and trademark of The PC Press, Inc.

Acquisitions Editor: Kim Fryer
Project Editor: Stuart J. Stuple

Dedication

I'd like to dedicate this book to my son, Nicholas,
who's been fatherless for the last four weeks.

Steven Kent

Acknowledgments

I would like to thank Steven Kent for writing such an enjoyable book
about a truly fascinating game. I also wish to thank the many others
who contributed, behind the scenes, to the creation of
Age of Empires: Inside Moves:

At The PC Press, Inc.: Lance Elko, Project Editor;
Kim Davis, Art Director; Kathleen Ingram, Book Coordinator,
and David Jackson, Editorial Assistant.

At Microsoft Press: Our valued colleagues,
Kim Fryer, Acquisitions Editor and Stuart Stuple, Project Editor.

And lastly, Steven and I would like to thank the entire Microsoft Games
group, as well as the people at Ensemble, for letting us
participate in their tremendously cool game.
At Ensemble, our warmest thanks go to Rick Goodman
for his assistance, Bruce Shelley for his inspiration, and
Chris Rippy for his round-the-clock patience.

Robert C. Lock,
President and Editor-in-Chief, The PC Press, Inc.

Contents

ANCIENT EMPIRES

Modern society has a special fascination with creatures large and dangerous. In the 1970s, Peter Benchley made a fortune writing a simple story about a great white shark—*Jaws*. Twenty years later he repeated this feat with a similar story about a giant squid—*The Beast*.

Benchley isn't the only author to cash in on this fascination. *Jurassic Park* would not have rocked the world if it were about geckos, chameleons, or even Gila monsters. Even velociraptors, the real villains in Michael Crichton's book, lacked the charisma to create a bestseller. Crichton turned to the Tyrannosaurus Rex for star power.

The ancient empires of the world have this same dangerous appeal. Some of them were vast, even by modern standards. Alexander the Great conquered nations from Egypt to India, and the Romans went even further.

Many of the great empires had a certain fierce quality, too. The word "decimate" comes from the Roman practice of lining up entire villages and killing every tenth person. That practice was mild compared to destroying civilizations by killing or enslaving entire populations.

It is because of this fascination with large and dangerous entities that I found myself intrigued with Microsoft's Age of Empires the very first time I saw it. In April, 1995, Richard Brudvik-Lindner, the man in charge of communications for Microsoft's consumer division at the time, invited me to visit his office and have a look at his company's Christmas line-up. He showed me Microsoft's *Monster Truck 'Rally'*, *Deadly Tide*, and *Close Combat*.

Sometime between discussing the new features on the latest version of *Microsoft Golf* and telling me about *Full Court Press*, Richard leaned forward and said in a quiet but excited tone, "We have a product that we haven't announced yet." I half expected him to roll up his sleeve and show me an armful of watches that he could sell at a really good price.

"We have a new product that won't be out this year. It may be out for next Christmas, or it may not come out until '96. It's called *The Dawn of Man*.

AGE *of* EMPIRES

Blizzard Entertainment's *WarCraft II* had recently been released at that time, and I was a huge fan of this style of gaming. There was a television in the room, and Richard showed me videotape footage of a Stone Age battle and some villagers foraging for food.

Though the game that Richard showed me lacked the polish that makes Age of Empires so slick, I could see a certain winning style in the game footage. Great computer games have a hard-to-describe magic about them that outweighs the sum of their various elements. Dawn of Man, redubbed Age of Empires, clearly had that spark of magic.

Richard may have regretted showing me the game. I lost interest in his other titles and asked only about Dawn of Man. I wanted to know when it was coming out and how soon I could get a playable version. He wanted me to write about his 1995 lineup, but the only game that sparked my curiosity at the time would not be released until late '97.

Two years later, after playing through the scenarios on every difficulty level, I am even more impressed with this game. Age of Empires' combination of fast-paced, strategic play and historical information give it a depth that I would never have expected to find in a game.

Chapter One

An Introduction to Time

Whether you believe in Adam or Darwin, you're bound to accept the notion that technology and society have evolved. Adam may not have been an ape, but the Bible never mentions him owning a Ferrari. The Bible does mention a skyscraper, the Tower of Babel, but there is nothing to suggest elevators. Talk about your primitive circumstances—these people built a tower that reached the sky, then they had to use the stairs to get to the top.

Priests and professors may disagree about who occupied the earth during the Stone Age, but just about everyone agrees that there was a Stone Age, a Tool Age, a Bronze Age, and an Iron Age. Microsoft's Age of Empires presents rough approximations of the technologies of those ages to depict the wonder (and in a one sense, fun) of ancient combat. Of course ancient combat wasn't so fun 3,000 years ago when your life was in the balance; but society has evolved to the point where brutality is more acceptable when it's happening on your computer screen.

The Ages

In Denmark, in 1836, the curator of the National Museum in Copenhagen, Christian Jurgensen Thomson, devised a method for classifying historical objects by ages. He classified crude tools as being from the Stone Age, early metal items as being from the Bronze Age, and more advanced metal work as the Iron Age.

Even though Thomson did not have grand ambitions of changing the way mankind views history, his system was adopted by historians and archeologists and it did change the way people view prehistory.

Archeologists embraced Thomson's system and expanded it. Today, terms like Stone Age and Iron Age are an accepted part of our everyday vocabulary. Fred Flintstone would not have been a member of an "average Stone Age

family" if it weren't for Thomson. Instead, the Flintstones would simply have been classified as cavemen.

The Stone Age

The Stone Age, which began approximately two million years ago, did not vanish all at once. The Middle East and parts of Asia emerged from the Stone Age in B.C. 6,000, while the isolated civilizations of the Americas did not emerge from Stone Age culture for another three to four thousand years.

Contrary to history as portrayed in the movie *2001*, the Stone Age didn't begin with a bunch of hairy beasts discovering how to smash each others' skulls in with bones at the foot of a mysterious obelisk. Archeological evidence shows that Neanderthal and Cro-Magnon men were present in the Stone Age, but recent DNA tests suggest that modern man is not related to Neanderthal. In other words, if the obelisk advanced Neanderthal man, it wasn't enough, because Darwinian evolution still chose Homo Sapiens to join the winning team.

When Age of Empires refers to the Stone Age, it is referring to the Mesolithic or Middle Stone Age. Humanity still gathered food by hunting and gathering during the Mesolithic Era, but their hunting activities broadened to include fish and shellfish, as well as the animals and berries that have sustained humankind for the last two million years.

Men already had clubs and sharp stones that were used as knives during the Paleolithic (or first) Stone Age. Mesolithic man improved these instruments by imbedding rows of sharp stones into them. When you see clubmen whaling away at each other in Age of Empires, they're not just pounding each other, they're hacking each other to bits.

The Tool Age

The period that Age of Empires refers to as the Tool Age is more correctly stated as the Neolithic or New Stone Age period. This was the final era of the Stone Age, a time characterized by the beginnings of agriculture and specialized tools. By the Neolithic Period, ancient man abandoned the sharp rocks and began making hammers, axes, spears, and other tools sporting polished stone blades.

Improved tool-making wasn't the only marked change of this period; this was the era in which certain societies began farming, making pottery, and domesticating animals. It is widely held that Egypt and Sumer led the way in this evolution, closely followed by Greece.

The Bronze Age

The civilizations in Age of Empires slide over a grade. In real history, most civilizations had a copper age before they started working with bronze. Soft and malleable, copper does not require melting; you can simply pound it into shape. Bronze, an alloy created by mixing tin and copper, may have been a serendipitous accident.

Bronze changed the way wars were fought. Soldiers' helmets became more protective and lighter, and weapons once used for clubbing enemies suddenly became rigid enough to hack and slice.

Bronze was not the only innovation of the Bronze Age. Trade routes grew during this period, and great nations such as Babylon and Greece rose to power.

The Iron Age

The Iron Age would have preceded the Bronze Age if iron had been easier to make. Iron is actually more common than copper or tin, the minerals that form bronze; but working with iron requires melting raw ore, a process that requires a strong source of heat.

The first people to perfect the use of iron were the Hittites, who developed this talent shortly before they were wiped out of existence by invaders known as the Sea People.

Learning about working iron offered societies several advantages. Iron was more rigid than bronze. Iron helmets could deflect blows that would cause a bronze helmet to cave in. Iron was also more plentiful, meaning that it could be used for other purposes, such as building structures, and not just for weapons and ornamentation.

The Need for Food: Foraging to Farming

Early man was known as a hunter/gatherer, meaning he looked for fruits, nuts, berries, roots, and vegetables as well as hunted small animals. Tribes could find enough food to feed themselves during good years, but hunting and gathering

could not produce sufficient food during droughts. As mankind searched for more efficient means of providing for itself, both changed—hunting evolved into animal husbandry and gathering slowly became farming.

Of course, this didn't happen overnight. During the Neolithic Age, hunters slowly switched from chasing animals that traveled in herds to hunting forest animals.

The success of agriculture shaped society forever. People became less nomadic as they developed dependable sources of food, and the people inhabiting the lands that became Egypt, Greece, and Babylon all were among the first Neolithic farmers.

Scientists have traced wheat and barley farming in the Middle East as far back as B.C. 8,000 and sheep farming in Iraq, anciently known as Sumer and Babylon, as early as B.C. 9,000. The Sumerians dug canals and developed irrigation.

The Art of Weaponry: From Clubs to Catapults

There really is a logical sequence to the evolution of weapons. First, pre-Paleolithic man discovered that hitting enemies with sticks and bones did more damage than hitting them with fists. Next, pre-Paleolithic man discovered that clubs worked better than simple sticks.

Paleolithic man then discovered that clubs lined with sharp rocks did more damage than clubs without rocks, which led to the development of several ways to deliver blows with rocks. You could hit people with small rocks by throwing them with a sling, and you could hit people with sharp rocks by launching them on spears. (All of this is, of course, pure speculation since the actual inventors were too busy killing each other with sticks and stones to document their process on their notebook computers.)

Apparently, knives and swords came from sharp rock weapons. Neolithic man decided that lining clubs with sharp flint chips was not as clever as grinding rocks down and making a stronger, more polished blade. These blades ended up on prehistoric scythes that were used to thresh wild wheat, and they also ended up on prehistoric knives that were used to thresh wild neighbors. They also discovered that spears could be reduced, balanced, and fired from bows.

Metal weapons began to appear about B.C. 3,000, as a new Neolithic society began entering the Bronze Age. Several ancient Middle Eastern nations led this evolution. They used bronze to manufacture maces, swords, bows, arrows, axes, spears, and armor.

When it came to delivering rocks, the greatest weapon was the catapult. The first catapults were really enormous crossbows called "ballistas." These "double-armed" catapults fired darts three-feet long. The Greeks and Romans improved upon this technology by creating stone-throwing catapults that hurled 10-pound rocks.

Religion: Something to Believe

Only an uninformed fool would try to explain the influence of religion on the history of man in a few short paragraphs. So here goes.

Menes, the unifier of Ancient Egypt and arguably the world's first great ruler, convinced his followers that he was the son of a god. It was a good strategy because being the son of a god has a lot of great advantages. People join your army when you are the son of a god because any cause you wish to fight for instantly becomes a holy issue and, presumably, your father will help your men win your battles.

Having gods as parents also offers peacetime dividends. It means that your laws are inspired and your justice is divine. As the pharaohs discovered, it also means that your subjects will work slavishly to make you great monuments.

Egyptian and Sumerian rulers continued to claim divinity for centuries, but later rulers were not so bold. This did not mean, however, that they abandoned religion as a means of unifying their people. Many ancient kings said they were selected by the gods to be kings.

Being selected by the gods also has many great advantages. It means that the gods favor your authority and will presumably support you in times of battle. Conversely, it means that your enemies are not favored of the gods, except in battles such as Greece vs. Troy in which some of the gods liked the Greeks and others preferred the Trojans.

The advantages of having the gods on your side has not escaped modern leaders. Abraham Lincoln quickly discovered that more people were interested in fighting a holy war to end slavery than in fighting a pragmatic war to preserve the Union; and the Japanese were willing to sacrifice themselves

in combat during World War II because of the belief that their Emperor
was divine.

Creating Alliances

In his book *Leviathan: or the Matter, Form, and Power of a Commonwealth,
Ecclesiastical and Civil*, Thomas Hobbes described the natural state of humans
as "nasty, brutish, and short." He argued that big people picked on little people,
who in turn picked on anyone they could terrorize.

According to Hobbes, the only way for mankind to preserve itself was to
create the "Leviathan," a monster that was bigger than anything that got in its
way. The Leviathan was society—small men formed alliances that made them
more powerful than big men.

Hobbes' theory should not be overlooked when considering the history of
diplomacy. Take, for instance, the Yamato Clan of Ancient Japan. The Yamato
were in and of themselves no more powerful than any of their neighbors. What
made them special was their ability to forge alliances.

The leader of the Yamato Clan might form alliances with Clans A, B, C,
and D while intentionally keeping these clans from forming alliances among
themselves. These alliances state that if anyone attacks one of the clans in the
alliance, the other one will protect it. Hence if Colony E attacked Colony D, the
Yamato would come to D's defense.

Colony E would be a fool to attack Colony D because if the Yamato came
to defend D, Colonies A, B, and C would come to defend the Yamato. This also
served as a warning to Colony D not to break the alliance. In the end, the
Yamato made so many alliances that they were able to steamroll any clans not
wanting to join their league.

Having allies was not always advantageous. Having allies during the
heyday of Ancient Assyria sometimes meant that you had to join your friends in
a losing campaign against a nearly undefeatable nation. Fighting against
Assyria meant that you would lose most of your army. And losing to Assyria
meant pain and death.

Chapter Two

FEARED IN THEIR TIME

Egypt's might is tumbled down
Down a-down the deeps of thought;
Greece is fallen and Troy town
Glorious Rome has lost her crown,
Venice pride is nought.

—Mary Coleridge

The ancient Egyptians created beautiful artwork and developed complex mathematical concepts; and the ancient Greeks wrote wonderful literature and founded democracy—but you don't make these historical realities into a game like Microsoft's Age of Empires to demonstrate the cultural contributions of these great civilizations. The nations in this game terrorize their neighbors, make mincemeat out of armies that challenge them, and establish empires that last for centuries.

As you might imagine, terrorizing neighbors and grinding the bones of enemy soldiers does not win many friends. On the other hand, ancient friendships often failed when world powers marched into town.

The four empires featured in Age of Empires are Egypt, Babylon, Greece, and the Yamato Dynasty of early Japan. You can't begin to understand these empires without also considering their respective rivals, the nations that helped make them great. Without the Assyrians, the Babylonians may have been satisfied with developing new farming techniques, and without Troy and Persia, Alexander, the Greek who conquered the known world, may have only been Alexander the Good.

To put things in perspective, here are brief looks at the four powers in Age of Empires and the nations that made them strong.

Egypt: Ruled By a God

Egypt was ancient even to the ancients. It was a great nation a thousand years before the Minoans of Crete built their palace at Knossos; about 900 years before the Israelites followed Moses out of bondage. It flourished when tribesmen still dwelt in huts above the Tiber. It was viewed by Greeks and Romans of 2,000 years ago in somewhat the same way the ruins of Greece and Rome are viewed by modern man.

—Lionel Casson, *Ancient Egypt*

Egypt, older than human history as we know it, has existed in one form or another since approximately B.C. 3200. It was nearly 4,700 years old when Columbus sailed over the edge of the Earth and found the other side and 4,900 years old when American Puritans hunted witches in Salem. When the United States proudly celebrated its 200th birthday, Egypt was nearly 5,200 years old.

According to most sources, it was the Nile River that brought several tribes together and caused the formation of Egypt. Mankind was slowly emerging from its hunter-gatherer days and experimenting with a more dependable meal ticket: agriculture.

The Nile, which floods every year, churned up some great farmland, and several tribes moved in to share it. Inexplicable by modern reckoning, these tribes decided to cooperate rather than kill each other, and two early nations (Southern, or Lower, Egypt and Northern, or Upper, Egypt) were born. A while later, Menes, a ruler of Lower Egypt, conquered Northern Egypt and forged Upper and Lower countries into a single nation.

Menes, the first king (but not the first pharaoh) and his immediate successors formed what is now known as the first dynasty. The Egyptians did not start calling their kings *pharaohs* (meaning "he of the great house") until the New Kingdom period, 1,700 years and 17 dynasties after Menes' reign.

As it turned out, Menes was not only a king of the sword, but also something of a diplomat. To create harmony among his people, he located his capital, Memphis, in the north. He also included the white crown and lotus flower, symbols of fallen Upper Egypt, into his royal motif.

Though it was certainly the world's greatest superpower in its time, early Egypt did not have a standing army. From the days of Menes all the way into the Old Kingdom period (B.C. 2700, the 3rd through 6th dynasties), the king of Egypt called his men to arms during times of war, then allowed them to return to their farms in times of peace.

Even after later pharaohs created a standing army, they continued to hire mercenaries to supplement their forces. Archaeological evidence suggests that Egyptian soldiers carried spears and shields. Their army was strengthened by archers from Nubia, a small nation to the south.

Known for personally leading their troops into battles, pharaohs generally went to war surrounded by personal guards known as "retainers." After they returned, the pharoahs (most of them, anyway) wrote the history of each battle to suit their taste. According to Ramses II's recollection of the battle of Kadesh, the great pharaoh smashed the Hittite army, sending a shock of fear throughout the world. According to Hittite records, Ramses II fled the battlefield, leaving his men to be caught in an ambush. The fact that the Egyptians avoided further conflicts with the Hittites suggests that the Hittite version of the battle was more accurate.

When they won at war, pharaohs were not known for sportsmanship. They celebrated victorious battles by ceremonially hacking the leaders of opposing armies to pieces to demonstrate the achievement and totality of their victory. Many of the kings of Egypt did not get to enjoy such power, however, during eras of deterioration; several pharaohs made peace with their enemies and married their daughters rather than go to war.

Egypt did not emerge as a world-threatening imperial power for several generations. It flourished culturally in its Old Kingdom period (B.C. 2755-2255), emerged from a period of disunity that lasted from B.C. 2255-2134, and began its Middle Kingdom period, only to be conquered by Hyksos in B.C. 1700.

Described as an Asiatic Semitic people also known as the "Shepherd-Kings," the Hyksos army deployed a new weapon for which Egypt was unprepared—the chariot. The Hyksos chariot was a sturdy unit with heavy construction and four-spoked wheels.

During their years of captivity, a group of Egyptian princes in Thebes modified this design to fit the arid Egyptian terrain. After 120 years of occupation, an Egyptian army led by men in lightweight chariots with six-spoked wheels defeated the Hyksos army.

AGE of EMPIRES

The royal power of Egypt suddenly centered around Theban princes, marking the beginning of the imperial 18th dynasty. During the time of this dynasty, the dynamic Hatshepsut, Egypt's greatest ruling queen, usurped power from Thutmose III, who was both her nephew and son-in-law (the son of her husband's concubine, who married Hateshepsut's daughter), and ruled Egypt.

After 20 years of unwillingly sharing the throne with Hatshepsut, Thutmose laughed last after her death. He had Hatshepsut's name removed from all of the temples and monuments she had built. Consumed with preventing further invasions, Thutmose took the offensive and became Ancient Egypt's most militaristic leader.

Egypt had two kinds of fighting units during Thutmose's time: chariots and foot soldiers armed with bows, clubs, shields, and axes or spears. Two soldiers usually drove chariots; one's job was solely to drive, and other's role was to assault enemies with arrows and javelins. Contrary to the Hollywood image of a line of chariots following swarms of foot soldiers into battle, it was the charioteers who usually led the way.

The chariot itself was a relatively new military device, used much as tanks and armored vehicles are in modern warfare—as a screen behind which the infantry could advance.

During the 20th dynasty (approximately B.C. 1180), Egypt added another weapon to its arsenal: fighting ships. When a group called the Sea People (possibly the Minoans) attacked Egypt, the Egyptians developed a navy and fought back, eventually defeating the invaders.

The pharaohs of Egypt, who were seen as god-kings, led a society completely obsessed with death. They created huge cities of death monuments known as necropolises to themselves, had their bodies specially embalmed, and had priests create elaborate ceremonies to help them pass into their netherworld. The ancient Greeks counted the great pyramids of Giza among the Seven Wonders of the World.

The last Egyptian pharaoh was Cleopatra VII, a woman of Greek descent who tried to preserve her power by courting two great leaders of Rome—Julius Caesar and Mark Antony. When her plans failed, she killed herself rather than see her country fall. After Cleopatra's death in B.C. 30, the politics of the 3,000-year-old Egypt changed forever.

Greece: Democracy That Ruled the World

*Do not trust the horse, Trojans. Whatever it is, I fear the Greeks even
when they bring gifts.*

—Virgil, *The Aeneid*

When Greece entered the Bronze Age, around B.C. 3000, it consisted of two
very distinct nations—the Cretan and the Helladic peoples. Greece remained
fairly disorganized until B.C. 1500 when Indo-European invaders from the
north moved into the area. A unified culture evidently resulted shortly after this
invasion—thereafter most historians claim that the Trojan War took place
around B.C. 1250, based on the art found on the pottery of the time.

Virgil's *Aeneid* and Homer's *Iliad*, the two best known accounts of the
Trojan War, offer surprisingly different conclusions. According to Virgil, the
Greeks gained entrance into Troy through the use of a hollow statue of a horse,
which they pretended to give to the Trojans as a tribute. Homer mentions no
such device.

Between 800 and B.C. 650, the small autonomous city-states of which
Greece was comprised saw the rise of the "tyrants." This word refers to the
aristocrats who overthrew the existing monarchies. Though the term has come
to refer to abusive leaders, the original tyrants, all too aware of their tenuous
situations, were generally popular with their subjects.

In B.C.546, Cyrus, the destroyer of Babylon, took his conquering act to
Greece and captured most of the country in the name of Persia. After Athens
and Eritrea revolted in B.C. 499, Cyrus destroyed the Greek town of Miletus
and demanded complete obeisance.

When Sparta and Athens revolted in B.C. 490, Cyrus sent a huge army to
teach them a lesson. Unfortunately for Athens, Sparta was too busy with a
religious ceremony to help when the Persian army arrived. Athens had to attend
to Cyrus alone. Surprisingly, the Athenian army defeated the Persians, and
earned independence without Spartan help.

In 480, Xerxes I, the son of Cyrus, decided to deal conclusively with the
Greeks, so he dispersed one of the largest fighting forces ever assembled in
ancient times. Severely outnumbered, the leader of the Spartan army met the
Persians with a much smaller force in a narrow pass. Because of his choice
of battlefields, the Persian's numerical strength was negated. Only a small

number of men could attack the Greeks because the pass admitted but a few men at a time.

This plan might have worked, but a traitor revealed to Xerxes the back door. To give most of his men time to withdraw, the heroic Spartan general and 1,000 men held off the Persians as long as possible. They fought to the last man and perished.

The Persians were not so successful in their naval assault. As Xerxes watched from a safe mountain location overlooking the battle, the 1,200-ship Persian navy took on a 400-ship Grecian armada and lost.

After staving off the Persians, Greece, led by Athens, had a brief period of unchallenged world supremacy, but within 120 years, matters changed. In B.C. 359, Philip II was crowned king of a small neighbor to Greece's north: Macedonia.

Philip, who spent part of his youth as a prisoner in Thebes, had leaned the Theban war technique of the *phalanx*, a formation consisting of two rows of eight men with overlapping shields and long pikes. Philip used this technique to win some impressive skirmishes with Greek city-states, then used it again to punish a combined Athenian-Theban army in the Battle of Chaeronea in B.C. 338.

While this victory left Philip II the undisputed leader of Greece, he did not have long to enjoy it. Two years later, while preparing to invade Persia, Philip was assassinated.

Philip's son, Alexander (later known as the Great) replaced his father and took the empire to new heights. He conquered Persia and Tyre. In Egypt, greeted warmly, he established the magnificent city of Alexandria.

And his world tour continued. Alexander made his way through Asia Minor, even attacking regions of India before dying of natural causes in B.C. 323 at the age of 33.

Since Alexander left no heirs, his generals carved up his empire among themselves—Antiochus Epiphanies took Palestine, Ptolemies received Egypt, and Seleucid held Syria. This was the golden age for the spread of Greece's enlightened Hellenistic culture. Alexander the Great had been tutored by Aristotle, and his generals imbued their conquered nations with Greek culture.

Greece remained under Macedonian control until B.C. 197, when Rome conquered the Macedonians and set the Greek city-states "free"—meaning that the Romans became their new masters.

Babylon:
The Wonder That Disappeared Over Night

4 They drank wine, and praised the gods of gold, and of silver, of brass, of iron, of wood, and of stone. 5 In the same hour came forth fingers of a man's hand, and wrote over against the candlestick upon the plaster of the wall of the king's palace: and the king saw the part of the hand that wrote. 6 Then the king's countenance was changed, and his thoughts troubled him, so that the joints of his loins were loosed and his knees smote one against another.

25 And this is the writing that was written, MENE, MENE, TEKEL, UPHARSIN. 26 This is the interpretation of the thing: MENE; God hath numbered thy kingdom, and finished it. 27 TEKEL; Thou art weighed in the balances, and art found wanting. 28 PERES; Thy kingdom is divided, and given to the Medes and Persians.

30 In that night was Belshazzar the king of the Chaldeans slain.

—The Book of Daniel, chapter 5

Thousands of years ago, a fertile belt of farming land stretched across most of the territory we now know as the Middle East. Referred to as the Fertile Crescent, this land became the cradle of civilization, and the birthplace of the first great empires. Stretching from the Nile River on the west to the Persian Gulf on the east, it gave birth to such future nations as Assur, Palestine, and Egypt.

Though the city of Babylon existed on the eastern end of this crescent as early as B.C. 3000, it was the Sumerians, not the Babylonians, who carved out that region's first empire. Abraham, the patriarch of both the Islamic and Hebrew peoples, once lived in the Sumerian city of Ur, and many scholars believe that the Tower of Babel described in the Old Testament was a *ziggurat*—a massive religious tower first built by the Sumerians and later the Babylonians. In later times, ziggurats came to stand as high as seven stories. This would, as you can easily imagine, have left quite an impression on the early nomadic Israelites.

Living in an area that is now southern Iraq, the Sumerians created a remarkable culture that greatly valued religion and learning. These were basically a farming people with three distinct social classes—aristocracy,

commoners, and slaves. They recorded their learning in writing called *cuneiform*, which takes its name from the Latin word for wedge, referring to the wedge-shaped markings that formed the characters used in the writing. The Sumerians wrote on clay tablets, not paper.

The history of Sumer is marked by losses, not victories. But even while being conquered by one empire after another, the captive Sumerians managed to thrive under new regimes. Around B.C. 2400, a Semitic people known as the Akkadians conquered Sumer. The mighty Akkadian king, Sargon, expanded his power by attacking the known world of the time-the territory between the Persian Gulf and the Mediterranean Sea. Though his reign lasted for 55 years, Sargon's empire fell quickly after his death, when several of the nations he conquered revolted. Within 100 years, the Guti, a fierce tribe from the north, replaced the Akkadians as the rulers of Sumer.

After the Gutians came the Amorites and years of chaos. It was from this chaos that a great man of order arose: Hammurabi. Credited as the one who established the first Babylonian Empire (his reign lasted from B.C. 1792-1750), Hammurabi created a special code of law that was inscribed on huge stone tablets. The laws were fierce and clear cut. Some of Hammurabi's code was remarkably enlightened for its time, although certainly primitive by modern standards. For example, thieves, surgeons charged with malpractice, and boys who hit their parents had their hands cut off; innkeepers who overcharged for drinks were drowned.

Over the next 500 years, the Assyrians, Babylon's once docile neighbors, emerged as a great power. Few leaders had the nerve to challenge them. The Assyrian army had mighty weapons, such as enormous battering rams for destroying city walls and mobile towers manned with archers. If you fought against this massive force and lost, your entire army (and sometimes your entire population) would be subject to torture and death. The following is an excerpt from a letter written by an Assyrian leader: *"Many captives from among them I burned with fire, and many I took as living captives. From some I cut off their noses, their ears and their fingers, of many I put out the eyes. I made one pillar of the living and another of heads, and I bound their heads to tree trunks round about the city. Their young men and maidens I burned in fire."*

Obviously, empires do not elicit loyalty from their defeated enemies by amputating their noses and cutting off their heads for tree ornaments. A few defeated countries tried to break free of Assyrian rule, but it wasn't until

Nineveh, the capital of Assyria, fell in B.C. 612 that anyone successfully challenged the empire's power.

Once Assyria fell, the Chaldeans raised Babylon to new splendor. Under the leadership of Nebuchadnezzer II, the heir to the Chaldean throne, Babylon returned to world-power status, sacking nations and building a splendid fortified city.

This new Babylon was strong and beautiful. The largest city in the world in its day (2500 acres), Babylon was built on both sides of the Euphrates River and had walls so thick that it was said a four-horsed chariot could drive along the top. In the center of the city were two magnificent structures, a 250-foot ziggurat featuring three staircases and the palace of Nebuchadnezzer II.

Nebuchadnezzer II was married to a Median, Nitocris, who missed the gardens of her homeland. In an effort to please her, he created enormous gardens along the terraced roofs of his grand palace. The ancient Greeks counted Nebuchadnezzer's "hanging garden" among the Seven Wonders of the World.

Despite its might and thick walls, the city of Babylon was captured in a single night. During the reign of Nebuchadnezzer's son Nabonidus, King Cyrus, the man who united the Medes and Persians, attacked the great city on a Babylonian high holiday.

Rather than warn the Babylonians of his arrival by assaulting the city's thick walls, Cyrus had his army reroute the Euphrates so that they could wade through its bogs. The Persians quietly entered the city without disturbing the Babylonian's celebration. Cyrus' men quickly murdered the few citizens who saw the army enter the city. When the Babylonians shouted for help, Cyrus' men joined in shouting along with them, as if they, too, were merry makers, then killed them when no one was watching.

According to the Old Testament, the only warning the Babylonian royalty received was a vision received by Prince Belshazzar. During the festivities, he saw a hand appear from nowhere and write words upon a wall. Daniel, a Hebrew prophet serving in the palace, interpreted the vision as a message from the Hebrew god. He said that his god had judged the Babylonians and found them unworthy, and that they would fall that very night. By the end of the night, Belshazzar was dead. The Babylonian Empire never regained its glory.

AGE of EMPIRES

The Yamato Dynasty: The Clan That Would Be King

In the old days of the shogunate, an advisor who advocated a policy that failed was expected to redeem his honor by disemboweling himself. Understandably, this led to a certain reluctance to take responsibility.

— Jonathan Rauch, *The Outnation*

It is absolutely amazing how little is known about Japan's early days. Not until after World War II did anyone come to know that Japan had a Paleolithic occupation. Now thousands of sites have been located, dating ancient populations back as far as B.C. 28,000.

The Yamato Clan, named after the Yamato prefect on the main Japanese island of Honshu, does not date back that far. In fact, most historians believe that they rose to power sometime in the third century A.D. By the time the Yamato rose to power, Egypt had ceased to be an empire, and no one remembered what the Babylonians looked like.

At the time the Yamato rose to power, Japan was a quagmire of power struggles, ruled by an estimated 100 rival tribes. The Yamato emperor created a power base by setting up strategic alliances with other tribes. As he grew more powerful, his partners gradually found themselves in subservient positions. He further promoted his position by promoting the Shinto religion, in which the highest deity was a sun goddess of whom he claimed to be an heir.

Having unified much of Japan, the Yamato leaders expanded into the Korean peninsula, where they set up an alliance with the kingdom of Paekche in their struggle with the Silla, a Korean state with northern Chinese allies. As it turned out, the Paekche were weaker than their enemies, needing constant help. The Silla defeated the Paekche and helped the Chinese send the Yamato forces packing.

While the Yamato expansion into Korea was eventually frustrated by the Silla and their allies in the Chinese Shang Dynasty, it led to the introduction of both new technologies and Buddhism into Japan. Around this time, approximately 500 A.D., the Yamato also focused their efforts on local rivals in the provinces of Izumi and Kawachi.

Little is known about Yamato battle techniques, except that they prized warriors and warrior skills. It should be noted that the Yamato disappeared long

before Samurais and the Shoguns rose to power. The defeat in Korea signaled the beginning of the end for the Yamato clan. Despite a brief return to power in around 600 A.D., the Yamato Clan was unable to maintain its hold over the islands of Japan.

Dangerous Neighbors

The Egyptians, Babylonians, Greeks, and Yamatos all had one thing in common—dangerous neighbors. Granted, not every nation was as horrifyingly fearsome as the Assyrians, but you wouldn't want to take the Hittites or Persians lightly. Following is a brief look at some of the empires you'll have to deal with in Age of Empires.

The Assyrians

The most feared army of its time, the Assyrian army included chariots, archers, slingmen, spearsmen, battering rams, mobile towers, and spies. As high priest to the god Ashur, Assyrian kings were assigned the task of enlarging their lord's holdings. Thus the Assyrian expansion was, to them, a holy war.

Unlike Greece and Babylon, Assyria was not a gracious master. Nations that did not surrender to Assyrian expansion were massacred. Those that gave up without a fight were required to pay huge tributes and to submit to military service.

The Hittites

No one knows who the Hittites were or where they came from. Because they spoke an Indo-European language, many scholars speculate that they came from somewhere north of the Black Sea.

The Hittites were known as fierce warriors. They were the first civilization in their region to domesticate horses, and they had chariots before most of their neighbors. They also had superior iron weapons.

A lengthy feud broke out between the Hittites and the Egyptians when the bereaved widow of Tutankhamun asked the Hittite king to send her one of his sons for a husband. The king reluctantly agreed, but the boy never reached Egypt. The queen fell from power, and the young man was murdered in transit.

The feud erupted into an enormous battle in which the Hittites used a stratagem to surprise the Egyptians and gain the upper hand. Egyptian reinforcements arrived, however, and each side claimed the battle as a victory.

Around B.C. 1200, Hittite civilization disappeared as mysteriously as it began. The Mediterranean "Sea People" defeated and destroyed the Hittite city of Hattusa. Shortly thereafter the Hittites disappeared.

The Paekche

The Paekche were a third-century Korean people that established diplomatic relations with both Japan and China in a vain effort to establish themselves against more militaristic Korean kingdoms. It was through the Paekche that Japan was first introduced to Buddhism.

The Persians

Ancient Persia was located in what today is Iran. Under the leadership of Cyrus, the Persians and Medes banned together and conquered the known world—from the Indus River to the Euphrates Valley and to the Aegean Coast. To maintain this empire, Cyrus' descendants set up an elite 15,000-man royal guard that managed a much larger regular army including recruits from conquered nations.

The Silla

Silla was a highly warlike third-century Korean kingdom that, in conjunction with the Chinese Shang (or Tang) Dynasty, ran the Yamato Clan out of Korea. With the Yamato no longer there to protect them, the Paekche and Koguryo kingdoms fell to the Silla.

Chapter Three

Alone, Allied, and Embattled

When Sega released the 16-bit Genesis game console in 1989, one of the first titles it released was a peculiar cartridge game named *Herzog Zwei*. In this strange game about war at sea, players, in order to wage the battle, had to find fuel for their ships while hunting for enemies. Notably, it was the first real-time strategy game. Sega did not sell many Genesis consoles in 1989, and very few people noticed when *Herzog Zwei* disappeared from the market.

In 1991, the computer and video-game publisher Virgin purchased the interactive game rights to *Dune*, Frank Herbert's exceptionally popular science-fiction/fantasy novel. Virgin executives approached the French software company Cryo and a Las Vegas development group Westwood about making a game based on the license.

A year later, both Cryo and Westwood showed Virgin such terrible works in progress that Virgin executives threatened to cancel both projects. Westwood continued to work with Virgin's blessing while Cryo went on to develop the game on its own. When Cryo returned with the finished product, Virgin was stunned—the game was an amazing combination of strategy and role playing with gorgeous graphics and a very *Dune*-like plot.

Westwood then returned with its version of Dune. In this game, players controlled one of three armies vying for control of a planet. In order to build your army, you had to mine spice while building your cities and sending forces to locate and engage your enemies. The game's interface bore a stunning resemblance to the by-now forgotten *Herzog Zwei*, but improved upon it greatly.

Even though Virgin had already agreed to publish Cryo's *Dune*, the company found it impossible to say no to a game like the one Westwood showed them. To achieve the best of two worlds, Virgin bought it and named it *Dune II*. It won several gaming awards in 1992.

Virgin was very slow about following up on *Dune II*'s success; so in 1994 a company called Blizzard Entertainment stepped into the picture with the game

WarCraft. The programmers at Blizzard never denied their fondness for *Dune II* and openly admitted that they had imitated it.

The most obvious difference between the two was that *WarCraft* took place in a fantasy world. A more important difference, however, was that *WarCraft* was network- and modem-compatible. In *Dune II* you only battled computer opponents; in *WarCraft* you could declare war on your friends.

WarCraft was moderately successful, but no one could have predicted what would happen in 1995 when Blizzard released *WarCraft II* and Westwood released *Command & Conquer*, the true heir to *Dune II*. (*Command & Conquer* was not a sequel. It did not feature the same story, characters, or setting as *Dune II*; it simply had similar play mechanics.)

The sequel to a flagrantly copied imitation of an enhanced version of a forgotten Sega Genesis cartridge, *WarCraft II* topped the "best computer game of the year" lists of most every computer entertainment publication. *Command & Conquer*, which featured more realistic armies, also sold extremely well and had stronger appeal with military gamers. The critical and entertainment successes of both games inspired several new companies to enter the real-time strategy game market.

One of those companies was Ensemble, a Texas-based computer consulting firm that just happened to have a very creative staff. Ensemble teamed up with Bruce Shelley, a history buff who helped Sid Meier create *Civilization*, one of the most popular computer games of all time. Shelley and the rest of the Ensemble team then devised a historically based real-time strategy game, which we now know as Microsoft's Age of Empires.

Real-Time Basics

Real-time strategy is a euphemistic term describing games that get you so angry you'll want to spit on your mouse pad. Believe it or not, this is a good thing. We're faced with too many wishy-washy adventure games that test your intellect but leave you sitting detached from your computer.

Real-time strategy games elicit emotional involvement, passion, and anger. You spend time developing strategies only to discover that they don't work, or you develop an entire civilization only to have a herd of mongrels crush it into dust. You scream, cuss, and hate life, but you *love* your computer!

The trick to beating real-time strategy games is learning to juggle several tasks at once. You begin most missions with civilian units, the most basic kind in the game, known as villagers.

Villagers are not good fighters and it doesn't take much damage to kill them, but they are the single-most important kinds of people in this game. You need villagers to cut wood, forage for food, mine gold and stone, erect buildings, and repair ships. Very few items or components can stop you from rebuilding armies and cities in Age of Empires, and running out of villagers is one of them.

You will begin most missions in this game with a couple of villagers and a town center (a town center is an all-purpose building that can store wood, food, stone, and gold, as well as create new villagers).

As you start your missions, you should have your villagers collect wood so that they can build barracks, houses, and other structures. You should also have them build farms or forage berries so that you can create more villagers or train soldiers. One of the defining elements of the real-time strategy genre is that you have to gather food and resources—as in real life—to build your civilizations and armies.

You must also learn how to budget these resources. If it costs 50 units of food to create a villager and 100 units of food to train a cavalry scout, you may be tempted to build the villager. After all, it's cheaper. Not only that, but only villagers can gather food—and if your village runs out of food, you run out of luck.

Another defining element about Age of Empires as a real-time strategy game is combat. As you look at your screen during the game, you'll notice that large portions of the playing map have been blacked out. This is called the "fog of war." Again, a realistic touch, since you see only areas that your men have explored; the rest of the map is hidden from you. The fog of war can be problematic—just because you can't see enemies hiding in the fog of war doesn't necessarily mean they can't see you. Once your enemies have explored your area, they will be able to see your buildings.

Also, some units have a longer line of sight than others. Catapults, archers, and priests can see much further than such nearsighted ninnies as swordsmen, axemen, clubmen, and villagers. There will be moments when you may think you're alone, but in reality, a catapult is preparing to splatter your men.

Real-time strategy games involve hunting for enemies. As you build your civilization, you'll need to send armies to explore the uncharted areas of the map in search of enemy cities. This, of course, exposes your armies to all kinds of ambushes and other dirty tricks. And the fog of war is an added complication.

The final element that separates real-time strategy games such as Age of Empires from traditional combat simulations is that you do not take turns. In traditional war simulations, including the most basic ones (checkers, chess, and Risk, for example), each side takes a turn either striking at the enemy or arranging a defense. In real-time strategy games, both sides fight it out without pausing.

Game Mechanics

Age of Empires has a smooth and friendly user interface. Here are the basics.

Loading

It's time to discuss the fundamentals of playing Age of Empires. First, you have to load it into your IBM-compatible personal computer. Don't bother loading it into a Macintosh—Age of Empires requires Microsoft Windows 95 or Windows NT version 4.0, Service Pack 3. You do this by placing the CD-ROM into your CD-ROM player—that's the little sliding tray that first-time users sometimes mistake for a drink holder. (No, I did not make that up. Ask a repairman at your local computer store.)

Click on the top icon on the left to load Age of Empires on your computer.

The Age of Empires CD-ROM utilizes the Windows 95 AutoRun feature, meaning if Windows 95 is your operating system, it will recognize the disk when you place it in your CD-ROM drive and automatically walk you through the loading process.

The first screen will ask if you want to install Age of Empires, exit the installation program, or connect to the World Wide Web. The answer to this little multiple-

choice quiz is A) Install Age of Empires. Click on the little round seal beside that selection.

Before beginning the loading process, the installation program will display a window describing the legal ramifications of loading software onto your computer. It's all very standard—just respect Microsoft's copyright and don't worry about it. Click "I agree" unless you plan to sell illegal copies of the game, in which case you should probably click "I do not agree."

The next special window will inform you that you need to place Age of Empires in a directory (or folder) in your computer. Unless you have a better idea, the installation program will automatically create a folder named Age of Empires, which will be located in the Microsoft Games directory in your computer. If this is acceptable, click on the Continue button on the bottom of your screen.

The next screen lets you decide how much of Age of

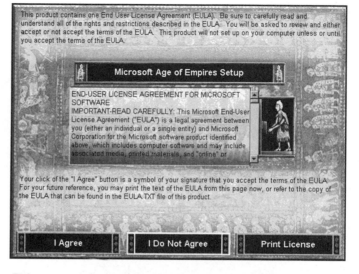

This screen informs you of the implicit legal agreement that comes with installing a game on your computer.

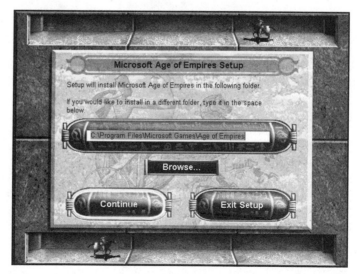

This window informs you that Age of Empires is creating an Age of Empires folder on your computer.

AGE of EMPIRES

This screen lets you decide which Age of Empires files you want to load into your hard drive.

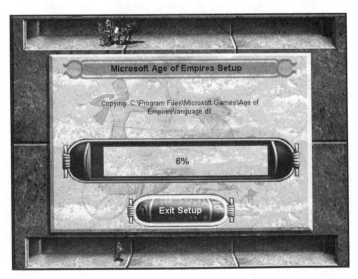

This screen shows you how much of the loading process has been completed.

Empires you want to install on your computer. The Minimum Setup option places only those files needed to run the game on your hard drive. The Typical option places the same files as the Minimum option, but also places online help files on your hard drive. The final option, Full Setup, places help files and cinematic files on your hard drive. (The only reason for installing these files is so that they display quickly when you come to them in the game; you only see these cinematic sequences as you start the game and when you begin or end an entire campaign.) You don't need to load these files into your computer to see them, so you should probably select the Typical Setup option.

You will next be shown a screen with a large oval meter; this is simply Microsoft's way of showing your computer's progress as it loads Age of Empires into your hard drive.

Next, you're asked if you would like to register Age of Empires electronically. If you have a modem in your computer and an Internet connection, online registration is a very easy option. If you'd rather get playing, click on the Continue option and your computer will complete the installation process.

Once you've registered or opted to Continue, you are returned to the help screen you saw after first placing the CD-ROM in your computer. Note that the screen now has three new options: Play Age of Empires, Reinstall Age of

Here's where you register your copy of Age of Empires online.

Empires, and Uninstall Age of Empires. At this point, you probably would rather play the game than reinstall it or uninstall it. Believe me, fun as the uninstall protocol may be, the game is a lot more engaging—so click on Play.

Starting Up

Age of Empires opens with an animation depicting an ancient battle. Glorious and cinematic as it is, you may get tired of watching this animation after you've seen it a dozen times. You can skip it by clicking the left button on your mouse or by hitting the Escape key.

After the animations, you'll see a screen with buttons for accessing single and multiplayer games, online help, and the scenario builder. With the exception of single-player games (below), each of these options will be discussed later.

Single-Player Games

Most people will begin Age of Empires by playing the single-player game. Age of Empires has campaigns—a collection of 36 carefully crafted and thoroughly diabolical scenarios designed to reflect historical situations while smothering

the player's will to live with a combination of nasty surprises and enjoyable frustration; a random map generator—an option that lets you create scenarios in which you go head-to-head against the computer; death matches—an especially competitive option for playing against the computer; scenarios—an option providing access to any of the 24 multiplayer scenarios that make up the campaigns; and saved games—an option that lets you resume your progress in a scenario that you previously quit and saved.

Campaigns

Most first-time players will want to begin their time with Age of Empires by jumping into the campaigns. Going through the campaigns is probably the best way to familiarize yourself with the game since the early campaigns are designed to work like a tutorial.

A window will open asking you to type your name after you click the Campaign button in the single-player menu. Type in your name and click the OK button, and you'll enter the campaign selection screen.

There are three windows inside the campaign selection screen. The first

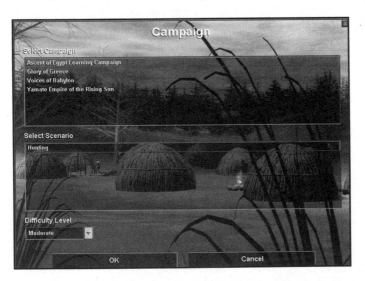

There are four campaigns with 36 missions in Age of Empires. Use this screen to select your campaign and enter the missions.

window lists the campaigns available—Egyptian, Greek, Babylonian, or Yamato. First-time players should select the Ascent of Egypt campaign since it was designed as a tutorial to teach players about Age of Empires.

The next window lists available scenarios. The Egyptian campaign has 12 scenarios, and the other campaigns have eight scenarios each, but you must proceed through these missions in sequential order—you don't get access to the second mission until you beat the first one. (Once you beat a scenario you can replay it whenever you choose.)

Bruce Shelley, one of the evil geniuses who created Age of Empires, wanted the game to contain scenarios with historically factual story lines. With this in mind, he simplified 36 pivotal historical junctures and worked with such cutthroats as Chris Rippy to immortalize these historical moments as challenging missions.

The third window sets

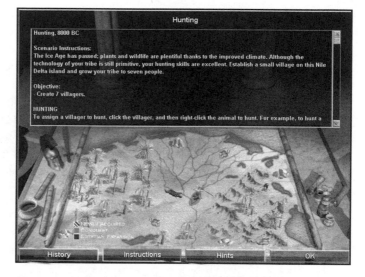

Once you've started a game, clicking Menu and then Scenario Instructions will trigger a scenario description screen.

the difficulty level for each scenario. Do not take the choices in this window lightly. On the easier settings, Age of Empires lets you cruise along, building your civilization and attacking your enemies whenever you feel ready. On the hardest settings, the game sends enemies to stomp your town into the ground on a regular basis. Beginning players who attempt the hardest levels will be terribly frustrated, and experienced strategy gamers should avoid easier levels to avoid boredom. Once you've selected your campaign, mission, and difficulty level, click the OK button on the bottom of the screen to launch your mission.

Before each scenario, you'll be shown a mission summary screen. These screens explain the circumstances of the scenario and list your objectives. You can also access hints and histories through this screen. Once you understand your objectives, click the OK button and begin the scenario.

Campaign Differences

Each of the four campaigns in Age of Empires has a unique flavor. The Egyptian campaign is a tutorial. It gets steadily tougher as you move through it, and you never face any real danger until you get to the seventh mission.

The Greek campaign begins with defensive missions and shifts into an offensive posture. You go from helping the Athenians struggle against other Greek city-states to joining Alexander the Great as he conquers the world. The later missions are characterized by large freewheeling battles sometimes fought against multiple enemies.

The Babylonian missions are similar to the Greek missions except that many of them are based more in defensive strategy. Much of your Babylonian experience will be about defending you country rather than trying to expand it.

The Yamato campaign is largely about getting revenge. In one mission, you send assassins to kill the leader of a clan who has challenged your allies. In two other missions, you go out to collect treasures that have been stolen from your leaders.

Single-Player Death Matches and Random Maps

Death matches and random-map games are almost exactly alike. Unlike campaigns, which are stories relayed through a series of missions, single-player death matches and random maps are stand-alone missions in which you slug it out with up to seven computer opponents.

In single-player random-map games and death matches, you control how many opponents you face, who they are, and how they're allied. You also control the map settings, victory conditions, and difficulty level.

You begin these games by defining the situation via a screen that enables you to select how many nations you wish to compete against; how those nations will be allied; whether you wish to compete in a mountainous area, an inland area, along a coast, or at sea; and at what level of difficulty the game should be played. Although you'll face the same number of enemies on the hardest difficulty setting as on the easiest, your enemies will play far more aggressively on the harder settings.

Unlike campaigns scenarios, death matches and random maps do not have story lines. Once you click OK on the setup screen, you launch into your mission.

The only difference between death matches and random-map games is in start-up resources: death matches always give you 20,000 units of wood, 20,000 units of food, 10,000 units of gold, and 5,000 units of stone, and random-map games offer you some control over your opening resources.

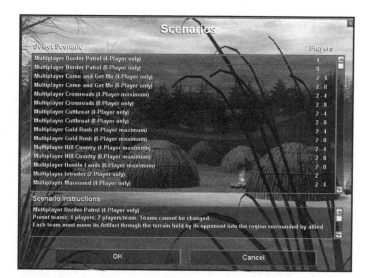

The scenario screen offers quick access to two dozen multiplayer missions.

Scenarios

Once you've completed the campaigns, you may wish to try your hand at the individual missions listed on the Scenario screen—there are 81 missions in that menu. The Scenario screen lets you access all 36 missions from the campaigns.

Nobody knows Age of Empires like the guys at Ensemble, and clearly a few of them have played it a bit too much. As you browse through the list of games available in the Scenarios menu, you'll see games named after the people who created them. There are missions with names like "tim-mp-6," "Sean's Multiplayer 8player free for all," and "Ian-come and get me," which reflect just how much the Ensemble development team has invested in the game.

Age of Empires

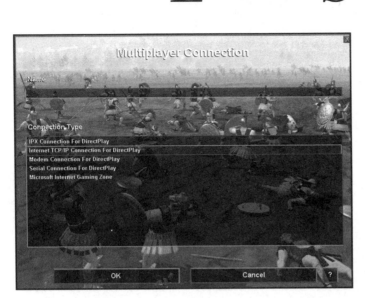

Age of Empires supports network and head-to-head competition. Set up your connection using the Multiplayer Connection screen, available through the game's main menu.

Multiplayer Games

Age of Empires is a great single-player game, and Ensemble has invested a great deal of time into creating intriguing campaigns for the single-player mode; but to get the most out of this game, you're going to have to play against live opponents.

First, the mechanics of multiplayer games. Age of Empires supports four kinds of connections for head-to-head and team games. You can play on a TCP/IP (Transport Connect Protocol/Internet Protocol) network. Take a couple copies of the game to your office and play a death match during your coffee break; I'm sure your boss won't mind.

If you don't have an understanding boss, you can set up a modem-to-modem connection or connect two computers together via your serial ports for a little DirectPlay head-to-head action. Microsoft has also opened an Age of Empires site in its Internet Gaming Zone.

Ensemble has put a lot of effort into providing every conceivable option for multiplayer gaming. Two people can play Age of Empires head-to-head, or as many as eight people can play it as a group. The game also supports IPX if installed or other direct-play service providers. You can play a cooperative game in which players form alliances, a battle royale in which every player vies for total domination, or a team game in which players control the same civilization.

Doing Unto Others: Team Play

The cooperative modes in Age of Empires allow players to match their strengths so that they can build truly impressive teams. The multiplayer modes allow players to select a nation to control. Matching a productive nation such as

the Shang with an aggressive nation such as the Assyrians is one of the best ways to produce a balanced team.

Each of the 12 nations in the game has unique strengths and weaknesses. The Shang, for instance, have the least expensive villagers. (It generally costs 50 units of food to build a villager, but Shang villagers cost only 35.) Babylon is a great choice for players who like to trap opponents. The Babylonians have the deadliest towers. If you ally the Assyrians and the Babylonians, you can send Assyrian armies to attack you enemies while having the Babylonians fortify your cities against attack.

One of the nice touches included in Age of Empires is the ability of allies to send private messages. This not only allows you to plan secret strategies and discuss important tactics, but it also lets you spread hurtful lies about your opponents without giving them a chance to defend themselves.

An Eye for an Eye: Working Alone

Of course, sometimes it's fun to fight alone against the world. And it's even more fun when you win. There are several ways to emerge as victor in Age of Empires. You can win by building a wonder of the world and protecting it for 2,000 years. (That's 2,000 computer years—better known as 20 minutes in real-world terms.) You'll find artifacts hidden throughout the map in some scenarios. Finding all of the artifacts and keeping them in your possession for 2,000 years also results in an instant victory.

But the surest route to victory is the old-fashioned way—kill absolutely everybody else. This can be very challenging in multiplayer games because many opponents, being only human, hold grudges and remember who killed their villagers. Get too aggressive in an eight-player game, and you may find yourself in the unenviable position of having to fight off seven other armies.

Chapter Four

WHAT EVERY EMPEROR SHOULD KNOW

You may believe in the divine right of digital kings to rule as they may, but your reign will end quickly and unceremoniously if you do not observe a few conventions. You need to get to know your subjects and what they can do if you plan to conquer the world; and let's face it, if you're not interested in conquering the world, you should be playing *SimCity*.

Villagers:
The Basic Building Blocks of Society

Villagers are both your most basic unit and your most valuable unit. You need villagers to erect buildings, gather food, mine stone and gold, chop wood, repair buildings, fix ships after and during battles, tend farms, and hunt. Your society stagnates when you run out of villagers and no longer have any way to create more villagers. Conversely, as long as you have villagers and 120 units of wood for a storage pit or 200 units of wood for a town center, you can always rebuild your society.

You need villagers to construct buildings, cut wood, hunt gazelles, and forage for food.

Most villagers are useless soldiers, but once you enter the Iron Age, you can turn them into fighting machines. If you purchase the Jihad upgrade through your temple,

you'll give your villagers "warrior strength." With their newfound strength, your villagers will be able to go toe-to-toe with axemen and archers; and because villagers are so cheap to make, you'll be able to send hordes of them to overwhelm such expensive units as cataphracts and phalanxes.

While it will not make your villagers any better at hand-to-hand combat, you can also purchase siege ability for them. This turns them into wall-breaching, tower-razing demons. You can only find the siege ability upgrade in Iron Age markets, and it's rather expensive. But it really pays off when you attack cities fortified by towers and walls.

Since clubmen are the only fighting units available in the Stone Age, the only way to win those battles is to have a larger army than your enemy's. (All icons appear on units in the scenario builder; they don't appear in gameplay.)

Axemen hit a little harder than clubmen and can absorb a little more damage.

Foot Soldiers

When you have a Stone Age village, you can only train one kind of soldier-clubmen, big-hearted troglodytes who tend to stand around and smack each other like kids in pillow fight. Because they are the only combat units available at the Stone Age level, battles tend to be decided by numbers.

Once you reach the Tool Age (assuming you've already built barracks), you may diversify your army by building stables and an archery range. You may also upgrade your clubmen to axemen through your barracks and upgrade their fighting ability and armor through your storage pit.

Once you enter the Bronze Age, you'll be given several new options for building your forces. You can upgrade your barracks to create short swordsmen and broad swordsmen. (You have to upgrade from axemen to short swordsmen and then from short swordsmen to broad swordsmen.) These units are much more durable than axemen, but you must have gold to train them.

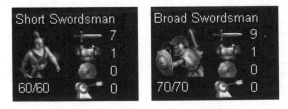

The Bronze Age answer to the Tool Age axeman, the short swordsman and broad swordsman give and take a lot more damage than their earlier counterparts.

Bronze Age villagers can also build academies, buildings that train fierce foot soldiers who use spears instead of swords. The first units you'll get from your academy are hoplites, aggressive soldiers who can absorb 120 units of damage—more damage than some buildings. Hoplites are not particularly fast, but they can smash their way through rows of short swordsmen.

Once you enter the Iron Age, you can upgrade your broad swordsmen to long swordsmen and then to legions, which buys you a few more damage points and a slightly fiercer attack. You can also upgrade your hoplites to phalanxes and then to centurions. Centurions are great to have around since they can absorb 160 damage points and possess an attack rating of 30 points.

Hoplites are the basic academy fighting unit.

Long swordsmen can take 80 damage points, and they have a slightly higher attack rating than broad swordsmen.

Phalanxes have better armor and a stronger attack than hoplites.

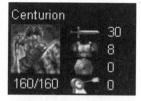

The ultimate foot soldier, the centurion both gives and takes excessive amounts of damage.

Bowmen

At first glance, bowmen may seem to be rather useless units. Don't be deceived. They can be used quite effectively in certain situations, and upgraded archers are among the most effective soldiers in the game.

You cannot even build an archery range and train bowmen until you advance into the Tool Age, and then you get only basic bowmen with an attack rating of 3 (actually lower than clubmen). It's useless to send bowmen to attack enemies; they don't have the firepower to kill anything fiercer than a gazelle, and they can't withstand much more damage than a villager.

They do, however, work well in a group. Have four or five bowmen attack the same clubman, and they'll kill him quickly. Bowmen are also effective when attacking enemies from cliffs or from behind walls. It may take them a while to kill their enemies,

With very low attack and hit points, bowmen should mostly be used in groups or from behind protective barriers.

Composite Bowman
5
0
0
45/45   7

Composite bowmen are a marked improvement over regular bowmen. They shoot farther and inflict more damage per shot.

Chariot Archer
4
0
0
70/70   7

Don't spend a lot of money on chariot archers; they're neat-looking but they don't do a lot of damage when they attack.

Elephant Archer
5
0
0
600/600   7

Elephant archers don't have much of an attack, but their 600 hit points provide strategic value.

Horse Archer
7
0
2
60/60   7

Horse archers have reasonably strong attacks, but their hit points are low.

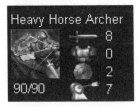

Heavy Horse Archer
8
0
2
90/90   7

The ultimate bow-and-arrow unit, heavy horse archers may not have the strongest attack, but their speed and durability make them a great asset.

Scout
3
0
0
60/60   0

The basic mounted soldier, scouts are inexpensive to build, and they're fast.

but they'll get the job done if they have a barrier protecting them.

Once you enter the Bronze Age, you can upgrade to improved bowmen and then to composite bowmen. This breed has longer-range weapons, higher hit points, and a slightly stronger attack. Place a group of these warriors behind walls or around a tower, have them focus on a single target and they'll wear it down quickly.

If you purchase wheel technology from your market, you can also build chariot archers during the Bronze Age. Chariot archers can sustain more damage than composite bowmen, and they're able to get to trouble spots quickly. The downside: a low attack rating—4 points.

There are three specialized Iron Age archers who can completely change the tide of battle. The first is the elephant archer. While not as fast as chariot archers and owning a fairly weak attack rating, they can absorb a worse beating than a tower and make perfect bait for luring enemies to your priests.

Horse archers have reasonably strong attacks and a decent firing range-but are weak in taking damage. Bolster them with the missile weapons upgrades from your government center, and they'll make a good mid-line defense unit. You cannot upgrade to heavy horse archers without having horse archers first.

Once you spend all of the gold and food required to start making heavy horse archers, you'll have an excellent

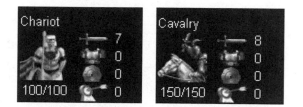

fighting force. Heavy horse archers may not be able to inflict damage as quickly as phalanxes and centurions, but they can ride to trouble zones quickly. Catapults can't hit them—they move too quickly—and with an eight-point attack rating, a group of two or three heavy horse archers can wear down most enemies very quickly.

Cavalry

You can build stables during the Tool Age, which will enable you to train scouts, fairly weak mounted soldiers who attack with no more force than a clubman. They have strength in hit points, and they're fast and inexpensive to train. But it's their speed and eyesight that makes scouts so valuable. They're excellent at overwhelming archers and catapults, and they're so inexpensive that you can send them on high-risk mapping expeditions.

Once you enter the Bronze Age, you can upgrade your stables to train chariots and cavalry. The difference between chariots and chariot archers is that chariots do not shoot arrows; instead, they use lances for jabbing at enemies. Chariots have much stronger attacks than chariot archers and can withstand more damage.

Cavalrymen take horseback attacks to an even higher level. With 150 hit points and an attack rating of eight points, they can rush and annihilate platoons of bowmen and caravans of catapults. They're effective only in close quarters, however, so avoid sending lone cavalrymen to destroy towers or attack walls.

One final cavalryman deserves mention—the cataphract. You won't see many of these mounted menaces, and you should be grateful (unless they're

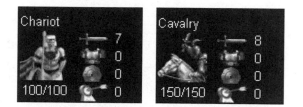

Chariots and archers are more durable and destructive than chariot archers and horse archers, but they're effective only at close range. The second most powerful mounted soldier is the heavy cavalryman. With better armor, a very powerful attack, and slightly more range than others of his kind, heavy cavalrymen can even attack over walls. They may not be well-suited for battling war elephants and towers, but they can burn through a row of chariot archers or a line of composite bowmen.

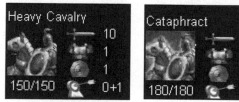

Heavy cavalrymen not only have a powerful attack, but they also have more range than other combat soldiers.

The cataphract is the ultimate mounted soldier, and his horse is pretty cool, too.

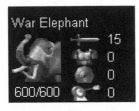

Nothing can stand in a war elephant's way. While overwhelmingly powerful, they move so slowly that most enemies walk away from them unharmed.

yours). Cataphracts have the same range as heavy cavalrymen, but they have a 12-point attack rating, stronger armor, and can absorb 180 damage points. They can also destroy nearly any other unit in the game.

One of the most powerful but least versatile weapons in Age of Empires is the war elephant, an enormous and slow creature that wanders up to enemies and butts them with its head. The beast is too slow to attack priests without being converted. It's attacks are so slow that mounted units and even archers can walk away from it. War elephants can be used to destroy catapults, and they're capable of taking out towers and walls. Elephants can hurt any unit, trampling it easily.

Catapults and Missile Weapons

You cannot build a siege workshop until the Bronze Age. Once you have a siege workshop, gain access to the most powerful line of weapons in Microsoft's Age of Empires—catapults and ballistas.

Stone throwers and other siege weapons are perfect for clearing walls and towers out of your way. Because of their long range of vision, they are also excellent at sneaking up on unsuspecting enemies.

The basic siege weapon is the stone thrower, a miniature catapult that has limited range and power by catapult standards, but definitely scores well compared to any non-siege units. Stone throwers are powerful enough to kill bowmen, axemen, priests, and scouts with a single shot. They can hurl loads of stone farther than most towers can shoot arrows, so they can usually attack towers without being hit.

Stone throwers and catapults have three Achilles heels, however. First, they're slow. It takes stone throwers and catapults five seconds to aim and fire a load of rocks—more than enough time for priests to begin converting them or for scouts to rush and attack them.

Second, catapults and stone throwers are completely defenseless against close-range attacks. They're too slow to run away from attackers, and they stop firing altogether once the attacker is at close range.

Their final weakness is that they tend to shoot indiscriminately at any enemies appearing within range. This can be a problem, for example, when two of your very expensive centurions attack an enemy phalanx and your catapult fires two or three shots at the phalanx, destroying it—and your centurions.

The nations in Age of Empires possess different siege weapons. Some have ballistas, which are giant crossbows on wheels. While not as powerful as catapults and limited in range, ballistas have a much faster rate of fire and do not kill fellow soldiers with friendly fire.

Ballistas are not as powerful as catapults and stone throwers, but they're easier to control.

Built to blast through towers, walls, and buildings, heavy and massive catapults are the ultimate siege weapons.

The most powerful weapons are heavy and massive catapults. These fighting behemoths can destroy houses with a single shot. They are weapons with an extremely long range, able to decimate armies from deep within the fog of war. Towers cannot possibly defend themselves against them. Massive catapults can even destroy fleets of fighting ships too far offshore to threaten towns or soldiers.

Like other siege weapons, however, these units are worthless in close combat and must be carefully guarded.

Expensive and powerful as they are, catapults have a major flaw: no way to defend themselves once attackers get in close.

Some nations, such as the Shang, for example, have mega-ballistas called *helepolises* as their ultimate weapon. Helepolises have neither the power nor range of a catapult, but their rapid rate of fire makes them deadly and an excellent weapon for attacking walls. Best of all, you can shoot them into a crowded battlefield without injuring your own men.

The helepolises' rate of fire and range make it a good weapon for guarding your shores. It's also good for laying sieges and defending against them.

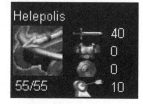

The helepolis has a rapid rate of fire and shoots a reasonably long distance.

Priests

There are two compelling reasons for training priests in Age of Empires—conversions and healings. Use your priests wisely in this game, and they'll be more potent than an entire army of soldiers.

Three heavy cavalrymen attack two priests. The priests convert two of the cavalrymen, who then kill their former comrade. Good strategy, no?

When enemy soldiers come within range, you can have your priests chant to them. They generally respond by trying to kill your priest, so you may lose priests if you have them convert, say, archers; and you should be careful not to leave your priest in one spot for too long when converting catapults.

Priests run out of faith the same way athletes run out of energy. Your priest is going to need several seconds to regenerate his faith after every conversion, so be sure not to place him in front of 10 angry centurions and expect him to convert his way to safety.

Priests are important for healing your troops. They not only heal soldiers and villagers, but they can also heal ballistas and catapults.

Healing wounded soldiers does not tax your priest's faith, so you may want to have your priest heal them between conversions.

Buildings

As an imperial leader, you'll have to build your nation while attacking other nations. This is a very important strategem because the buildings you erect determine the flavor of your mission, and very few missions have the kinds of unlimited resources that let you build one of everything. You'll need what your enemy has.

There is a decided economy in the pacing of Age of Empires; it's not the kind of game that lets you sit and ponder as you play, so you should probably learn what every building type has to offer so that you can construct your cities on the fly.

Proud soldiers such as the Ancient Greeks and Babylonians may never have crawled on their bellies, but they still cared about their next meal. In order to make your armies and empires larger, you'll have to build some civilian shelters as well.

Houses

You must have a sufficient number of houses for your troops before you can train them. You're allowed 50 men, so plan on building 12 to 13 houses in every mission. Even the cataphracts are used to tract housing, so don't worry about creating homes with a view.

If you have enough time and supplies, it's a good idea to build a little suburb in some out-of-the-way nook on the map. That way you won't have to worry about building new houses during a heated battle.

Once you build houses, they serve very little purpose. You can use them as barriers to stop enemies from entering your cities, but houses have are no upgrade possibilities, and they're easily destroyed.

Your enemies have the same city-planning problems that you have—they too can only train soldiers if they've created houses to put them in. Destroy your enemies' houses, and they'll have to expend resources to build more houses before they can train additional or replacement soldiers.

Granaries

Granaries are buildings that hold food. You can speed up your villagers' work by erecting granaries by berry bushes. Your villagers won't have to carry their food far to store it. The same holds true with farms. By building farms around granaries, you can speed up farm production.

You also need granaries to build guard towers and walls. Once you reach the Tool Age, you'll see upgrade windows along the bottom of your screen when you click on your granary.

Perhaps the most versatile building in Age of Empires, storage pits are used to hold wood, gold, stone, and meat.

Most scenarios begin with this scene: a town center with a group of villagers waiting for orders.

Storage Pits

Storage pits are the Swiss army knives of Age of Empires architecture. Your villagers use them to store gold, wood, stone, and meat from animals they kill.

Building storage pits is also essential to your war effort. Storage pits hold combat and armor upgrades for your soldiers, cavalry, and archers.

Town Centers

The town center is the most basic unit in the game. It serves three purposes— building villagers, storing food and resources like granaries and storage pits, and advancing to new ages. In the latter case, it's a matter of clicking in your town center's menu—you advance once you've constructed enough buildings and saved up enough food and gold.

While town centers are durable and can withstand a great deal of abuse, you should always keep soldiers and towers around your centers to protect them. (You won't have to be quite so protective once you enter the Iron Age. Villagers from this Age can construct town centers.)

One last point of strategy. It costs 200 units of wood to build a town center (80 units more than it costs to build a storage pit or a granary), but town centers do the work of granaries and storage pits. Build town centers when you set up new colonies, and you'll save yourself some wood.

Farms

Farms can provide a stable food source for your cities. Unlike fishing, hunting, and foraging, which require food and produce on the hoof, you don't have to depend on nature to farm. (At least you don't have to depend on nature to farm in this game.) You only need land and wood.

You can upgrade your farm production with every new Age to which you evolve. These upgrades are fairly expensive; if you don't purchase them early in your missions, you'll be wasting your food and resources.

Farms provide a steady source of food, but you'll have to commit villagers to work them. If too many are farmers, you'll weaken your army.

You can purchase upgrades for your city's production capabilities through markets.

Markets

You cannot build farms until you have a market, and once you have a market you can use it to upgrade your farms' productions. Through markets, you can upgrade all of your city's economic activities, plus woodcutting (which also improves your missile weapon range), gold mining, stone mining, and your villagers' siege abilities. Wheels help too, making all villagers faster.

Under normal circumstances, markets should be the first building constructed when you enter the Tool Age.

Civic and Government Buildings

Some of the buildings in Age of Empires do not have a direct military purpose but are not made for economic or agricultural purposes. These buildings can play unbelievably important roles during your missions, so don't skip them until you know what you are missing.

Temples

Priests are probably the single most effective weapon in Age of Empires. They can convert catapults, cataphracts, heavy cavalrymen, centurions, phalanxes, long swordsmen, transports, and villagers. In fact, you begin one of the more interesting missions in this game with nothing but a priest and 200 units of wood.

So what does that have to do with temples? You need temples to train priests and to upgrade them to do several things. (The coolest upgrade is monotheism, which enables your priests to convert enemy buildings and priests.)

Docks

You can build several kinds of ships throughout all of the Ages if you have a dock. During the Stone Age, you can build fishing boats capable of catching up to 15 units of food per trip, and trade boats that barter wood, food, or stone for gold.

During the Tool Age, you can add scout ships—small, light, combat

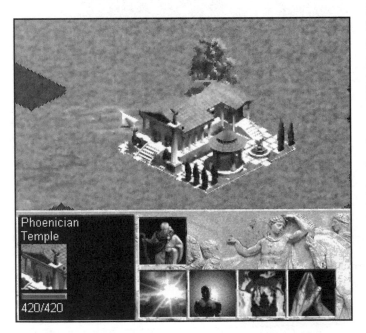

You need to build temples to train and upgrade your priests.

vessels—to your fleet. You can also build five-man transports to take your villagers and soldiers across the water.

During the Bronze Age you can upgrade your scout ships to galleys. You can also upgrade your fishing boats to fishing ships and your trading boats to merchant ships to increase fishing and trading efficiency.

It's the Iron Age, however, when your navy really gets going. It's here that you can upgrade your combat ships to triremes—huge fighting boats with ballistas, catapult triremes, and juggernaughts.

Government Centers

In terms of importance, government centers are deceiving: they serve no military purpose during the Bronze Age (they will allow you to build a town center), but become vitally important to your siege technology during the Iron Age.

The only upgrades they offer during the Bronze Age are trifling little peace-loving deals that let you erect buildings quicker and help you establish trade routes. No big deal.

During the Iron Age, however, they offer upgrades for your hoplites and phalanxes, make your catapults more deadly, and enable you to build catapult triremes and juggernaughts. Building a government center may not be as juicy as constructing a siege workshop, but you simply won't become a world power without one.

Having a government center increases cavalry hit points.

Military Buildings

Military buildings are made for one reason: killing. They don't teach dance in hoplite academies.

There's really not that much to barracks; they exist simply to make soldiers.

Age of Empires features a wide variety of types of archers, each with special attributes. The only possible exception is the basic bowman, who is so cheap to train that he's totally expendable.

Barracks

During the Stone Age, you are allowed to erect only one kind of military building-barracks; and you only get one kind of soldier-clubmen. Stone Age architects had such a prehistoric mindset.

You can upgrade your basic soldiers from clubmen to axemen during the Tool Age; from Axemen to short swordsmen and even broad swordsmen in the Bronze Age; and from broad swordsmen to long swordsmen in the Iron Age.

Archery Ranges

Archers may not do much damage on their own, but put a group of archers in a strategic location and they can obliterate an entire legion of enemy foot soldiers. Even more importantly, archers come in all kinds of shapes and sizes. And you can train them on the ranges.

There are basic bowmen, who are cheap to train and painless to replace. There are chariot archers and horse archers, who can get to trouble spots quickly and defend shores against invasions. There are even industrial-strength archers—elephant archers—who are slow and lumbering, but can take all kinds of damage.

Like archers, cavalry and mounted soldiers come in all shapes and sizes.

The weapons manufactured in siege workshops are great for finishing missions. They were designed to shatter walls and remove towers, and they're especially good at destroying wonders.

Stables

Stables create a line of fast-moving soldiers who specialize in close combat. Like archers, these mounted soldiers come in all shapes and sizes. For the most part, cavalrymen and scouts suffer from being jacks of all trades. They're not as fast as archers and not as tough as phalanxes and hoplites, but the mounted militia is wonderful at tackling catapults.

Siege Workshops

If there's an irresistible candy store in all of Age of Empires, it's the siege workshops. There's something wonderful about such death-dealing machines as massive catapults, ballistas, and helepolises—and the only place that has them is the siege workshop.

The only weapon offered by siege workshops during the Bronze Age is the stone thrower, but several additional weapons become available during the Iron Age.

Academies

Academies are specialized training centers that produce soldiers with lances. These soldiers move at an irritatingly slow gait when you send them to stop an

Three phalanxes await orders in front of an academy.

These sacred ruins look a bit like Stonehenge.

Who says that wonders never cease? A few catapult shots erased this one.

invasion, but they're especially fierce fighters who can take a beating.

Ruins

The Greeks, Egyptians, and Babylonians may be ancient, but they weren't the first inhabitants of their worlds. Some missions feature sacred ruins from long-extinct civilizations. You can even win certain missions by finding all of the hidden ruins before your opponent.

Wonders of the World

The greatest, most satisfying achievement any nation can have in Age of Empires is to destroy its enemy's wonder of the world. Your enemies sink 1,000 units of wood, stone, and gold into their wonders, not to mention thousands of man-hours. Think how cleansing it feels to wash all of that effort down the drain with a few pleasing shots from your catapults.

Actually, there's a different reason to destroy your enemies' wonders of the world. A 20-minute clock starts ticking the moment they complete these colossal-but-useless monuments. If the wonder is not destroyed within 20 minutes of completion, the nation that built it automatically wins the war.

Chapter Five

....➤

THE EGYPTIAN SCENARIOS

The Egyptian missions of Microsoft's Age of Empires may be considered a unique tutorial designed to acclimate players to the overall game. It's nearly impossible to lose the first few missions, but the scenarios quickly become more challenging.

Players unfamiliar with real-time strategy games should take this opportunity to do some experimentation and familiarize themselves with how these games are played. In short, for example, if you have never built farms while mining gold and fighting off invading armies, get used to it: you'll need to think in terms of multitasking.

Experienced players may want to experiment on the early scenarios as well, This will provide a chance to get a feel for the interface and design of the game. Age of Empires has an extremely intuitive interface that will make most gamers feel right at home in a matter of moments, but Egypt especially offers the chance to learn the ropes in a relatively safe environment.

Mission 1: Hunting

There's not much to do in this level and not much room for experimentation either. The goal is to increase the population of a Stone Age village from one person to seven. To accomplish this, forget about biology and rely on your town center.

You only need food and dwellings to create villagers. (In later missions you will need to harvest trees to build houses, but in this mission there's no need to worry about wood since you start off with 50 units of wood and it takes only 30 to build a house.) Thanks to the tremendous efficiency of the times and good chemistry among villagers, you will only need one house for all seven of your cavemen to cohabitate.

You begin this mission with one villager and a town center. The most effective way to get through this mission, and later missions, is to assign your

By placing your hunter near his prey, you can herd gazelles toward your village as you spear them. This helps you harvest more meat from every kill.

Alligators slowly follow your villagers in the hopes of grabbing a bite to eat. You can lure them to your town center and spear them. They're good for 100 units of food.

villager to get food as soon as the mission begins. As he increases his food supply to 50 units, you create more villagers and assign them to tasks.

In this case, the only task besides hunting food is building one house. You may assign your second villager to build that house while your first villager continues hunting. Once the house is finished, your second villager should join his neighbors in the slaughter of gazelles. You will need 300 units of food to create six more villagers; the more hunters you send out, the faster you will have enough food to complete the scenario.

Gazelle Hunting

As the mission begins, there is a large herd of gazelles just west of your town center and a few stray gazelles just to the east. To hunt gazelles, left click on your villager, then right click on the gazelle you want him to hunt. Primitive as he is, your Stone Age hunter will know enough to start hurling

spears at the gazelle as soon as you click on it. It generally takes three hits to kill the animal.

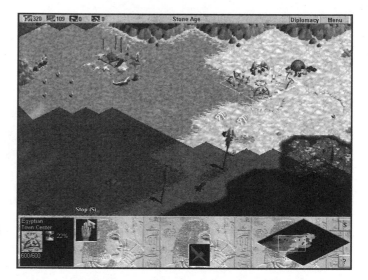

Gazelles contain 150 units of food, but they decompose rapidly. Once your village kills the animal, he begins skinning it and carrying its meat back to the village. Since he can carry only 10 units of food at a time, some of the gazelle will waste away while your villager is transporting the meat. One way to increase your net meat supply is to go after gazelles grazing near your town center.

The two alligators on this level are near the water. Keep your eyes peeled (metaphorically speaking) or your evolution may get nipped in the butt.

If a hunter kills a gazelle next to the town center, he should get nearly 90 units of food from it. If the gazelle is farther away, he may get 65, maybe 70, units of meat before it decomposes. One of the tricks, then, is to guide gazelles near your town center before killing them.

To do this, have your villager walk around the outside of the herd so that the gazelles are between him and the village. Don't worry if the gazelles start to run, they won't go far.

Next, select a gazelle positioned directly between you and the village. Have your villager spear the gazelle once or twice. It will run toward the village. Follow it and spear it a third time when it is near your town center. Now you're practically dining in instead of carrying take-out back to town.

This reduces the commuting time between your kill and the place where your villagers store their meat: the less time wasted, more food harvested from every kill. You can further reduce decomposition by having your villagers hunt in a group, gaining more than 120 units of meat from a single gazelle by having four villagers skin it.

As your food supply increases, you should create more villagers—and that is the goal of the mission. Once your first villager kills a gazelle, it will take

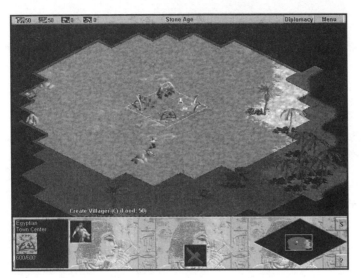

two trips between the kill and the town center for you to have 50 units of food— enough to begin creating another villager.

To create a villager, left click on your town center. A button displaying a villager will appear on the lower-left side of your screen. Left click on that button and work will begin on your next villager.

Ways to Lose

Once you have 50 units of food, you can create a new villager. Click on the villager button and he will appear beside your town center.

The only plausible way to fail this mission is to kill your first villager before he collects 20 units of food—the amount needed to add a second villager. This can be accomplished by having your villager meander aimlessly around the island until he is caught and killed by either of the two tremendously slow-moving alligators residing along the shoreline.

You will probably encounter the first alligator, who is relaxing by some palm trees west of your village. The second alligator is a bit harder to find; it's located on a narrow peninsula northeast of the village.

Alligators indeed have some value—100 units of meat. Besides making great prehistoric purses, they are great little followers. If one of your villagers should encounter the first alligator, have him lead it back to the village by walking ahead of the beast, then pausing for the alligator to catch up. Once the alligator is near your town center, kill it and skin it.

One word of caution—unlike real alligators, the ones in this game have great eyesight. Have your villagers keep their distance so that they don't get bitten. It takes four spears to kill an alligator, and they provide less food than gazelles.

Additional Hints

Do not worry about gathering wood; you are given enough at the beginning of this mission to survive.

Do not concern yourself about gathering enough food to move on to the Tool Age. This is a Stone Age mission; you will not be able to move to the Tool Age by gathering 500 units of food. You will not be able to erect any buildings other than houses, so it's impossible to make ships and leave the island. This mission is strictly about killing gazelles and creating villagers—experimentation beyond these tasks will yield nothing of future value.

Mission 2: Foraging

While the purpose of this mission is to acquaint you with gathering fruit from edible bushes, you are required to build a granary, a storage pit, and a dock to complete it. To do this you will need 370 units of wood—120 to build a storage pit, 120 to build a granary, 100 to build a dock, and 30 to build a house so that you can create more villagers. (To accomplish this mission in a reasonable amount of time you will need a crew of villagers.)

You begin this mission with three villagers and no materials. Fortunately, there are two palm trees and two bushes within sight of your town center. Start this mission by assigning all three of your villagers to pick berries—this will facilitate the creation of a fourth villager. As soon as you have 50 units of food, you can create a villager and assign him to cut down wood. (You can also assign one of your original villagers to cut down wood, too, so that you have quick progress

Assign all three of your original villagers to pick berries. You'll have enough food for a fourth villager in no time.

There is a grove of trees hidden by the fog just west of your town center. Send woodcutters to this forest and set up a storage pit there. There's more than enough wood to finish the mission.

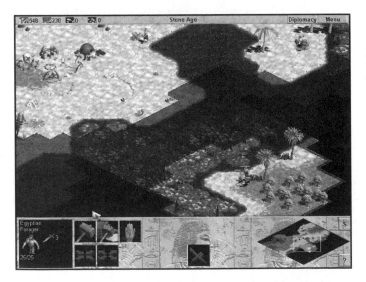

You may run into a stray berry bush or two north of your village, but your hunters were referring to this veritable orchard when they said they saw abundant food.

on both wood and food. You'll need a lot of wood to finish this mission.)

You will need to build a house before you can create a fifth villager. Once your woodcutters finish chopping down the first palm tree, assign one of them to build a house. By the time he finishes, you will have more than enough food to create more villagers and to start looking for more trees and food.

Though it's no Yosemite National Forest, there is a nice grove of trees just east of your village. As you create more villagers, begin sending some of them to this grove for wood. Once they have gathered 120 units, you can build a storage pit by the forest. (You may be tempted to build your storage pit by the eastern tip of the forest. If you walk around the southern edge of the trees, you will find a more central location. This will shorten the distance your woodcutters have to travel to store their work.)

With a team of three or four woodcutters shuttling wood to a nearby storage pit, you will quickly accumulate more than enough wood to successfully finish this mission. The next job is to locate a large cache of berries and build a granary beside it. There is a sandbar southeast of your village. Send two foragers across the sandbar, where they will find enough berries to feed all of Stone Age Cairo. Build a granary beside the berries, and you will have more than enough berries to build a villager army.

Set up a granary beside the berry bushes and your mission is essentially finished. All that's left to accomplish Is placing a dock in the river.

The last task is to build a dock. You can put that dock in any body of water on this map, even in the alligator-infested lake north of your village. It doesn't matter. There are no fish in the waters and no foreign ports to trade with. This dock is simply for show. Once you build the dock, the mission is over.

Ways to Lose

You would have to try very hard to lose this mission. There are three alligators on this map, one in the lake to the north, one at the bottom of the map, and one across the river; but with no enemies to fight and no dangers other than the alligators, your villagers are very safe.

Additional Hints

This mission will not allow your village to advance to the Tool Age. You will only be allowed to erect a granary, a storage pit, a dock, and houses. There aren't even any gazelles to eat. If your villagers get hungry for meat, they'll have to be satisfied with roast alligator.

Mission 3: Discoveries

Contrary to what the mission instructions suggest, winning Mission 3 is not a simple task of looking around the map and finding some old ruins. Unlike your Egyptians, the Libyans have domesticated horses, so they're faster and tougher than your forces. (It's not quite historically accurate, but roll with it.) More importantly, this section of Ancient Libya isn't open for tourism, so don't expect them to roll out the red carpet.

Your job here is to find five hidden sacred symbols before the Libyans do. But before you can look for it, you're going to need to establish a village. Think of the village as a factory for creating more men. There's a certain yin and yang to this mission—the Libyans kill your men, you make more and keep exploring.

The element that makes this mission doubly challenging, however, is an implicit race against the clock. Not only do you have to build a village with sources of food and men as quickly as possible, but you must also find the five sacred sites before the Libyans do, and you can bet the Libyans have a head start.

There are three berry bushes southeast of your camp, just beyond the edge of the fog. Harvest these quickly and you will have enough food to last the rest of the mission.

This is where you start learning about strategizing and multitasking—real-time, strategy-game styled multitasking. You start this mission with a single villager, 15 units of wood, and 90 units of food—more than enough food to create your next villager. Assign your town center to create a villager, then send your first villager to chop down the nearest tree.

When your second villager appears, send him southeast of your town center. There he will find

three berry bushes. Have him start picking the berries from the first bush.

As soon as your villager drops his first load at the town center, begin creating a third villager. (You began the scenario with 90 units of food, so you will have 40 remaining after making your first villager.) Assign that villager to the same bush as you did the first one. Remember, do anything you can to save time.

You should have three or four men before the first Libyans show up at your front door. The good news is that this first group of Libyans are hunters who will not cause any problems. The bad news is that they are looking for sacred sites. In other words, the race has already begun.

With any luck, the first Libyan hunter to pass through your village will be killed by a lion as he walks through the unmapped regions southwest of your town center. If you hear angry growling, chances are that there is one less Libyan hunter in your world.

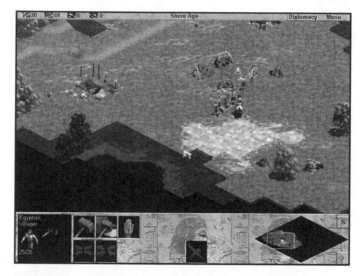

The Libyans will send scouts to attack your villagers. Remember, there is strength in numbers. Send one or two villagers after the Libyans and he may kill them first. Send four or five and you may get all of them back.

The fourth sacred site is right in front of the Libyan's town center. You know they will find that one quickly. They are also likely to notice your forces as they come by and leave a flag to mark that they were there.

A lion guards the first site, just southeast of your village. Have several villagers kill it, then send one man to the site to mark it.

Libyans will begin wandering through your village in search of food and sacred sites very early on. Ignore them. This first Libyan will find a sacred site and a lion guarding it. He doesn't get a roundtrip ticket.

Whether he lives or dies, do not go after this first Libyan. You need to create villagers, gather food, and build a couple of houses as quickly as possible. Assign one of your berry pickers to build a house, create more villagers, and keep the raw materials pouring in. You need villagers, and fast!

Once you have two houses, you can stop chopping wood and concentrate on food. It is very possible to complete this level with eight villagers.

As you progress, you can expect to be visited by armed representatives of the Libyan cavalry. When Libyan scouts ride in and attack, group your men together and create an all-peasant army. It does not take a band of five angry peasants long to beat a basic cavalryman and his horse into humus. As soon as the threat is gone, have your men resume their jobs.

Remember, you will likely lose men on each of these attacks, so keep a steady production of new villagers coming from your

town center. Food equals villagers, and villagers equals survival.

Speaking of survival, remember that first Libyan hunter who (probably) became cat food just south of your village? The first sacred site is just below the stand of trees to the south of your village. Send a group of villagers to kill the lion guarding the site, then have a villager walk over the site to mark it. A blue flag will appear. (There should already be a red flag on the site signaling that the Libyan made it there, too.)

You may want to abandon your village at this point in the mission. Its only purpose is to produce more men should your existing army be destroyed, so why waste valuable resources leaving men to defend it? Throw all your efforts into locating sacred sites. Fail to find at least one of the sites before the Libyans and you forfeit the mission.

The second sacred site is in the southeast corner of the map. Send four villagers to this site. If you send a single man, he may fall prey to the

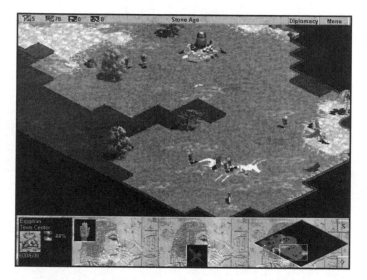

The second site is in the southeast corner of the map.

The third site is just north of your village. A herd of gazelles grazes between the site and your town center. You can kill them if you need the food.

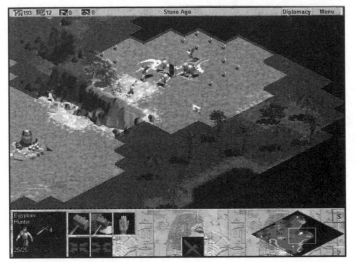

The fourth sacred site is on the cliffs overlooking your village. Several Libyan woodcutters are hard at work around the site, but they will ignore you.

There's no point in fighting this Libyan. Let him kill your villager while your other men hunt for the sacred site. Victory is literally around the corner-and so is a lion, so you had better have a few men to spare.

Libyans. Leave a marker on this site by walking over it and move on to the next site.

The third sacred site is north of your village. You will pass a small herd of gazelles on your way there. If you are short on villagers and need more food, you may wish to have one or two of your men kill a gazelle and skin it while the others move on. Look just north of the gazelles for the sacred site. The Libyans will discover it before you get there, but don't worry, you're still in the race.

There's no point in dawdling. Have your men mark the site by walking over it, then move on to the next site. Have your hunting party move east to the top of a cliff slightly northeast of your village.

The fourth site is in the middle of the map just beyond the stony ledge of that cliff. Send your party to the center of that sacred site to mark it. Do not worry about the Libyan woodcutters chopping trees along the ledge; they won't hinder you.

Now you're on the home stretch. The fourth site is right in front of the Libyan village, so don't expect to leave this area without a fight. (Actually, if you are playing on an easier level or you make it up to Libya Central very quickly, you may pass without meeting a cavalryman, but don't count on it.)

Should a Libyan scout attack you as you pass the town center, do not stay to fight. There's no advantage in fighting at this point in the mission—you're too close to the end. As he attacks your villager, send your other villagers toward the grove of trees to the east. The last site is right beyond the trees.

Ignore the lion and the cavalry and get to the fifth sacred site beyond the trees due east of the Libyan town center. You accomplish your mission the moment you reach this site.

You must send more than one villager on this last leg of the mission because there's a hungry lion guarding the site. Should a lone villager stumble into the lion, he will likely become an hors d'oeuvre before marking the site.

Remember that you do not need to capture this site, just have one villager walk across it and you accomplish your mission. If the lion attacks one of your villagers, send the rest to the sacred marking and the mission is ended.

Ways to Lose

The easiest way to lose this mission is to spend too much time trying to decide what to do next. Wasting time and resources building extra houses will slow you down, but the error is not fatal. Waiting too long to build houses so that you have to stop creating men while your villagers cut down trees and build two houses will slow you down too, but you can recover from that. Waiting too

long to create new villagers and hesitating before you send your villagers to attack Libyan horsemen will leave you too weak to win.

The most important decision in Mission 3 concerns sending your men out to find the sacred sites. The fifth site, the only one you are likely to find before the Libyans, is very close to their village. The moment they find it, all is lost, so send out your first hunting party as soon as it is big enough to defend itself. A group of four to five should do the trick.

Additional Hints

Do not bother trying to defend the southwest site even if it is just below your village. You will need too many men too quickly, and it will distract or stop your all-important race to forage for food and create more men.

You will not be able to build a stable, an archery range, or barracks in this mission. So don't bother chopping wood, and get used to the idea of attacking cavalrymen with a team of villagers.

A cavalryman can kill several villagers in one-on-one fights, but if attacked by four or more villagers at once, he generally dies before killing a single enemy.

If you prefer the sure-fire method, have two villagers continue cutting down trees until they collect 120 units of wood. Once you have these, you can build a storage pit near the trees and speed up your wood production, or you can build a granary near the bushes and gather food more quickly.

Even though the bushes will run out of berries before the forest runs out of wood, you should go with the granary. Gathering food and increasing your population should be your top priority. Building the granary will enable your villagers to harvest berries more effectively.

Do not try to accumulate enough food to move on to the Tool Age; that option is not available in this mission.

Mission 4: Dawn of a New Age

It's evolution time. Your society is finally going to cross the bridge from a village of Stone Age hunter-gatherers to a Tool Age town of fisher-hunter-gatherers. That may not seem like much of a change on paper, but wait until later, when you have to find ways to exist without berry bushes and gazelles while waging wars.

Evolving your society to the Tool Age is more expensive than creating peasants. First, there's the much stiffer requirement of 500 units of food. (Later evolutions are far more expensive, so don't complain just yet.) That means this mission is mostly about gathering food and wood as quickly as possible.

You begin this mission with three villagers and no supplies. Your first task is to decide a career path for your village—you can begin this rather leisurely paced mission by chopping down trees and building houses, a dock, and fishing boats, or you can stick to the old methods and hunt for food.

If you decide to hunt for food, forget about foraging: there are no berries in the vicinity. Instead of foraging, you will have to hunt mammoth-sized food supplies-i.e., there are two elephants near your village. The good news here is that elephants represent 300 units of wholesome food, and they are more than happy to come toward your villagers and your town center. The bad

This elephant represents plenty of food on the hoof, so to speak, but he's not a very cooperative or happy meal. Notice the dead villager decaying at the top of the screen; he didn't get that way from old age.

You can only place docks on a relatively straight stretch of shore.

Where there are whales, there's food. If you see a whale dive into a tile, lead your fishing boat there and you'll catch up to 250 units of food.

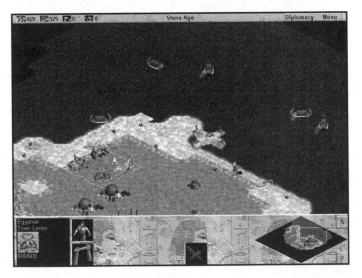

Fishing boats are efficient and economical vehicles for catching food. Unlike hunters, you don't need food to make them, and they can carry up to 15 units of food at a time. To finish this level and get to the next, make four or five boats.

news is that they are tough and usually kill one of your villagers before they die. In this case, the safest bet is to gather enough wood to build a fleet of fishing boats and leave the enormous and ill-tempered pachyderms alone.

Either way, you should build a dock in this mission and experiment with fishing as a method of gathering food. One experiment you might perform is to try to discover what is making the grunting noise you hear as soon as the mission begins. It sounds like an elephant clearing its trunk, but the sound is coming from the ocean. (Here's a little hint: It's a whale, it's worth 250 units of food, and it doesn't hit you with its trunk.)

You need 100 units of wood to build a dock, and an additional 50 units of wood for each fishing boat you construct. In order to build boats, like villagers, you will need houses, so have your three villagers continue chopping wood. You should build three houses by the halfway point of the mission so that you can construct a large fleet of fishing boats.

Once you have 100 units of wood, you can begin building a dock. Erecting docks is no different than building houses except that they must be placed in the water with one edge touching a straight edge of land.

As you gather more wood, build at least four fishing boats. The goal of this mission is to build two Stone Age buildings and gather 500 units of food so you can evolve to the Tool Age. Each fishing boat can carry up to 15 units of fish per load, so the more boats you send out, the faster you will reach your 500 units.

You beat this mission the moment your society advances to the Tool Age. Notice that the houses are no longer huts and the town center looks like a structure instead of a pile of elephant bones.

Boats are controlled like woodcutters or foragers. Look around the water for fish or whales. When you find some, left click on your boat to select it, then right click on a tile in which you saw the fish or whales to send your boat fishing in that area. The boat will automatically shuttle between the dock and the tile until it has caught all of the fish in that area.

Watch your food unit totals. Once you have 500, left click on your town center, then click on the Tool Age icon along the bottoms of the screen to evolve to the Tool Age. This nifty bit of evolution could take a few minutes.

Ways to Lose

The only way to fail in this mission is to coax the elephants into killing your men before you have enough food to create more. There's an elephant grazing just a little west of your village. If you send your villagers to kill him, he will probably kill one of them and seriously injure another before he dies. On the other hand, skin that elephant quickly and you will be halfway to your goal of 500 units of food.

Should you still wish to go elephant hunting after losing villagers on the first elephant, there's another one in the southwest corner of your map. There's also a lion on a small island, but your men cannot reach him.

Additional Hints

There are no other nations in this level, so don't bother building a trading ship—you'll just waste wood and time. Once you launch your fishing boats, your landlocked woodcutters become unimportant. Do not create more villagers; it will needlessly prolong the mission.

Mission 5: Skirmish

Don't expect your problems to become easier now that your village has entered the Tool Age; they're about to become more complex. You have the misfortune of having become the envy of your neighbors. Your people have food and stone for making tools, and the Upper Egyptians want to share in your wealth, but they are taking without asking. They've sent a band of thugs to raid your land. Now is the chance to test your newly created Tool Age army in combat.

Actually, this "skirmish" doesn't offer much of a test. The king of Upper Egypt must not be in too big a rush to confiscate Lower Egyptian land or he would have staged a full-scale invasion instead of sending three archers and four axemen.

As it turns out, this is one of the few missions in which you have exact parity with your opponent. You begin with three archers and four axemen. Hopefully, you will have more than they do by the end of the scenario.

Since you and the Upper Egyptians have identically matched units, this mission could turn into a battle of attrition in which your army slugs it out with the enemy until only one man walks away. That might be a fun way to play the mission, but tying your future on a flip of the coin is no way to run an empire, especially when a little strategy will guarantee that you have the last men standing. Besides, this is one mission you can win without losing a single man.

Begin the mission by separating your men into two groups—axemen and archers. Holding down the left button on your mouse, drag your cursor over the axemen to select all four of them. Now click the "Group" button along the bottom of the screen (it's the one with the four arrows toward the center). Next, select and group your archers.

As you move into battle, you want to keep your axemen in front of your archers. Axemen can absorb more punishment and deal out more damage at close range. If an enemy axeman gets too close to your archers, he is liable to kill two or even all three of them before they can kill him. Use your axemen to protect your archers, and employ your archers to soften up the enemy at long range before your axemen confront them.

Once you've grouped and arranged your army, march them toward the northern edge of the map. When they come to a large lake; have them travel along the east shore until they reach the top of the map.

They will arrive at a spot where there is a small grove of trees just east of the lake. Send your axemen around the top of the grove and have your archers move around the lower edge of the trees.

Just beyond the lower edge of the trees is a stone ledge, guarded by an Upper Egyptian axeman. Have your archers get close to the edge and shoot arrows at him. If

Rather than fight your enemies face-to-face, pick them off. Have your archers needle this unsuspecting axeman from below the ledge, where he can't possibly reach them.

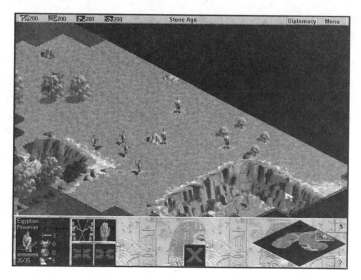

This axeman will try to walk out of the ledge and get your archers, but even if he makes it out, he'll be too injured to hurt them.

f you have your archers attacking the Upper Egyptian axemen from far away, and your axemen attacking their archers from up close, you'll win this fight quite easily.

you position your archers so that they face northwest of (rather than parallel to) the axeman, you will pin him against the ledge, prohibiting him from escaping. If your archers are parallel to him, he'll probably be able to walk away before they kill him (but he will be injured and easier to kill when you see him again).

Once you have shot the defenseless Upper Egyptian, have your archers join your axemen at the top of the trees. You will find that they are standing in front of a pass leading to the top of the ledge. The pass is large enough for your entire army to climb through. Have your archers stand at the left side of this ramp while your axemen march up the right side. That way your archer's superior visual range will enable you to see farther in case any enemy soldiers approach.

You will find a crevice just beyond the top of the ramp. Have your archers march to the edge of the crevice and shoot the axeman below. He will walk out of range and attempt to climb out of the crevice and attack your archers. Have your archers retreat and your axemen kill him.

Two Upper Egyptian archers will follow him. Have your archers take out one of them, and have one of your axemen kill the other. With two axemen and two archers dead, the rest of the Upper Egyptian army will be child's play.

You will find the last Upper Egyptian archer minding his post along the stony ledge of the cliff. Have all three of your archers shoot him. Because their three arrows will hit him for every shot he fires, they will annihilate him while only absorbing minor damage.

The final Upper Egyptian raider is an axeman hiding in the easternmost part of the crevice. Have all four of your axemen attack him. When he falls, the mission ends.

Ways to Lose

Do not rush into this battle. If you charge into the Upper Egyptians head-on, they may pepper your axemen with arrows from on top of the cliff. Lose your axemen and your archers won't stand a chance. Remember, the key to this mission is a rounded attack—your archers neutralize their axemen, and your axemen neutralize their archers.

Additional Hints

Do not let your archers follow that first Upper Egyptian axeman if he walks away. He will lead them toward the two enemy archers guarding the cliffs to the east, and you may lose an archer if you try to shoot it out with them.

Try to herd your axemen so that they are always in your archers' line of sight. That way your archers can inflict additional damage upon the enemy if attacked.

Attack enemy axemen with your archers while they arc far away, then lead them toward your axemen. By the time they get to your axemen, they'll be ready to drop.

Have your archers attack when enemy soldiers are in geographically vulnerable spots, such as on ledges and in crevices, from which they cannot fight back.

Match up your forces so that your archers attack their axemen from a distance and your axemen thrash their archers at point-blank range.

Don't expect later fights to be this easy.

Mission 6: Farming

There are two distinct objectives to this mission: finding the fabled ruins and building farms. These goals are not connected in any tangible way, except that you will need to face the Nubians to gain control of the ruins, and farming will become markedly easier without the Nubians coming by and killing your farmers.

You begin this level with a Tool Age village, three villagers, three clubmen, and 100 units of wood, food, gold, and stone. You also have a granary and three foraging shrubs (each shrub has 150 units of food) on the western edge of your village. Your first task at the beginning of this mission should be to assign all of

Upgrade from clubmen to axemen as soon as possible by clicking on your barracks then clicking the axe icon toward the bottom of the screen.

your villagers to pick the food from those shrubs.

You also begin this mission with a barracks. Select the barracks by clicking on it with your left mouse button, then left clicking on the axe icon on the bottom of your screen. This will upgrade your soldiers from clubmen to axemen. Axemen are tougher than clubmen, and your sworn enemies, the Nubians, have axemen. It costs 100 units of food to make this upgrade, but it's worth it.

As your foragers collect food, create one villager to speed your food-gathering efforts and three soldiers to guard your village. You'll need those extra soldiers shortly.

The first party of Nubians will attack from the north. It will consist of a hunter, who poses no threat, followed by a lone clubman, followed by four axemen, followed by a fifth axeman, followed by another clubman. The axemen pose a significant danger, but if your foragers continue to gather food while the battle goes on, you will be able to create additional soldiers should you need them.

Once this initial battle is over, the Nubians will not attack for a while. Use this time to store up food and build your village. The three bushes by the granary represent only 450 units of food, so don't create an extravagantly large army at this time.

Build two more villagers (you will have a total of six), and assign two of them to chop down the palm trees closest to your town square. Once you have 150 units of wood, assign one of your villagers to build a market. Building a market will enable you to build farms; it's part of the Technology Tree.

By the time the market is finished, your villagers will have picked all of the berries from the bushes near the granary. Assign them to cut down wood. You'll need 75 units of wood for each farm. In this level, there are no fish in the waters, so the only way to keep your food supplies high once your foraging areas are depleted is to farm.

Have your villagers clear the trees away from your granary and build a ring of three farms around it. The only difference between building farms and other buildings is that the villager who erects the farm automatically becomes a farmer and maintains it. You want to have up to six farms up and working before too long.

Now that the Nubian threat is stalled and you have a steady supply of food, it's time to rebuild your army and take the offensive. Tool Age farms are a good source for food—not overabundant, but fertile enough to upgrade your army. Build a storage pit north of your village around the area where you fought the Nubians. Once it is erected, your woodsmen will harvest more quickly.

Next, select the storage pit with your mouse. You will see a row of buttons

The Nubian's first attack will come in waves. It begins with a single clubman followed by several axemen. Have your army ready, and build more axemen as the battle progresses. Lose this fight and you'll most likely have to restart the mission.

Build farms close to your granary. That way your farmers will not have to walk far to store food they produce.

Upgrade your army's fighting ability by clicking on your storage pit, then clicking on the spear icon. You can also upgrade their armor from this menu.

If you do not seal off the bridge in the center of the map quickly, the Nubians will try to settle in your territory. Stop them. If they create a stronghold on your side of the river, you will waste time and energy winning you own land back.

along the bottom of your screen. These buttons allow you to upgrade your army. The Tool Age spear icon on the left lets you improve your soldiers' hand-to-hand combat skills. Invest 100 units of food in this upgrade as quickly as possible; it will prove invaluable.

While you have been building and strengthening your army, the Nubians have made a modest attempt to expand their territory. There is a river running through the middle of the map in this scenario, with a shallow land bridge halfway up the map. Send your axemen to destroy the houses constructed by the Nubians on your side of the river and to guard the bridge from further Nubian encroachments. (A small party of Nubians have been sent to challenge your men, so make sure you have at least seven healthy axemen when you seal off the bridge.)

This will not be the last time you see the industrious Nubians, however. By this time they have also built a dock just north of the land bridge. You can take care of this dock in one of two

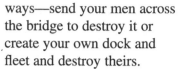

ways—send your men across the bridge to destroy it or create your own dock and fleet and destroy theirs.

The safest bet is the latter. This not only allows you to eradicate their naval threat, but also enables you to control the center of the map. You can guard the land bridges with your ships and prevent their transports from bringing soldiers to your shores. Create a dock (100 units of wood) and at least one scout ship (135 units of wood each), and destroy the Nubian dock.

You should expect to be attacked by at least one Nubian and possibly several scout ships while destroying the dock. You may even decide to send your men over the land bridge to attack the dock during the naval battle. After the dock is destroyed, take out their scout ship, fishing boat, and transport.

With the Nubian navy out of the way, the time has come to march your army across the river and into Nubia. The Nubians do not have a large standing army, but they have several archers

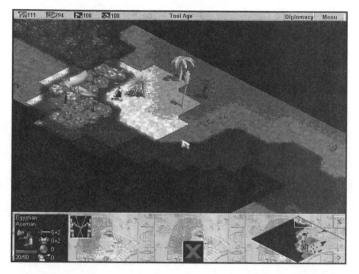

The Nubians' first scout ship will head north and hide at the top of the map.

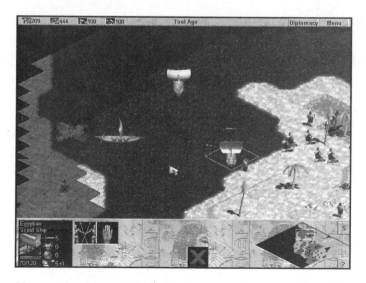

You need only one ship to destroy an entire enemy fleet if you post a repairman beside it for repairs. This scout ship will destroy three Nubian scout ships and their dock.

Controlling this bridge means controlling the entire mission. Once your forces are sufficiently strong, cross the bridge and take the war to the Nubians.

The Nubians' fight for life begins as Egyptian forces fly into town.

who will quietly snipe at your soldiers while they destroy buildings. Nubia also has a guard tower.

Assign your men to destroy military targets first—stables, archery ranges, and barracks. Also, assign four scouts to destroy the tower at the east end of the city. If you leave it alone, it will serve as an attack source for picking off your men while you are not looking.

As the battle progresses, keep an eye out for more archers. When they appear, send your axemen to destroy them.

Once you've annihilated Nubia's military targets, there's no need to kill the villagers and destroy their houses. They're not going to rebuild their civilization in this scenario. (Total annihilation is a good practice, however. All it takes is one villager with 120 units of wood or a storage pit to rebuild the entire empire.)

After you've finished massacring the Nubians, it's time to find the ruins. There are no forces guarding the ruins, so there's no need to send a large army. Just send

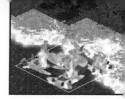

a single axeman or scout along the southeast edge of the map. Once he passes the ruins, they will change in color from red to blue, signifying that you have captured it.

The last objective in this mission is to accumulate 800 units of food. Once you have neutralized the Nubians and found the ruins, simply wait until your farms produce enough food.

With the Nubian town center in flames and their barracks, archery range, and stables undefended, the town is crumbling. The difficult part of this mission is over.

Ways to Lose

The first Nubian incursion poses a very serious threat. If you have thrown all of your resources into creating villagers and harvesting food, they will overpower your soldiers and destroy your village. Make sure you create additional soldiers and upgrade from clubmen to axemen before the Nubians arrive. Upgrade their fighting abilities at the first opportunity.

Additional Hints

If it looks as though your soldiers are going to lose that inaugural fight with the Nubians, have one of your villagers abandon the village and hide in the southern corner of the map. Have him return and resume picking berries when the Nubians are finished destroying your houses.

With any luck you will be able to resume this mission without restarting.

Tool Age markets let you upgrade your farm production, gold mining, and stone mining. These are expensive upgrades that you should only facilitate early on in your missions. They make a big difference, but they cost a lot and do not pay for themselves if you make them too late. Upgrade your farms before launching your invasion. (The cost will be 200 units of food and 50 units of wood.)

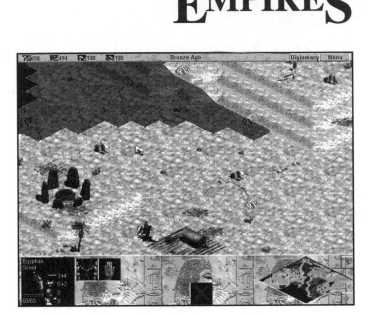

The ruins are along the southeast edge of the scenario map. Locate it, and it will turn blue, signifying that you control it.

Don't upgrade abilities you are not going to use. There is no reason to upgrade your village's stone and gold mining abilities in this mission since there are no gold or stone deposits on the map.

You can defeat an entire enemy fleet with one ship if you have the ship fight from along the shore. Post a villager beside the ship and have him make repairs as it takes damage. Enemy ships usually ignore peasant repairmen, so they will not shoot him.

Farms are not permanent structures. They run out of food. Make sure you have a constant supply of wood coming in throughout this mission and check to verify that your farms are still intact. If you lose track of your farms during the battle, you'll have to wait while your farmers build new ones and save up food before you can accumulate 800 food units and finish the mission.

You do not have to destroy every Nubian building and kill every Nubian to win this mission. Once they are too weakened to thwart your progress, concentrate on finding the ruins and producing food.

During the battle, watch for Nubian builders. They will try to reconstruct barracks and archery ranges. Stop them and destroy their construction sites quickly to avoid having to deal with completed buildings.

Don't bother building an archery range; this is a hand-to-hand kind of mission. Build a stable and send scouts into battle instead.

Mission 7: Trade

The pharaohs dearly loved their monuments. In this mission, a pharaoh needs you to contribute 1,000 units of gold and 1,000 units of stone to help him build a monument. You've got the stone supplies near your village, but you'll have to trade with your neighbors for the gold. The good news here is that they will trade, whether they like you or not.

You begin this mission with a Tool Age village, three villagers, a dock, a granary, and a storage pit. Your resources include 200 units of food, 200 units of wood, and 200 units of stone. There are four berry bushes in your village and more are nearby.

Start this mission by assigning two of your villagers to forage for food while your third villager chops wood from the forest by the storage pit. As you create new villagers, assign them to chop wood and forage. When you have enough wood, build a fishing boat and two trading boats.

You'll need lots of villagers to cut wood for this mission. To reach your objectives, you'll need to trade 1,250 units of food or lumber for more than 1,250 units of gold. (It should have been 1,000 units, but you automatically pay 25 percent of the gold you receive as a tribute, and it does not go into your storage.)

Don't worry about the menacing-looking ballistas guarding the yellow port. They won't shoot at you unless you shoot at them. By the way, don't shoot at them. In fact, don't even build any ships that can shoot at them.

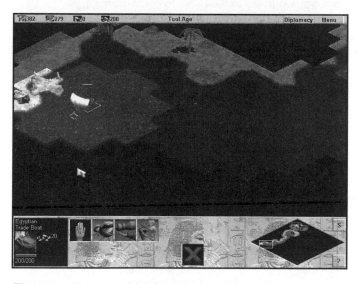

Thutmose II's port, which is yellow in color, is in the westernmost corner of the scenario map.

Once you've built two Tool Age buildings and have enough food, you can advance your village to the Bronze Age. The biggest benefit of Bronze Age technology in this mission is that your fishing boats will be able to catch more fish and your trading boats will be able to carry more cargo.

The stone deposits in the western desert hold more than the 1,000 units of stone you need to meet your objective.

While there are three nations existing in this mission (excluding yours) only two of them have ports—Nebuchadnezzar's Babylonians and Thutmose II's Egyptians. The Babylonian dock is located on an island southeast of your village. The Egyptian dock is in the southwest corner of the map.

Once you have trading boats, you should send them to these ports to trade lumber for gold. Left click on a trading boat to select it, then click on the "trade wood for gold" icon along the bottom of the screen—it has a picture of a wooden spindle and a knife. Once you have configured your trading boats, lead them to the Babylonian and Egyptian docks, right click on the docks, and the boats will automatically shuttle from your dock to your trading partners.

Along with 1,000 units of gold, you need 1,000 units of stone to complete this mission. There is a large deposit of stone in a desert west of your village. Be careful sending villagers into the desert—a lion is hiding near the trees. Before sending villagers after the stone, assemble a hunting party to kill the lion.

Once you've killed the lion, send three men into the desert, where they will find a gentle hill. The stone deposit is at the top of the hill. Have your men build a storage pit beside the deposit. Once the pit is finished, they can begin mining the stone.

There's not much left to do once your men begin mining the stone. You've set the mechanisms in order; now you have to sit back and watch them perform their jobs. As long as your woodcutters provide lumber, your trading ships will bring gold.

If you want to create more villagers and ships to speed the process, you'll need to provide more food. You can build farms in this mission, but fishing offers the most efficient way to get food. The waters along your coast are teeming with fish. Create several fishing boats and assign them to the various fishing spots.

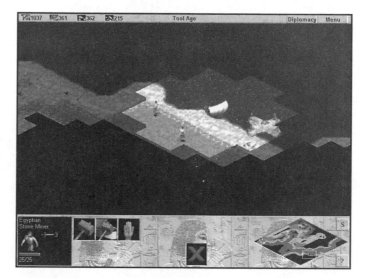

Archers guard the Babylonian dock, which is located on the Island southeast of your village.

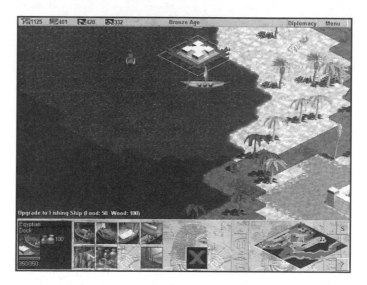

Your Bronze Age dock can upgrade all of your ships.

AGE of EMPIRES

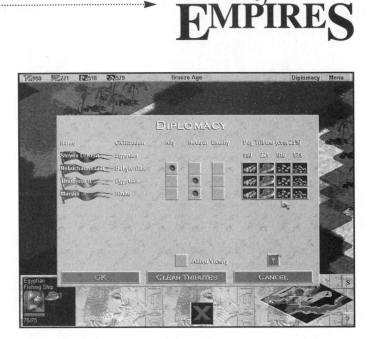

The "Diplomacy Screen" shows whether you are friendly or ambivalent toward other tribes.

Who knows why Thutmose II built this dock? He doesn't use it. The only ships in this mission belong to you.

With no enemies to invade you, the key to winning this mission is setting up a steady supply of logs and food to trade for gold. Create lots of fishing and trading boats, and keep your routes hopping. You'll have ample supplies soon enough.

Ways to Lose

Thutmose II has ballistas and several archers guarding the Babylonian port, but these forces will not attack you. The surest way to lose this mission is to get spooked by your trading partners. If you do not build an armada of scout ships and do not attack their ports or people, your relationships will be profitable for all parties. The only way to lose this mission is to cut off the trading routes. Destroy those ports and you're out of luck.

Additional Hints

Have your first villagers forage for berries so that you can create more villagers to chop wood. The key material in this mission is wood. You

need wood to build boats and to trade for gold. Don't waste time and materials building lots of farms; they won't help.

Upgrade your village to the Bronze Age, then upgrade your trading ships so that they can carry more materials. You'll reach your objectives more quickly.

Upgrade woodcutting and stone mining productivity in your market. The investment will pay for itself by bringing a speedier conclusion to this mission.

Upgrade your fishing fleet so that your boats can obtain food more quickly.

Mission 8: Crusade

It's time your village learned the power of proselytizing. The Libyans have a big gun (it's actually a big bow-and-arrow known as a ballista), and you want it. Attacking it won't do any good—you'd only destroy it. What can you do to make it yours? Send a priest out and convert it.

You begin this mission with 100 units of wood, 100 units of food, a Bronze Age village, four villagers, and a priest. The village has bushes for foraging, a temple, a barracks, a storage pit with nearby forests and stone deposits, and a granary. There's a small gold deposit (300 units) a little southeast of the village, just beyond the fog of war.

Begin by building two more villagers and assigning three to gather food. Send the fourth villager to mine gold. When your new pair arrives, send them to join him. Use this gold to purchase the speed and conversion upgrades your temple offers for your priest. You may not like spending 270 units of gold on clerical upgrades, but these talents are important when looking down the barrel of an angry ballista.

As your foragers store more food, train eight axemen. Once you have

This small deposit of gold is located just south of your village. Send three villagers to mine it as soon as possible.

The temple has four icons—the first sells you a new priest, the second makes your priest more effective at converting enemies, the third doubles his hit points, and the last icon makes him move faster. Use the gold outside your village to make your priest faster and better at proselytizing.

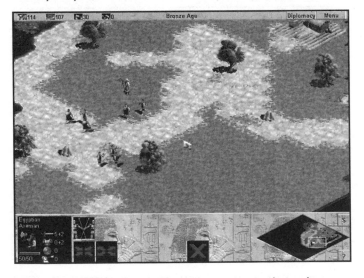

With eight axemen and a faster, more persuasive, priest, you're ready to collect the ballista.

upgraded your priest and created your axemen, your ballista—conversion team is ready to collect its prize.

Your village is built along the northern edge of a lake. Libya's town center, complete with a ballista and several archers, is in the center of the map just south of that lake. Have your raiding party follow the edge of the lake toward the Libyans—your axemen should walk a few paces ahead of your priest. When you get to the south shore, assign your men to charge into the darkened area.

You will see the ballista before you see the archers. As soon as you see an archer, assign your axemen to attack him. Your priest should still be by the shore of the lake. Left click on your priest to select him, then right click on the ballista to begin the conversion process. Your priest will begin chanting and waving his arms.

As soon as the ballista turns blue, signifying its conversion, left click on it to select it, then assign it to move toward your

town center. Your axemen will keep the archers busy as it leaves, but if it should get struck with arrows, your priest can heal it. Just left click on the priest and right click on the ballista.

Have your priest and the ballista return to your town center. Your mission is accomplished when they arrive.

Ways to Lose

This is a combat mission, meaning there are lots of pitfalls and traps. If your priest dies, you will be unable to convert the ballista, and destroying it doesn't earn any points. Do not send your priest after the ballista alone, with too small a guard, or ahead of your axemen. Any one of these mistakes can result in failure.

Once the ballista is converted, the Libyans will attempt to destroy it. You'll have to start over again if they succeed, so make sure that your axemen keep their archers busy while the ballista escapes.

Have your priest stand by the lake and convert the ballista as your axemen attack the Libyan archers. Expect casualties.

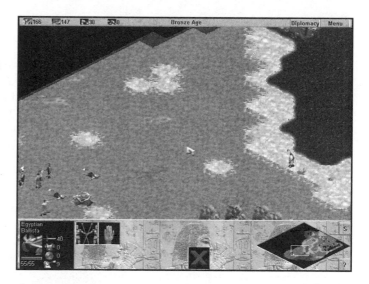

Once the ballista is converted, the Libyans will try to destroy it. Move the ballista from the battlefield as your men slug it out with the archers.

Having fled from the bloody field of honor, your freshly converted ballista awaits your every command!

Additional Hints

Don't bother upgrading your priest with double-hit points. When you're dealing with super weapons such as ballistas, double-hit points mean nothing.

Once you've collected 270 units of gold and upgraded your priest, the gold deposit becomes meaningless. Assign the gold miners to help forage for food.

If you decide to wreak some havoc on the Libyans with the ballista, a foolish waste of time, make sure that you do so at long range. Even archers can overwhelm a ballista from point-blank range.

While priests can convert enemies from far away, they need to get close to their target when they heal people. Bring your ballista to your priest so that both are far from the battle should you need to heal the ballista.

This is a particularly fast mission, requiring only between 20 and 30 minutes to complete. Do not waste time building too big an army: it's unnecessary and it can even work against you. If you have too many axemen around the ballista before it's converted, one of them is bound to attack it.

Mission 9: River Outpost

The Nubians are back and more powerful than ever. The Pharaoh doesn't want to fight them; he just wants to regulate those who come roaming along the Nile by setting up a stronghold. This might have been a simple architectural lesson if the Nubians weren't stubborn about being regulated. They're not the only Nile inhabitants that will resent your presence on the island. Other native inhabitants will also try to prevent your men from making themselves at home.

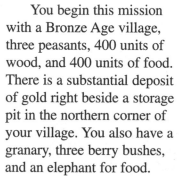

You begin this mission with a Bronze Age village, three peasants, 400 units of wood, and 400 units of food. There is a substantial deposit of gold right beside a storage pit in the northern corner of your village. You also have a granary, three berry bushes, and an elephant for food.

The first priority in this mission is to establish a fleet. Assign one of your villagers to build a dock while the other two mine gold.

Start creating more villagers while the first villager builds the dock. You'll want at least ten villagers before long. You should have eight cutting wood, while two others build houses and a government center.

Once you have an ample supply of wood coming in, build two scout ships, then upgrade your dock and fleet to war galleys. The primary use for your navy in this mission is to destroy enemy towers. War galleys can shoot their arrows farther than towers can, so your ships will be able to sweep the towers out of your

You will need a large team of hunters if you want to kill and skin this elephant without losing villagers.

You begin this mission with more than enough wood to build a dock. Make building the dock a top priority.

AGE of EMPIRES

The enemy has a ring of towers guarding its island. Have your war galleys attack the towers from long range.

Your galleys can also kill the island's lions and alligators to clear the way for your villagers.

villagers' way without sustaining damage.

You will be able to see the island from the shore. Once you have two galleys, have them attack the tower at the eastern tip of the island. Have your fleet destroy enemy towers and kill lions and alligators as they travel counter-clockwise around the island. By the time they finish, the only dangerous creature remaining on the island will be a lion.

As your fleet clears the island, build a transport boat. Make sure that you have at least 120 units of wood, have your villagers board the transport boat, then take them to the island.

To have your villagers board the transport boat, left-click on the men, then right-click on the boat. The boat will move in their direction to meet them. Once your villagers have boarded the boat, left-click on the boat, right-click on the off-load icon, then right-click on the eastern shore of the island, around the ruins of the first tower.

You will see the last lion as your villagers off-load. Select all five villagers and have them attack the lion. Once he is dead, have them build a storage pit.

As your villagers build the pit, send your transport back for the rest of your villagers. When they arrive, assign your first wave of workers to harvest stone while your second wave builds a town center. Once you have 300 units of stone, have your villagers build two towers. After they finish the job, you will officially control the island and win the mission.

Having just completed their town center, a group of villagers prepares to help some comrades build two guard towers.

Ways to Lose

While it probably would not cost you the mission, underestimating the danger on that island would be a serious mistake. Those towers may be no match for a couple of war galleys, but the towers would turn your peasants into cat food that the lions and alligators would be very happy to eat.

Make sure your galleys go all the way around the island as they destroy the

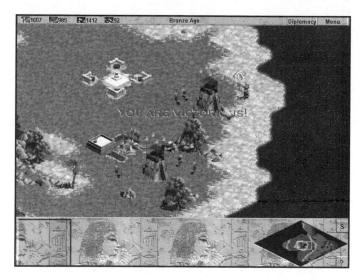

Once you finish the town center and the towers, the island and mission are yours.

towers and kill the animals. Your peasants won't have any problems killing a single lion or a couple of alligators, but too many lions or a remaining tower could be fatal.

Additional Hints

At this point in the game, you should be looking for efficient ways to run your campaign. The waters around the island have several fishing holes and a couple of whales. Don't waste your time and materials building farms. Create a couple of fishing boats and your food needs will be solved for the entire mission.

If you find yourself with a surplus of wood, build an archery range. An archer could offer your villagers good protection against lions and alligators on the island.

You need to build a government center before you can build a town center. Have one of your villagers build a government center early on.

Don't bother advancing your village to the Iron Age; it won't affect the outcome of this mission.

Don't get carried away gathering materials. You need 300 units of stone to build two towers. Once you have enough, stop mining and start building.

Mission 10: Naval Battle

Now they've done it! The Libyans have stolen the Pharaoh's tribute and he wants it back. That means that you will not only have to defeat the Libyan fleet, but you'll also have to take the battle to their homeland so that you can recover the stolen booty.

You begin this mission with a Bronze Age village, three villagers, a market, a granary with nearby foraging bushes, a stable, a storage pit, a dock, and 200 units each of wood, food, gold, and stone. Your first objective should be to gain control of the sea, so assign your villagers to cut wood as you begin building your navy.

Create one villager and assign him to forage while your first villagers continue cutting wood. Use your remaining food to upgrade your fighting ships from scout boats to war galleys. As soon as you have enough money, build two more villagers to help gather food, then upgrade your fishing boats. You'll want a good supply of wood coming in so that you can build a strong navy and a good fishing fleet.

Upgrading to war galleys will deplete your food supply, but the added firepower will pay off shortly. You'll be visited by a couple of Libyan scout ships almost immediately. They will attack your dock, but don't worry, it's a sturdy building.

As soon as your dock is finished, upgrade from scout to galleys to start building your navy. The enemy scout ships will engage your galley as soon as it appears, so send a villager to the dock to repair your ship as it fights. Two scout ships are no match for a galley with a repairman, so expect this fight to end in a first-round knockout.

Once the battle is over, you will have a brief time to rest and plan. Use this time to build up your labor force; you'll need lots of wood so that you can build three galleys and three upgraded fishing boats. If you do it early enough in the mission, upgrading your woodcutting ability at the market is a wise idea.

Once you have three galleys, your first task should

The first Libyan ships will arrive quickly. Upgrade your ships from scouts to galleys and build your first ship. It takes scouts a long time to destroy a dock; there's no need to hurry.

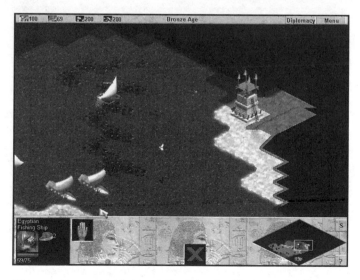

The westernmost tower on the island will try to attack your fishing boats and galleys. Make it your first victim as you take the fight to the Libyans.

The island to the west is covered with towers and lions; good thing there's no reason to land men on it.

Having thrown most of their fleet at your dock early on, the Libyans have few ships left for this war. You may encounter one or two scout boats on your way to the northern island, but they pose little threat to your galleys.

be to destroy the tower on the western tip of the island just off your shores. This tower threatens your fishing boats, so have your galleys attack it. Unfortunately, it's an upgraded tower, so send your boats back to your repairman when they've taken on too much damage. If you need to, have your boats shuttle back and forth between the repairman and the tower until the battle is over.

Once you've finished with the tower, take control of the sea by destroying the Libyans' dock. Group your galleys, then send them to the dock. Libyan archers will attack your ship as you destroy the dock. They pose a more immediate threat than the dock, so kill the archers as soon as they appear, then go back to work on the dock.

While your galleys are out making trouble, create more villagers and begin mining gold from the deposits near your village. If you keep your gold, food, and wood harvesting teams going while your ships fight the bad guys, you'll have more than enough supplies to last you for the rest of the mission by the time your galleys destroy the enemy's dock and towers.

Once you've destroyed the dock, keep your eyes peeled. Those persistent Libyans may try to build a new one. If you notice four stakes appearing in the water (that's what enemy docks look like when they're under construction), have your galleys fire in that direction.

Once the dock is destroyed, the next step is to neutralize any soldiers or towers on the Libyans' island. The Libyans have hoplites, cavalry, and other

Archers will shoot arrows at your ships as you attack their dock. Since the Libyans are unlikely to build more ships, their dock poses little threat. Take out the archers as soon as you see them, then finish working on the dock.

Iron Age threats. Use your fleet to destroy these tactical targets (including powerful infantry and cavalry units), and you won't need a major landing force. The mission will end faster.

If you created a large team of woodcutters, gold miners, and fishing boats early in the mission, you should have thousands of units of gold, lumber, and food by this time. Assign your villagers to build two Bronze Age buildings. (One of these should be a government center.) Once these buildings are up, you can use your food and gold to advance your village to the Iron Age.

As an Iron Age civilization, you can upgrade your dock to build triremes and catapult triremes—ships that fire large, projectile weapons instead of arrows. You can make these ships' weapons even more powerful by using the projectile weapons' upgrade available in your government center.

As your ships destroy the Libyans' coastal buildings, build one catapult trireme. With the upgraded catapult, this ship has such a long firing range that it will be able to destroy most of the buildings on the north island. Use it to kill any soldiers you find hiding from your other ships as well.

Note the tower just beyond the dock. Get too close to shore and it will sink your ships. Also, note that there is no siege workshop beside the tower; the Libyans will build one in that spot the moment you look away.

The Libyans will try to rebuild their dock. Catch it quickly enough and you can destroy it with a single arrow. Look for four posts sticking out of the water.

While your catapult is battering the island, build a transport ship. There's no need to upgrade this ship, once your catapult and standard triremes finish their awful work, there won't be enough enemies left to stop you. You need only one soldier or two villagers on this ship to finish your work.

Load a soldier or two villagers on the transport, and have it drop them near the site of the destroyed Libyan dock. Have your triremes go to this site as well, but keep your catapult trireme away. If it sees an enemy, it will fire and may inadvertently mash your men into mush.

The stolen tribute is just beyond the line of sight, stowed behind a brick wall. Have your soldier or villagers walk around the wall and approach the tribute. It will change color from red to blue to signify that you now control it. Return the tribute to your transport and ship it to your port. You win this mission as soon as you unload it on your island.

Ways to Lose

You will need to be far more careful of the buildings, such as the ones on the Libyans' island, in later missions. They will not use their siege workshop to build catapults in this mission, but a good rule to remember is this: "Where there are siege workshops, there are catapults." Catapults are long-range weapons that can sink a ship quicker than you can say, "Bring her to starboard."

The most dangerous mistake in this mission would be to train too large of an army and try to fight with the Libyans on their own territory with Bronze Age soldiers. Their hoplites and cavalry are tough and it would take a lot of time and materials to develop an army that can defeat them.

You can also hurt your chances of winning this mission by taking too long to launch your fleet. Start building and upgrading your armada as soon as possible. You win this mission by dominating the Libyan navy. After that, it's just a question of launching your land attack.

The Libyans have hoplites and cavalrymen. You don't want to fight them hand-to-hand. Have your ships destroy these units.

The tribute is behind a wall against the edge of the map. Have a scout lead the Libyan axeman toward your ships, then go back and collect your prize.

Additional Hints

Make sure you have a villager/repairman to fix your first galley. Two and possibly even three scout ships will attack it the moment it appears.

The are schools of whales in the waters off your shore. Don't waste your time on farms—make a fishing fleet.

Don't waste time developing an army. Your navy can wage and win this war with minimal land support.

Avoid wasting time clearing the island to the east. It's a good idea to destroy any towers endangering your ships, but you will not have any reason to travel along the eastern edge of this map, so attacking the towers on the far side of the island is a waste of time and effort.

Watch out for construction sites as you attack the Libyans. It takes but one arrow to destroy these sites when they first appear, but once a builder starts working, they're tougher to demolish than finished buildings.

Don't let your ships get too close to the enemy shore. Hoplites and cavalrymen will attack if they can reach them.

If you get to a construction site after a builder has begun, kill the builder. You'll have more success damaging the site once the builder is dead.

Advance your village to the Iron Age. The additional power this affords your navy is worth the cost.

Use a cavalryman to ride across the north island and gather the tribute—his speed will save you time.

There may be an axeman guarding the tribute. If so, have your cavalryman lead him to your triremes. He can return and gather the tribute while your ships annihilate the axeman.

Mission 11: A Wonder of the World

Okay, so the Pharaoh wasn't there when you took on the Libyans; don't get hung up on technicalities. Who's going to argue if he wants to say it was his personal victory and celebrate it with a wondrous monument? The problem is that he not only wants you to erect this great monument, but he also wants you to pay for it, and wonders of the world do not come cheaply. This one will cost you 1,000 units of wood, stone, and gold.

Keep an eye on your ships when they're near the Hittite coast, or you may lose them to catapults.

You begin this mission with a Bronze Age-village, four villagers, and 100 units of wood, food, gold, and stone. You've got a well-rounded village that includes a dock, a market, a granary and a stable. You'll need a storage pit, too; this mission involves acquiring a lot of materials.

The first problem, however, is that the Hittites aren't anxious to have you build a wonder to the world. In fact, they're downright tired of you. You won't even get your feet wet in this mission before Hittite scout ships come rolling in, followed by a transport loaded with swordsmen and archers.

Begin the mission by throwing all of your men into gathering wood. You need to build at least three scout ships as quickly as possible, not just to fight off the Hittites' scout ships but also to stop their transport. If that little five-seater lands, you can kiss this mission good-bye, because you don't have anybody strong enough to stop three Hittite swordsmen.

The Hittites won't be the only ones visiting you at the start of this mission, there's also a nosy little Minoan trading boat hoping to exchange gold for food. You need gold, so you don't want to hurt this ship.

What's the answer? Assign all of your villagers to chop wood. You need wood more than food so that you can stop the Hittite invasion. Once you've done that, build fishing boats. There are lots of fish in the waters off your dock, and by fishing instead of farming, you can keep your men cutting wood.

As you begin to accumulate wood and food, upgrade your scout boats into war galleys and send a fleet of four fighting ships to destroy the Hittites' dock.

A tower overlooks the Hittite dock. Be sure to keep your ships out of that tower's range.

A Hittite transport will pay you a visit early in the mission. Trap it and sink it with a fleet of scout ships. If it lands, you're toast.

This will allow you to trade with the Minoans and Canaanites without having to guard your ships against attack.

The Hittites' dock is below a cliff along the southwest edge of the screen. A tower overlooks the dock, so be careful not to get too close as you attack, or the tower will attack your ships.

Once you confine the Hittites to their island, you can establish bustling trade routes. Both the Minoans and the Canaanites have docks along the southeast edge of the map. Lead your trading boats to these docks and start your routes.

The next trick is finding stone. There's a small deposit of stone on the west site of your island, but it doesn't represent even half of the thousand units you need to make the Pharaoh's monument. You're going to have to hunt for a better source.

There's a huge deposit of stone on an island found in the eastern portion of the map. In fact, this vein is so large that you have to build your storage pit a short distance from it. Build a transport ship and send at least five men. At this point there is nothing left to threaten your mission, so you might as well accumulate your stone and gold as quickly as possible.

Only the Iron Age civilization can build wonders, so you're going to have to advance your people before you can start building the Pharaoh's monument. That's going to slow you down more than you might think since you need two Bronze Age buildings, 1,000 units of food, and 800 units

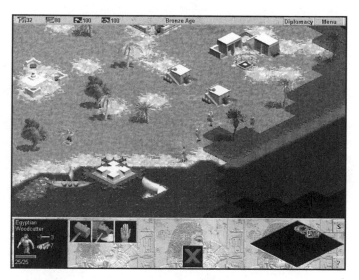

If the Hittites land their transport, they will attack with swordsmen and archers. With only villagers and 100 units of food, you won't have the men or resources to fight off the invasion.

of gold to make the jump from Bronze to Iron.

While your men mine stone and wood, construct two Bronze Age buildings. It doesn't matter which buildings you erect. Once you have the buildings, 1,000 units of food, and 800 units of gold, select your town center and click on the Iron Age icon.

When you have enough materials, begin building your wonder, then sit back and wait. Rome wasn't built in a day and neither, apparently, were any of the seven wonders of the world. You accomplish your mission when the wonder is built.

Ways to Lose

Your first opportunity at abject failure comes in the form of a Hittite transport. If that boat manages to land, you'll have to scramble to find some way to defeat its passengers. Make sure you have enough scout ships to trap and sink that transport before it arrives. Remember, this is one time that quantity means more than quality. Galleys may take more abuse and have more firepower, but the

Despite the fact that you want to save your resources to build the wonder, you're going to have to pay 800 units of gold to upgrade to the Iron Age before you can start construction on the Pharaoh's monument.

The stone deposit on the eastern island is so big that you will have trouble placing your storage pit. Assign lots of villagers to mine it so that you can finish that work and begin building your wonder.

best way to get this ship is to surround it and sink it quickly.

A nearly surefire way to lose this mission is to cause the Minoans and Canaanites to stop trading with you. The best way to do this is to attack their dock. Destroy their docks and your trading partners will have no way to share their gold with you, assuming they still want to.

You can still win without maintaining the trading relationship with the Minoans and Canaanites, but it won't be easy. You'll have to steal the Hittites' gold. They have a huge deposit on the edge of their island, near where you supposedly left their dock in ruins. (Please say you destroyed the Hittites' dock and not the Minoans'.)

The problem with taking the Hittites' gold is that they have lots of angry soldiers who really don't want to share. They have a siege workshop that pumps out catapults faster than GM makes automobiles, an archery range, and several very durable towers. You can destroy all of these dangers with your ships if you

upgrade from galleys to triremes, but it takes time and effort. In other words, don't touch your friends' docks.

That siege workshop, by the way, means that you should not leave ships unattended off the Hittite coast. Look away for just a minute, and they'll roll out their catapults.

Additional Hints

Wood is the key to everything in this mission. You need it to build fishing boats for food and to take the battle to the Hittites. As soon

Building wonders takes a long time; assign lots of men to build yours. Once they finish, the Pharaoh will be pleased (assuming he hasn't died of old age).

as you have a decent fleet of galleys and fishing boats, go to your market and upgrade your woodcutters.

Don't bother upgrading your farming ability or developing the wheel—neither will matter in this mission.

Don't bother making any soldiers in this mission. You'll be able to accomplish everything you need to do with ships and villagers.

Assign as many villagers as possible to build your wonder. It takes ten villagers a long time to build a wonder; one villager could take a digital lifetime.

Mission 12: Siege of Canaan

The Pharaoh loves his new monument, and he really appreciates the Canaanites part in your accumulating enough gold to build it. Unfortunately, he now wants to lay siege on the Canaanites and destroy their capital. Your empire exists in an ever-changing world.

You begin your conquest of the Canaanites with a Stone Age village, three villagers, three archers, three clubmen, and 200 units each of wood, food, gold, and stone. Your village consists of a few houses, a town center, and a barracks. There are bushes near your town center for foraging and trees just outside your village for wood.

The first priority is twofold: have your existing villagers forage and create more clubmen in case you have visitors. Make three clubmen and three new villagers. Assign the villagers to cut wood.

This opening setting is slightly tenuous—the Canaanites have a tower and archers on a cliff directly north of your village. Send your men in that direction, and they will alert the Canaanites to your whereabouts and get injured. (At this stage in the mission, the Canaanites soldiers are more powerful than yours.)

At this point, the most needful things are to protect your village and to advance to the Tool Age. You will not be able to build farms until you reach the Tool Age, and there aren't enough foraging bushes in your village to grow your population.

Create three villagers and five clubmen. Do not create more than this or you will not have enough food to progress to the Tool Age. You should not need the clubmen, assuming you do not inadvertently let the Canaanites know where you are hiding; but if they should find you, eight clubmen and three archers should be able to beat the small force on the cliff overlooking your town.

While your villagers collect food and wood, build a granary and a storage pit. Build the granary east of your village in a wide open area so that you can construct farms around it. Build your storage pit near trees.

As soon as you have enough food, advance your society to the Tool Age and build a market. Once you have a market, you can build farms. Build three farms around your granary. (Remember that the villagers who build the farms will remain at the farms to till them.) This will give you enough food to turn your clubmen into axemen and upgrade their hand-to-hand fighting and armor. They'll be able to defeat the Canaanites on the hill and destroy their tower.

Now's your chance to learn a new technology: building towers. Left-click on your granary to select it. Left-click on the guard tower icon along the bottom of the screen. In a few moments, your villagers will be able to build primitive towers.

Just east of your village, a pass leads up to the ledge where the Canaanites built the tower. Four archers and two clubmen guard that pass. You probably

won't lose any men taking the pass, but count on heavy casualties as you destroy the tower. Have your axemen rush it as your archers shoot it. Half of your axemen will die, but this location not only overlooks your village, it also overlooks a land bridge that connects your village to a Canaanite city.

Once you destroy the Canaanite tower, build one of your own. Your Tool Age-tower will look pretty sad compared to the Canaanites' stone tower, but evolution will help you catch up in the end.

You not only gained a good vantage point by conquering this plateau, but you also confiscated minerals. There are rich stone and gold deposits there, so have your villagers go up and build a storage pit. And make sure all of the hill's former Canaanite inhabitants are dead before sending your soldiers away.

Once your men have mined enough stone, you might want to develop the technology to build walls, then seal off the land

The last tower crumbles, leaving the Canaanite government center wide open to attack.

Once you've outgrown your protective wall, use your catapults to blow a hole in it.

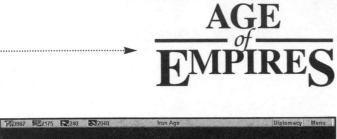

This is your final target as an Egyptian. It's heavily guarded, but it's no match for a well-managed catapult. Just make sure your soldiers guard the catapult during the siege.

This animation reveals the last image the Canaanites saw as their city fell.

bridge. You develop stonewall technology through your granary.

With the bridge walled off, you now have the opportunity to develop your society. Use this time to build farms and upgrade your farming and wood-cutting capabilities. You'll need two buildings to advance to the Iron Age, and you might want to build a temple and a siege workshop.

You'll need a temple if you want a priest to heal your wounded men and convert enemy soldiers. Having a siege workshop is important because it enables you to build important weapons such as catapults. You'll want both priests and catapults when you attack the Canaanite's city.

During this building period, you should upgrade your woodcutting and farming to the highest level. You should also upgrade your priests so that they have a greater number of hit points, move faster, rejuvenate more rapidly, and can perform long-range conversions.

There is a second gold deposit at the north end of your side of the map. Once you deplete the gold deposits on the plateau near your village, send three villagers to mine the other deposit. It has more than enough gold to enable you to build and upgrade your catapults and priests. (You need to build a government center to upgrade your projectile weapons. In missions like this one, in which you must destroy several towers, having powerful catapults is worth the expense.)

Arrange your farms around your granary. If you take every farming upgrade your Iron Age market has to offer, five constantly renewed farms will produce all of the food needed throughout this mission.

Once you have a big enough army (see Additional Hints below), you will need to cross the land bridge into Canaanite territory. Two towers guard the far end of the land bridge; have your catapults crush them from behind your wall. Also, have your catapults fire at any people standing beside the towers.

After destroying the towers, back your catapults and people away from your wall and have the catapults punch a large hole through it. Send your archers halfway across the land bridge, then send your chariots and swordsmen to the far shore. They will secure the shore as your archers join them.

Your priests and catapults should be the last units you send across. Though they have the broadest range of vision, they are extremely vulnerable to close-up attacks. You should always have four or five axemen or swordsmen stationed directly in front of each catapult. Priests should enter new areas only after they have been secured.

The Canaanites have built their city on a series of terraced ledges in the northern corner of the scenario map. There are sloped passes that lead to each ledge and multiple towers beside each pass.

Two towers guard the opening through which your soldiers must pass to attack the Canaanite city. Destroy the towers with your catapults, but be careful—there are soldiers nearby.

The Canaanites' town center is on the lowest terrace in their hills. Destroy the towers guarding the pass to this terrace, and you can destroy the town center.

Whatever you do, do not rush blindly up these passes. Assemble your foot soldiers at the bottom of each pass, out of the range of the towers. Then have your catapults close up behind your men and take out the towers. It's a gradual process.

The first terrace is guarded by towers along its western and southern slopes. It is not heavily populated, but it does include several houses and a town center. Two passes lead up to this ledge. Split your army in half and send one team to destroy the southern towers and enter the terrace through the southern pass. Send your other team to destroy the towers along the western slope. Wait until both teams have cleared their objectives and shot any visible targets on the next terrace before proceeding.

There is only one ramp to the next terrace, and it faces west. A tower and several soldiers guard this pass. Have your priest convert a soldier, then guide the soldier toward your army. The other Canaanites will chase the converted soldier. Have your catapults and archers kill them, then have your catapults destroy the tower at the top of the pass.

The Canaanites' city, with several towers and a strong wall, is at the top of this pass. There is an archery range just outside of it. Have your catapults destroy it. Then have them take out the towers inside the wall. Remember, you should have several soldiers guarding your catapult.

Your final target is the Canaanite government center, which is nestled inside the walls. Destroy it with your catapults and mighty Canaan will fall.

Build a wall to stop the Canaanites from coming across the river. This strategy will be far more important in later missions against more determined foes.

Ways to Lose

The trick to winning this battle is patience. The Canaanites start the mission with stronger, more advanced, soldiers; but by the end of the scenario, you will have both a numerical and man-for-man strength advantage. The surest way to lose this battle is to charge ahead before you develop that superiority.

If the Canaanites on the plateau detect your village before you are ready, they will pour down on your men. Do not go near their ledge. Work on the wood and berries near your town center, and build up your warriors until you have an army of axemen.

The same thing holds true with the Canaanite towers guarding the river. Wall off the river and wait until you have catapults to destroy them. They will simply cut down any other type of weapon.

Additional Hints

Do not bother equipping your priests with monotheism in this level. Though it's fun to watch them convert buildings, they are lame when it comes to converting towers. These nearsighted clerics insist on walking right up to buildings when they convert them, and walking right up to a tower full of archers is not a healthy venture.

Do not build a dock or develop a navy in this scenario. Your ships will not be able to attack the Canaanites' city—it's too far up the hill.

Do not upgrade your walls. This primitive wall is all you need to keep the Canaanites out, and it will be easy for your catapults to punch through them when you're ready to cross the river.

Always station archers behind walls. When troops come to destroy your walls, your archers can shoot them with their arrows.

Create strong, slow-moving armies to unravel the hill. Your catapults will do most of the heavy work in this battle, and there's no way to make those big boys rush. In fact, the last thing you need is for your fighting men to run too far ahead of your catapults. If enemies engage your army, your catapults will automatically fire, killing both your short swordsmen and the Canaanites' primitive clubmen at the same time.

Don't worry about destroying the Canaanites' houses and granaries. It's their government center that you're after.

Create two priests. Sure they're expensive, but if you have two priests they can heal each other. If you team them together, one can convert enemies while the other rejuvenates.

Chapter Six

THE GREEK SCENARIOS

Heroes are as old as mankind, but the term and its definition is inseparably tied to Greece. Greece's gallery of great heroes is filled with familiar names such as

Ajax, Hercules, Achilles, and Atlas. American school children learn about the Trojan War, and modern athletes run marathons and compete in the Olympics— modern events borrowed from Greece.

Greece was not always so glorious, though. The great nation that modernized the world was born of smaller nations that often struggled and fought with each other. In Microsoft's Age of Empires, you become a general in Greece's troubled days as a tribal land and its glorious days as an empire.

Led by Alexander the Great, the army of Greece conquered the world from the Mediterranean Sea to India.

Mission 1: Land Grab

Build your farms and destroy theirs.... This first Greek mission sounds more like a family feud than a war, but Greece had to start somewhere. After all, Athens wasn't built in a scenario.

Your job is to destroy five Dorian farms while building five of your own. This would be easier if the Ionians and the Tirynians weren't involved. They

Everything in this mission should be on a small scale—even the fighting should be only scattered skirmishes. If you start having large battles, you've waited too long to make your move and your job becomes much harder.

like the Dorians more than they like your people.

There's another problem too—the Dorians have towers and axemen; you have six clubmen, four villagers, and enough wood to build a town center. Finding the best location in this land grab is essential. To borrow a bit from Horace Greeley, "Go north."

Two thirds of the way up the map, you'll run into an area with lots of trees and three groups of foraging bushes. This would be the perfect place to build a town center except the Dorians have beaten you to it. Of course, this entire mission is built around the idea that you want to take land away from the Dorians, and this is a great time to start.

Build your town center beside the foraging area, then send your clubmen southwest. There you'll find the Dorians' barracks. Get there quickly and you can destroy it with little resistance.

Keep your eye on the ground just to the right of the barracks; the Dorians will try to build a tower there. Send a clubman over to ruin that project as soon as you see the stakes go in. If you're a bit late, kill the builder, then destroy the project. If that tower goes up, it will be a source of great pain.

You should expand your population while your men attack the Dorian barracks. Create lots of villagers and send them foraging and cutting wood. In Age of Empires, the only way to make food is to spend it—and that means building villagers, enough of them until you have a steady workforce. You want to advance to the Tool Age quickly, so use your wood to build a granary—you need two Stone Age buildings to advance, and having a granary will speed up your foraging efforts.

Once you have 500 units of food, select your town center and advance to the Tool Age. By this time, your clubmen will have destroyed the Dorians' barracks. Have them return to defend the village and kill any Dorians they happen to see.

Here comes the interesting part of this mission. You share this territory with three other nations, and all of them hate each other. The Ionians and Minoans may come to invade you, but they are as interested in killing each other as much as they are in killing you. Don't be surprised if you see invaders start to fight among themselves.

Once you advance to the Tool Age, upgrade your army from clubmen to axemen. This will give you an advantage over any future invasions, assuming you finish the mission quickly.

Having destroyed the Dorians' barracks and killed their villagers, you will have stopped the Dorians from building farms. If they happen to have any farms in existence, send your soldiers

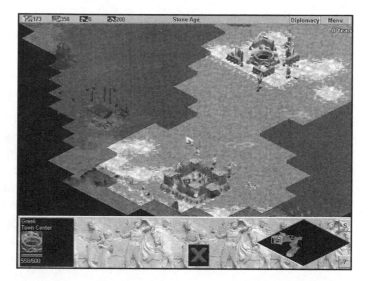

As soon as you locate a spot for your town center, send your clubmen to attack the Dorians' barracks. Get there quickly and they will not have guard towers or a standing army.

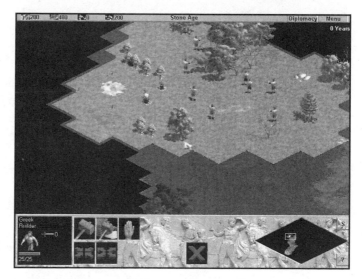

You will find a spot with lots of trees and bushes two thirds of the way up the map. Build your town center there, but know that the Dorians are right next door.

to destroy them. In the meantime, build a market. When it is built, have five of your villagers build farms. Once they are complete, you will have accomplished your mission.

Ways to Lose

Head north to build your town center. You still may beat this scenario if you go east or west, but your job will be much harder. By moving next to the Dorians, you nearly isolate all of the other nations from this incident. Build near the Ionians, and you give them a bigger role in the conflict while providing the Dorians with enough time to build an army and towers before you arrive.

This scenario should be played aggressively. Trying to conserve food to upgrade will actually slow you down and open the door to an invasion. Should the Dorians defeat your initial army and kill your villagers, you will have no way of rebuilding, so build lots of villagers and reinforce your army as often as possible.

Additional Hints

Build lots of villagers so that you can harvest food more quickly to build more soldiers and advance to the Tool Age.

If you see Dorians, Ionians, and Minoans attacking the same building, don't try to stop them. Those countries hate each other. Give them a moment and they'll start fighting, then you can kill the wounded survivors.

Attack the Dorians quickly so that they have no time to prepare. Kill their villagers and destroy their barracks.

Do not bother going after the other nations even if they attack you. Defend your village, but know that the only way for the Minoans and Ionians to affect the outcome of this mission is by slowing you down.

Mission 2: Citadel

The people of Thebes have their eyes on Greek land, and the best way to stop them is to give them a show of power. The Thebians are particularly proud of some ruins just outside their city; demonstrate your strength by capturing these ruins and building two guard towers beside them.

You begin this mission with a Tool Age village consisting of a town center, a market, barracks, a granary, a storage pit, and some houses. You have three

villagers, three clubmen, 400 units of wood, stone, and food, and 200 units of gold. Your village is in the southern corner of the map. The ruins are located along the northeast edge of the map across a large body of water. Start this mission by sending your villagers to forage from the bushes in the western end of your village and building your forces.

Upgrade your army from clubmen to axemen while your villagers collect food. A few Thebian invaders will enter your land from the north; position your axemen to meet them or they'll go after your villagers.

What's wrong with this picture? The Greek invaders have found the ruins and destroyed the towers. So what could possibly go wrong? Check the stone supply—this invasion was for naught.

The Thebians are entering your land by crossing a narrow strip of land near the eastern corner of the map. Send a villager to build a wall across that narrow neck of land and assign three axemen to protect him. (Make sure to build the wall across the narrow area. Use no more than 20 units of stone building that wall.) This will buy you time as you develop your forces.

The Thebians' land stretches in a ring from the southwest edge of the map, across the top of the map, and over to the northeastern edge. They have more land and resources than you; however, the southwestern part of their land has two deep waterways which they cross on a sandbar. Their dock is at the end of the northern waterway. If you attack it early enough, you will find it poorly guarded and you'll be able to destroy it with a fleet of three or four galleys.

If you are nervous about diving so deep into Thebian territory, you can stop their navy by clogging the mouth of their waterway; but they will be able to build up their fleet and challenge you if you pause too long before attacking.

Once you're finished with the dock, you might sail your fleet around the various waterways on this map. The Thebians have constructed several key

Seal off the narrow strip of land that connects your land to the Thebians, and you will temporarily stop them from invading your land. (The wall may even hold them out indefinitely on some difficulty settings.)

buildings along the edge of their cliffs overlooking the water. Your ships should have no trouble attacking these buildings, provided there are no catapults nearby.

If you have not advanced to the Bronze Age by this time, do so. This is not a leisurely mission; you have an important invasion ahead of you, and you'll want Bronze Age (or preferably Iron Age) weapons when you engage the Thebians.

A couple of things stand in the way of your entering the Iron Age—most importantly, you don't have enough gold. There is a large deposit of gold on a peninsula just north of your island. The peninsula is attached to the Thebes, so secure the area with your galleys and send villagers and axemen on a transport. Once your men get there, have them build a storage pit, stables, and a siege workshop. Taking this peninsula has put you well on your way to winning the mission.

The Thebians will have built at least one tower near the gold deposit, and there may be more depending on how quickly you get to it. Have your axemen destroy the tower. To save time, you can have your builders construct the storage pit, stables, and siege workshop while your axemen raze the tower. Between your galleys and the cavalrymen you create with your stables, your miners should be safe from attack.

Maintain control of this land; it will make a good starting point from which to launch your invasion. This is also where an upgraded fleet of triremes comes in. You already pulverized the Thebian cliffs with galleys; with triremes, especially catapult triremes, you'll eat up a third of their territory. You'll close down key buildings and kill dozens of villagers who might otherwise provide the food that powers the Thebian war machine.

Upgrade your navy to triremes and catapult triremes and start attacking the Thebians along their cliffs and southern coastline. When the Thebians reach the southern coast, they'll throw everything they have at your fleet, even though they won't be able to defend themselves as long as your ships do not stay away from the sandbar between the islands.

Your invasion, however, will be launched from the peninsula just north of your island. Build up a force with at least three stone throwers, ten scouts, and six villagers. Have your party go north to the top of the peninsula, then west to the edge of the map. If they run into Thebian forces (doubtful because they'll be busy dying at the hands of your navy), have your scouts swarm them as your stone throwers and builders continue toward the ruins.

If you use your galleys to patrol the cliffs along the Thebian coast, you'll get some good target practice. Later, when you upgrade to triremes, you can try your hand at hitting inland targets.

The ruins are guarded by two towers. Remove the towers with your stone throwers, then send your builders to construct two towers. Complete the towers and you win.

Ways to Lose

Some evil genius at Ensemble Studios concocted a brilliant and natural time clock for this mission, the mining of stone. In order to accomplish your mission, you have to construct two towers beside the ruins. You start the scenario with 400 units of stone; building the towers will require 300 of those units. Should you accidentally run low on stone, you can always mine more, of course; the problem is, all of the stone deposits in this mission are on Thebian land, and the Thebians have a penchant for building towers. In short, be

There are 1,500 units of gold sitting unmined in the middle of a peninsula just north of your land. Clear the area with your galleys, then send transports with villagers and axemen to claim the area.

The Thebians' dock is at the end of a long waterway in the west corner of the map. Go early enough and you will be able to destroy the dock and any scout ships guarding it.

economical with your stone supplies or prepare to invade the Thebians to steal stone because running out of stone means abject failure.

One more warning—learn to control narrow necks of land and land bridges. Depending on the difficulty setting you select, you can expect anywhere from a few minor invasions to a major influx of angry Thebians rushing down along the eastern strip. You can seal that strip with a wall and archers or possibly with a fleet of ships. Take too long sealing that pass, however, and the Thebians may well overwhelm your fledgling village.

Additional Hints

Don't build towers until you get to the ruins at the end. Building towers eats up 150 units of stone, and the only way you'll replace that stone is by launching an early invasion.

Watch your stone supply at the top of your screen as you build the wall to seal off your land. Do not let it dip below 300 units.

Watch out for archers as you clear the buildings along the coast with your ships. A single archer can do a lot of damage to a galley, especially if it is too busy shooting a building to fight back.

Keep your boats away from shores and sandbars. Left to their own devices, your ships may select a target and follow it. Sometimes they park themselves right on the shore or in the middle of a sandbar—places where axemen and cavalrymen can reach them. Whenever you hear the warning trumpet, check the small map in the corner to see if your ships are in trouble; they may have beached themselves.

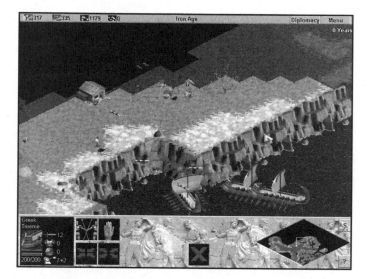

Lure the entire Thebian army south with your ships to clear the way for a light invasion to the north. Keep your triremes away from shores and sandbars and they will kill dozens of enemies.

The forces you send to take the ruins are not staging a regular invasion. Do not let them waste time attacking farms, houses, villagers, or even stables. Go straight to the ruins, destroy the towers with your stone throwers, and build towers of your own.

Mission 3: Ionian Expansion

"Win the war, starve your people"—isn't that how it always goes? You are hereby requested to wage a war on hunger by beating the tar out of the Ionians and commandeering Ionia.

You begin this mission with a Tool Age village, four axemen, four villagers, and 400 units each of wood, food, gold, and stone. There is a small forest near your village, and you have a granary and plants to forage.

Most importantly, you also have a dock. The Ionians seem to know your plans and they have a navy of their own. To win this mission, you will first

Do not let your men get clustered in a fight if you have catapults or stone throwers nearby. These weapons automatically fire at enemy units, killing everything around them. Let your men get in a tight group around the enemy and you'll lose more men to friendly fire than to hostile assault.

have to take control of the sea.

Assign three of your villagers to cut wood, then send the fourth to forage. Create new villagers to help forage, and begin building scout ships and fishing boats. (These waters are filled with fish. Even those little fishing holes along your shore hold 300 units of food, just as much food as areas with whales.) You need food and buildings to make the jump into the Bronze Age. Build an archery range and make the transition as soon as possible.

You score an instant win in this mission if you can locate and mark three sets of ruins. The first one is on your island along the western coast. Send an axeman to find it; your villagers are too busy to go.

As soon as you have three or more scout ships, send them west along the coast of your island. As they pass the peninsula at the north end of your island, they will spot an enemy scout ship. (It may be a galley if you wait too long before going after it.) Have your ships sink it and return to your dock. It's time to take control of the sea.

You do not have to enter the Bronze Age to go after the Ionians' dock, though galleys would make the job easier. Four or five scout ships should give you adequate firepower. It's on an island along the east edge of the map very close to the corner. Make sure to look for transports as well.

There are 600 units of gold on that beach, but the Ionians don't want to give it away. To take it, establish a picket line with your galleys along that portion of the shore and destroy any people, buildings, or towers within range of your ships. Send two transports, one filled with villagers, the other with axemen.

With your galleys forming a protective line along the beach, have your villagers build a tower and a storage pit. The tower will enlarge your field of vision giving you a little more response time when your enemies approach.

Have your villagers mine the gold as your ships and axemen protect them. When the Ionians send catapults, send your axemen to swarm and destroy them. It should not take long to get all of the gold.

The next step is clearing the island. Upgrade your horsemens' armor using your storage pits and build a stable and a siege workshop. Build three stone throwers and 10 to 15 scouts to protect them. You may even want to build a temple and a priest.

Once you have a full fighting force, work your way east and then north across the island. Kill everything and everybody as soon as you see them. In a scenario like this, you don't want to take a chance on some villager escaping and rebuilding everything.

The first step to winning this mission is taking command of the sea. The Ionian dock is near the eastern corner of the map. Invade it early.

Building a town center in the center of this clearing, which is located along the northeast side of the Ionia, is one of two ways to beat this mission.

There is a series of small islands with gold in the north part of the map. Don't bother with that gold; most of the islands are too small to hold a storage pit.

If you decide to play it safe, you can demolish all four towers and capture the last ruins with one catapult to finish the scenario.

You will find a rock wall along the edge of the map. The second set of ruins is inside that wall. Send a scout by it to mark that you were there. When you get to the northern end of the island, you'll find a spot marked by four red flags. There are two ways to beat this mission; building a government center in the space between the flags is one of the methods.

The other method, as mentioned earlier, is to find the three lost ruins. The first one is on your home island; the next one is on the island with the flags; and the third one is on a small island just off your original island's west shore. The path to the ruins starts on the island's eastern shore.

Getting to these ruins takes raw firepower; there are four towers guarding the island. The easiest way around having to deal with the towers is to sacrifice a cavalryman. Go to the other ruins first; that way it doesn't matter if your rider survives. As long as he reaches the ruins, you win.

If you are concerned with being a benevolent leader, you can send a stone thrower to the island. Unload it on the north shore first, where it will have a clear shot at one of the towers. Once that tower is down, move your stone thrower along the thin strip of shoreline and along the trees until you get within range of the next tower. Bombard that tower as well. When it's destroyed, load your stone thrower back on the transport, bring it around the island, and unload it in front of the path. Have your rock thrower destroy the remaining towers as it goes up the path; it will manage unscathed.

Watch for the Ionians to try to rebuild their dock. When you see the posts sticking out of the water, blast them.

Ways to Lose

This is a solid mission requiring nothing more than good skill. There are no unique elements threatening your success; all that's required is a little careful planning.

Additional Hints

Never run with scissors.

You can beat this scenario by building a government center in the flagged area on the Ionians' island, or you can look for the three sets of ancient ruins. Looking for the ruins adds a little flavor.

Mission 4: Trojan War

The Trojan War, immortalized by poets Homer and Virgil, and possibly the most famous ancient battle in history, was long considered to be mythological. Then archaeologists discovered the ruins of Troy. The Age of Empires version of this epic conflict is slightly different than the one you read about in the *Iliad* and the *Aeneid*. It lacks Homer's "red wine sea" and Virgil's Trojan Horse, but it does feature Hector, the hero of Troy.

The Trojans have stolen Helen, a Grecian woman so beautiful that it was written, "She had the face that launched 1,000 ships." Of course, she hasn't launched her 1,000 ships yet because those ships are yours. The king wants Helen returned to Greece, and he wants you to lead the largest armada in history to retrieve her.

The Age of Empires version of this battle is somewhat scaled down. In this game, Helen's face launches 10 or 12 ships, and you never get to see her. Your job is to build an army, go to Troy, have your men kill Hector, and capture a Trojan artifact.

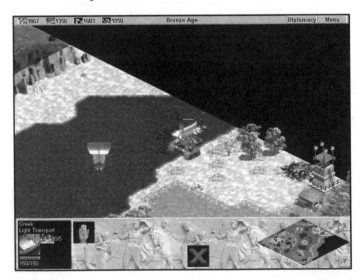

Begin your invasion of Troy by blasting the towers along the southern shore. You can hit the first one from the island across the channel, but you'll have to land on Troy to take out the other three.

You begin this mission with a large Bronze Age village that includes stables, barracks, and an archery range. You have 10 villagers, several archers, axemen, farms, a cavalryman, and 300 units each of wood, food, gold, and stone. All of this is nice, but it's not good enough. The Trojans in this war want to take the battle to you, and they have the navy to do it.

Assign one villager to pick rock, two villagers to forage, and one villager to tend a farm. Send five villagers to cut wood; you'll need wood for ships. Send

your last villager to build two guard towers along your eastern shore.

Your first concern is to fortify your coastline. You have a long and vulnerable shore to the east of your village and a small open beach at the north end of your island. Send your archer to seal off that beach until you have enough ships to patrol it.

Build your navy quickly and upgrade to galleys. As soon as you have four galleys, begin patrolling the waters just east of your island. You'll find a Trojan galley and a transport. Do not let that transport get past you. Sink it or the Trojans will cause untold damage to your village.

This is the crucial moment of this mission. You must destroy the tower, the wall, and all the people with your stone thrower, then send your cavalrymen in to collect your prize. This is not a fast operation, and you'll probably have to load your stone thrower and cavalryman back onto your transport several times before you've sufficiently softened the Trojan forces to make the heist.

Now take your fleet to Troy to destroy their dock. Keep on the lookout for more transports. If you get there early enough, you may catch them loading catapults into a transport. Sink that sucker. You really don't want them unloading cargo like that on your shores.

The Trojan island is located along the east edge of the map extending from the southern corner to the halfway point of the northeast edge. Their dock is directly across the map from your dock. Send your ships to destroy it, then leave them to patrol the island just out of the range of the Trojan catapults. Check back every few minutes, however, and have one ship to patrol the shoreline for new docks.

Between patrols, start mining for gold. There's a small island off your shore, in the southern corner of the map. It's filled with gold—and lions. Send a transport with four archers then a second transport with five villagers to the

| 114 | 609 | 300 | 550 | Bronze Age | Diplomacy | Menu |

Right click to attack this unit.

Greek War Galley
8
0
0
110/160   6+1

The catapults of Troy pose a threat to your ships. It's safer to destroy a catapult with one ship than with a fleet. The good news is that the Trojans will run out of gold if you destroy their dock. Then you won't have to worry about catapults and stone throwers.

island. Have the archers kill the lions and leave, then have your villagers erect a storage pit and mine the gold. If the gold on that island is not enough, there's a second island (just north of your base island) containing 1,500 units of gold and 600 units of stone. (This mission does not allow you to advance to the Iron Age, but if you want lots of wood, gold, stone, and food, this is a mission that provides it.)

After taking control of the seas, your next stop should be the small island off the northern coast of Troy. This island is separated from Troy by a channel. Transport a stone thrower to the southern shore of that island and destroy the tower guarding Troy's north shore. Now load your stone throwers back on your transport and unload it on the freshly cleared shore at the easternmost edge of the beach.

Once you unload the transport, you'll discover two more towers. Have your stone thrower attack them. You can't demolish the towers on your first try because your stone thrower will be close enough for the towers to shoot back. Inflict as much damage as possible to the first tower, then transport your stone thrower back to the island from whence it just came. Bring in a priest to heal it, then send the stone thrower back to Troy to finish the northern towers.

As you blast the towers along the north shore, you'll discover a wall surrounding a tower, barracks, a storage pit, and an artifact. One of your objectives in this scenario is to collect that artifact, and the easiest way to do that is to fulfill the other objective—killing Hector.

Station your ships along the northern coast of Troy and shoot everything and everybody. Cavalrymen will arrive and challenge your ships. Blast them

from off shore. Phalanxes will come. Kill them. Destroy the villagers, too; that will cut off the Trojans' wood supply. (Don't worry about catapults. You took away the Trojans' ability to make more catapults when you zapped their dock and stranded them on an island with no gold deposits.)

With your ships, continue killing anything that moves. When the coast clears (literally), unload your stone thrower and pummel the buildings inside the walls. You can also use your stone thrower to hit woodcutters and soldiers so long as they are not moving around.

Do not let your stone thrower stray far from shore and your transport. You'll need to load it back aboard quickly whenever cavalrymen or phalanxes come to destroy it.

Once you've smashed the buildings inside the wall, punch a large hole through it. When villagers come to repair the breach, adjust your aim to smash them, too.

The final step in this mission is to transport a scout or cavalryman to the

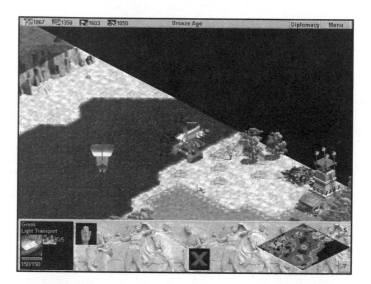

The Trojans will try to take the battle to you right from the start of the mission. Look for several galleys and transports. Stopping the Trojan navy and destroying their dock will be the most decisive blow of the mission.

Just east of your shores is a mine with more gold than you can possibly spend. It's guarded by lions, so send four archers to clear it before sending villagers to mine the gold.

＃

AGE of EMPIRES

You don't have to launch a full invasion in this war. The Trojans will send every available man, including Hector, to try and sweep you from their northern shore. Have your galleys slaughter these soldiers and you will accomplish half of your mission. The second half, the artifact, is waiting for you right behind this wall.

island. When your stone thrower has broken a big enough hole for your horseman to ride through, go collect the artifact. Reach the artifact and you win.

What about Hector? Apparently he was a hero after all. He was one of the soldiers your boats massacred while clearing the coast for your stone thrower.

Ways to Lose

As usual, you are most vulnerable at the very beginning of this scenario. The Trojans will send small high-powered parties to invade your shores. If they arrive, they will wreak havoc. Clog your northern shore with your axemen and archers while you build enough of a fleet to destroy the Trojan dock. If you place enough men there, the Trojans won't even have space to land.

Be aware that the Trojans did not become a major power by sending transports right into the laps of angry archers and axemen. These transports often show up in dark corners where you're less likely to place your men.

Cutting off the Trojans' gold is also important. They will spend their gold on catapults if they have it. Trojan catapults will make your invasion far more difficult. Your ships will not have enough space to maneuver in the channel between the islands, and your stone throwers will not be safe as they attack the towers and walls around the artifact.

While Trojan catapults will not necessarily prevent you from beating this scenario, the entire complexion of your mission will change. Instead of massacring their men from off shore, you will have to land, establish a

·124·

beachhead, and destroy several strategic targets. Sealing off their navy is a much easier proposition.

Additional Hints

Do not bother building farms or upgrading your farming capability. The foraging bushes and farms in your village will provide sufficient food until after you've destroyed the Trojans' dock. After that, get your food by fishing.

Other than storage pits, the only buildings you need to construct are a temple and a siege workshop.

Do not bother attacking the towers along the western edge of Troy; they are of no consequence.

If you want extra points, you can eliminate the nation of Pericles. It's located on a small island in the northern corner of the map. To knock Pericles out of the game, transport a stone thrower to the small island just south of Pericles and position it on the sandbar. Use it to bombard the towers guarding the shore and you eliminate Pericles—those towers represent the nation's only inhabitants.

Blast away the wall and send your cavalrymen in. The day is yours when you reach the artifact.

You can destroy the towers of Pericles, the nation's only inhabitants, by placing a stone thrower on a nearby island. With no army or navy, Pericles poses no threat.

Mission 5: I'll Be Back

Feeling rested after your relaxing invasion of Troy? Don't expect to feel that way after this next mission; this one will leave your nerves frazzled and your pulse running high. Of all the missions in this game, this one stands out as the one requiring the fastest reflexes.

The mission starts out with a betrayal. You begin with seven cavalrymen and four archers—and within seconds you find yourself down to one or two cavalrymen running for their lives. What causes this disaster? Mostly enemy priests.

Your supposed allies, the Minoans, suddenly turn on you. You actually have more cavalrymen than they do, but they have far more archers. They also have towers and swordsmen. Their best weapon, however, turns out to be priests. Try to fight the Minoans and they will convert half of your army and turn it against the other half. Your only chance is to quickly select all of your men by holding down the left button of your mouse and running your cursor across the screen.

This mission opens with your impressive fighting force being overwhelmed by their Minoan allies. There's no point in trying to fight back; your forces are outclassed and outnumbered.

Tell your men to run away by following the mountain trail leading away from the battle. Have them run east to the beginning of the trail, then turn north toward the top of the screen. They will pass archers and towers, and priests will line up along the top of the cliffs. Their chants will convert some of your men and arrows will kill others. If you're lucky, four or five of your cavalrymen will make it to the bottom of the trail.

The trail goes north, then takes a sharp turn and leads south. Once your men get to the bottom, they'll be met by

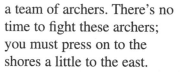

a team of archers. There's no time to fight these archers; you must press on to the shores a little to the east.

Get to the river quickly enough, and you'll see several Minoan ships sinking two Greek galleys. In the midst of this battle, you'll also find a transport. Load your men on that transport as quickly as possible. The moment the Minoan galleys finish sinking your fighting ships, they'll begin shooting the transport.

Have the transport head south and west to an island in the middle of the map. There are several trails

Begin your invasion by landing ballistas, horsemen, and a catapult on the Minoans' island. Use the catapult to destroy their towers and the ballistas to fight off the archers and soldiers they send to intercept you.

leading across the island, but the two most direct trails are marked by sandbars. These make good unloading areas.

The first of these trails, in the center of the island, is a little more narrow and more heavily guarded, but you can get to it quickly. Have the transport take your men to the first trail if there are enemy galleys in pursuit.

Don't breathe a sigh of relief just yet, there's more. The Ionians and Dorians control this island, and they don't like you. Run past them as quickly as possible. Follow the trail south, across the island. It will lead you past archers and towers, and you'll also come under attack from ballistas. Run past them. You may lose some of your men, but you don't stand a chance if you stay and fight.

There's a very thin shoreline leading west around the southern edge of the island. Parts of this shore may look blocked, but you can and must navigate it. Follow the shoreline west. The archers and ballistas are coming after you; there's no time to waste.

Three quarters of the way across the island, you'll find a friendly transport. Load your men on and head toward the southeastern or southwestern edge of the map.

AGE of EMPIRES

Converting Minoan galleys takes practice. The first galley is easy, the Minoans will send one to attack you. Once you've converted it, use it as a lure to attract other galleys, then have your elephant shoot them as your galley pulls out of range. Finally, have your priests convert the enemy ships as they fire arrows at your elephants.

The second trail, which is near the western end of the island, leads right to the bay where your transport awaits. You'll still have to run by archers and ballistas, but you'll have more room to pass them, and you won't have to deal with the difficult shoreline.

Either way, once you get in the transport, head south and have the transport drop you on the east or west edge of the island in the corner of the map. A ready and ferocious army awaits you there. Revenge is at hand.

Your new army includes two catapults, six composite bowmen, four ballistas, four heavy cavalrymen (tougher than those you originally had), four priests, six horse archers, six long swordsmen, four elephant archers, three heavy transports, two galleys, and the light transport which brought you to the island.

As commander of a new military machine, you should begin your revenge by taking your cavalrymen to the priests and having them healed.

Your next order of business should be to add more ballistas to your army. You don't have villagers or materials, but you do have priests, and there happen to be several ballistas available on the island in the middle of the map.

Transport two priests and a cavalryman or an elephant archer to the center of the island. Have the elephant archer or cavalryman lure and distract the ballistas along the two main trails while your priests convert them. Do not get overly ambitious; try to lure your enemies one at a time. Once you've converted both ballistas, heal your cavalryman or elephant archer and return to your base. Next send a catapult to the island to clear out the towers.

Once you clear away the fog of war, the center island looks like a maze covered with trees and towers. Use your catapult to destroy the towers and any archers that you see. Have your priests convert the ballistas. You will have quite an army by the time you clear the island. You will also control two thirds of the scenario map—not bad for a commander who just moments ago was running for his life.

With the island cleared, you can transfer your forces across the channel and prepare to take the fight back to the Minoans. Now comes the next challenge, the starting point. Remember, you cannot get your

Fast-firing, accurate, and powerful, ballistas should play an integral part in your final assault on the Minoans. You can add more ballistas to your forces by converting the enemy ballistas you encountered during your escape. Send a priest and an elephant or a cavalryman to the center island. Use the cavalryman as a lure to attract the ballistas, then have your priest convert them as they shoot at your other man.

transports and galleys around the center island; there are no waterways around or through it.

There's a good chance that the Minoan fleet never discovered your transport boat. Lead your men across the island and station them near the beach with your priests and elephants right on the water. Use your elephants as bait to lure enemy galleys toward your men. While they shoot at your elephants, have your priests convert them. Repeat this process several times and you will have converted enough of a navy to do the job.

Next, use your freshly converted galleys to chase Minoan transport boats toward your priests. Your original transport only held five passengers. Dropping off five soldiers near the Minoans would be the same as giving them the death sentence.

Having cleared the seas between your forces and the Minoans, it's time to begin your landing. Bearing in mind that the Minoans still have four archers

Once you get to the top of the Minoans' mountain, all you have to do is destroy the wall around the artifact to claim it, and destroy the Minoans' temple.

Four Minoan archers will attempt to stop your invasion as you land on the beach. Four archers against three catapults, five ballistas, and two elephants...wonder how that fight is going to go?

and a tower on the beach, your first ten invaders should combine power and fast shooting. Send two or three ballistas to clear out the archers, a catapult to destroy the tower, and elephants for protection, and you will clear the beach quickly. Send in cavalrymen and archers for reinforcements while your first party clears the beach.

After you destroy the first tower, have your ballistas form a protective barrier blocking the mountain pass, and send your catapult to destroy the two towers on the lower levels of the mountain. There are six towers along that pass; use your catapult to destroy all of them.

As you destroy the towers, the Minoans will send waves of soldiers to stop you. Your ballistas can chew through them before they make it down the mountain. The Minoans will also send priests down the path to convert your men. Have your catapult smash them and get ready for the faint-but-satisfying crunch.

As you make it along the last ledge of the path,

destroy the Minoans' stable along with their towers. With their archers and priests destroyed, the Minoans will attempt to rain heavy cavalrymen as a last effort to oppose your army. Destroying their stable will leave the final battle between your exceptionally strong forces and the Minoans' villagers.

When you reach the top of the hill, destroy the stone wall that surrounds the artifact to release it. Have one of your men approach it, and it will turn blue, signifying that it is now in your control. Finally, finish this mission by destroying the Minoans' temple. Do this and you avenge your betrayal.

Ways to Lose

The entire first half of this mission is one long opportunity to lose. If this is your first shot at playing this mission, clear your head and concentrate. You have only a few moments to select your men and flee. Staying and trying to win this fight is futile; the Minoans' seven priests will turn your best

Having narrowly escaped death, your men meander into this conclave of friendly military might. They may believe that they actually died and went to heaven.

In this mission, the Minoans call their priests the "seven yellow men." These are virulent priests that bravely challenge an entire army. Here a Minoan priest attempts to convert a ballista, unaware of the huge catapult load flying toward his head.

Pacing is everything as you make your way up the hill. Have your ballistas and archers clear the path of enemy soldiers as your catapult fires beyond them to demolish enemy buildings.

men against you, and their archers will thin your army to the last man. Try to win this fight, and the entire battle will end in a matter of seconds.

By the same token, you stand a better chance of escaping if you do not run with all of your men. Select the five cavalrymen positioned by the path down the mountain, and leave your other men to fight and die. (Hopefully, they will take a couple of Minoan priests with them.) If you select too few men to run down the hill, the Minoan archers and priests will overwhelm them, but if you take all of your men as you cut and run, you will not inflict any damage on the Minoans.

Whether you choose to take all of your men or just some of them, you have to get down that mountain as quickly as possible. The Minoan navy will already have launched its assault on your fleet before you arrive. Get to the shore too slowly, and the Minoans will sink your transport or chase it away.

The most obvious way to fail this mission, other than trying to win the opening fight, is running south along the top of the mountain instead of east and down the path. There's only one good way down that mountain.

The final way to lose this mission is to become stranded on the middle island. Remember to convert the Minoan ships, not destroy them. The Minoans' transport will not come by your shore naturally, so you will have to convert a galley and chase it. Allow your catapults to destroy all of the galleys and you'll have to start over from the last time you saved the game.

Additional Hints

Have your catapult creep across the island in very small increments as you clear the ballistas, archers, and towers from the center island. Your catapults have such good vision that you'll be able to see ballistas and archers well before they can see you. Fire a shot at these unlucky and unaware enemies and they will not move until the ball drops on their heads.

Make sure your elephants do not shoot back at the Minoan galleys when they attack. You can heal your elephants with your

Why are the priests in this game so dangerous? In this case, enemy priests converted a Greek elephant archer and a cavalryman. They turned on the Greeks' catapult. By the time the skirmish ended, the Greeks had lost two cavalrymen, two elephants, and a catapult.

priests, but you do not have repairmen or wood to repair the galleys.

Have your ballistas close at hand as you convert the enemy fleet. If the ships start firing at your priests, have your ballistas sink them. While this solution is not as good as converting them, a sunken convert is better than a floating enemy.

Have your priests heal each other as soon as one gets wounded. Priests only have 25 hit points; they usually die if you wait to heal them.

Only include one catapult in your party as you make your way up the mountain for the final fight. In their zeal to assault the enemy, catapults tend to kill everything in sight, including your men. Keep the other catapults in a transport off shore for safe keeping.

Keep your priests away from the action. With all of the archers on this mountain, your priests make too easy a target.

Mission 6: Siege of Athens

The Spartans have declared war on Athens. (At least the red Spartans have; the yellow Spartans and the gold Spartans are still on Athens' trade route.) Sparta has sent an enormous army with cavalry, phalanxes, and more.

The Spartans have a larger army than you, large enough to lay siege on any city in the game; but they also have the proverbial Achilles heel—their supply train. Far from home and with no convenience stores in the neighborhood, the Spartan army has had to ship its food in a caravan. If you can capture that caravan, you will cripple their effort, win the war, and accomplish your mission.

Before you can do this, however, you're going to face some very bleak moments. The people of Athens are tucked somewhat safely within their city walls, but their farms are outside. When the Spartans march through, they will cut the Athenians off from food and wood, and then attack the city's walls.

You begin this mission with an Iron Age city that includes two temples, a wall with five fully upgraded towers, a government center, barracks, stables, an academy, a market, an archery range, two docks that have been upgraded to make juggernaughts, two galleys, ten phalanxes, several archers, several cavalrymen, and lots of villagers. Most of your villagers are outside your city walls, however, standing beside their farms.

Your first act as ruler of Athens should be to abandon your farms. Call all but two of your villagers inside your city walls, then have the last pair seal the passages through your walls by building walls around your towers. These precautions

Athens wins the day by weakening the Spartans with long-range weapons rather than destroying them in close-combat. Once the Athenian army closes around the four artifacts to the left, the mission is over.

may well turn the tide of this battle and keep the Spartans outside your city walls.

Your next official act should be to have your villagers harvest every tree within your city walls. You only need 170 units of wood, but you need them quickly. You start the mission with 100 units, so you'll have to scrounge to find it.

Along with the navy that's based around your city, you also have a heavy transport that's loafing across the sea in the eastern corner of the map. (It's in the lighted area on the thumbnail map along the bottom of

Don't be lulled into thinking you can win this fight simply because you have an Iron Age city with towers, phalanxes, and heavy cavalrymen. Babylon fell in a day and so will Athens if you don't act quickly.

your screen.) Bring the transport to Athens, and have it carry ten peasants back to the island in the eastern corner.

Unload your villagers on that island and have them build a storage pit. This island is covered with trees, the raw material you need to rebuild the Athenian spirit, assuming the Spartans break through your city walls. You will also need stone so that your villagers can mend and thicken your walls during the siege.

Unload all of your villagers and have them build a storage pit. Have them cut wood until you have 120 units, then transport three of your villagers to the little island to the south, the one with the huge deposits of stone. Have those men build a storage pit and start mining stone.

The Spartans don't have a navy or catapults, so your ships will have free reign of the waters. Your triremes and juggernaughts will vex the Spartans if they stray within range, and your fishing boats can harvest mounds of food while your trading boats exchange food and wood for gold at the friendly Yellow Spartan dock in the southern corner of the map.

The difficulty setting you've selected determines the next phase of the game. If you've chosen a high level of difficulty, the Spartans will attack your

Your final battle will be a bloody one if you don't thin out the Spartan forces as they attack your city walls; but you can still accomplish your mission simply because you have facilities to train more soldiers while the Spartans do not.

If the Spartans break through your walls, they will kill the inhabitants then destroy its glorious buildings. Their phalanxes are vulnerable only to your archer while they are outside your city walls.

walls and you very well may lose the entire city. Their phalanxes will storm your walls. Aggressive and able to absorb 120 damage points, they flood in an attempt to destroy your new walls and attack your towers. (If you're playing on an easier level, the Spartans may be discouraged to find that you have walls and return to the countryside to attack farms.)

What they have in numbers, however, the Spartans lack in diversity. With no catapults or ballistas among their ranks, the Spartans lack the firepower to tear through your walls quickly. With your villagers cutting wood on that other island, you will have enough wood to build two triremes. Send them to the western corners of your city to shoot the phalanxes as they storm your walls. Your triremes will thin the enemy's numbers; and without barracks and stables on your island, the Spartans will not be able to replace their lost men.

Now is your chance to administer the knockout punch. Build up your army

with phlanxes, cavalrymen, and two or three helepolises. (Athens doesn't come with a siege workshop; you'll have to build one.) You'll want as many as 20 men, and possibly a priest to heal them between battles.

You can load your men into transports to take them to this battle, or you can blast a hole in your city walls and do a transcontinental march. Either way, you will find the last remnants of the Spartan army huddled in the western corner of the map.

Do not take them lightly. Though their numbers are diminished and they are on

Weakened but still tough, the Spartan cavalry will be all that remains of the enormous army that stormed your walls if you send ships and archers to protect your city during the siege.

the defense, they still have phalanxes, composite bowmen, and heavy cavalrymen. Keep your forces in a tight formation with your helepolises in the center and your phalanxes in the front, and head west until you run into a group of phalanxes, then stop and let your helepolies dispatch them.

March forward again until the first ring of cavalrymen come into range, then do the same thing. They will charge your formation. Your helepolises will cut most of them down, and your phalanxes will eliminate the rest. Continue this forward march until you reach the Spartan's supply train (represented by four artifacts), then claim it and you accomplish your mission.

Ways to Lose

This is an easy mission to lose if you approach it with the same mindset you used in other missions. Trying to slug it out with the Spartans is the surest way to lose the day. They have more than enough men to overwhelm your towers and your forces, so don't trade blows with them. Look for alternatives.

By the same token, you can't stay walled up in Athens forever. Sure, there are a couple trees and a few empty spaces in which you can build farms, but

AGE of EMPIRES

The Spartans will look for weak spots along your wall as they try to break into your city. If you run out of stone before walling off your towers, place farms around them to slow the Spartans down but know that they will break through it eventually.

you'll run out of wood quickly, and once the wood stops, so does your food. Build transports and harvest raw materials from other islands, trade with friendly nations for gold, fish for food, and send ships to harass the Spartans.

Even with their numbers shorn, these Spartans are deadly opponents. March an army of swordsmen (or axemen if you're into wholesale blood) into their territory and they will destroy your army.

Additional Hints

In some ways this mission is actually easier to beat on the harder levels. The Spartans will throw so much of their might into attacking your walls that you'll have less of an army to confront at the end of the mission.

If you are worried about food, send two of your villagers to hide in the northern corner of your land while the Spartans attack your walls. Kill enough Spartans outside your walls and they'll leave without finishing off your farms.

Place archers along the inside of your wall to shoot the enemy.

If you run out of stone before walling off your towers, build farms and houses in front of them as barricades.

There are several good fishing spots south of your city and just a little north of the yellow port. Send several fishing boats out to harvest this food and you'll have enough food to begin trading food for gold. (You'll need gold to rebuild your army. Phlanxes, heavy cavalrymen, and other soldiers that require gold for training have high hit points and very aggressive attacks.)

Helepolises and triremes will protect your men. Unlike heavy catapults, they will not kill your men with friendly fire.

If you decide to clear pockets of enemies with catapults, pull the catapults away from close-combat situations and make sure they do not attempt to fire.

You can end this mission quickly if you follow these steps:

Building a juggernaught or triremes to attack the Spartans as they maul your city walls will reduce their numbers greatly.

1. Build walls in front of your towers to protect them from the Spartans

2. Send a full load of villagers to the eastern island to cut trees

3. Build triremes and station them where they can shoot lots of Spartans as they attack your walls

4. Amass large trading and fishing fleets to bring in food and gold to build your army

5. Use long-range weapons to thin the Spartan army during your counterattack to wound their soldiers before they reach your line

Mission 7: Xenophon's March

Remember all the times your parents told you not to meddle in other people's affairs? You should have listened. Instead, you decided to butt your way into the Peloponnesian War and you backed the wrong horse. Now you have to fight your way home to Greece with only eight phalanxes, four villagers, two helepolises, and a priest. Or do you?

You begin this mission with 120 units of wood and no other materials. Why not build a storage pit and increase your wood supply right from the start? Once you have enough wood, you can even build a town center and farms so that you can build your food supply. By the time you leave your starting point,

4515   2166   900   0   Iron Age   Diplomacy   Menu

Greek
Centurion
30+4
8+6
0+2
160/160   0

Just because you're struggling to get home doesn't mean you can't have a big enough army to conquer the Old World. Using the gold and wood you've acquired, built a dozen phalanxes, five or six helepolises, and a heavy catapult. Who's going to stand in your way?

you should have more than 1,000 units of wood and food.

Leaving a town center also insures your survival. If your army is ambushed and slaughtered as it travels across the map, you'll be able to create villagers and start rebuilding your forces.

Moving ahead in small increments, begin to lead your men north, out of the valley. Have your phalanxes lead the way, moving nearly to the edge of the unfogged area, then move your helepolises behind them. Move your priest and villagers last, and keep them a short distance behind the line.

The first creature you'll meet will be a lion, who watches your men from a ledge. Pay no attention to him; he cannot reach them. You will encounter two more lions on the valley floor not far from the spot where you saw the first one. Line your helepolises together and have them each shoot a lion at the same time. You'll get them both without taking any damage.

Now that you've paid your disrespect to the local wildlife, it's time to move on. The valley will lead you to the western corner of the map then turn northeast and end. The Persians have a small town with barracks, stables, houses, and a town center just past the mouth of the valley. Your priest cannot convert buildings, so have your helepolises destroy the entire town.

Several broad swordsmen will attack your army as you destroy their buildings. Make sure your phalanxes are stationed in front of your helepolises to protect them, and have your priest convert two of the enemy soldiers. Once the battle is finished, have your priest heal your wounded.

Once you destroy the buildings, you'll find that you have come to a crossroad. If you want more food or wood, you can build a storage pit and start cutting. There are several gazelles trapped in a valley to the north. If you want food, have your villagers hunt them. The Persians will send elephants and swordsmen to attack you while you while you collect wood and food, so stay alert.

There is a river behind the town you just demolished. Build a harbor and a transport to get across it, and a trireme to sail along the river and attack enemy

Kill the towers and guards, then punch a hole in the wall, and the artifact is yours. Once you get it, the race is on and you have 20 minutes to take your artifact to its final destination.

towers and archers. You will find both to the south.

The Persians have composite bowmen who can absorb three shots from your trireme and damage it badly, so be sure to monitor the damage it takes in each battle and send it back for repairs as needed. You will need to return for repairs several times before you can clear the river, but your prize will be a large enough supply of gold to build more phalanxes.

This is also your chance to add some heavy horse archers to your army. Send your priest in a transport and place him across the river from the gold. He will be able to reach the horse archers with his chants while remaining out of the range of their bows. You'll be pleased with how many soldiers the Persians give you. Once they stop throwing soldiers your way, destroy their town, then transport your helepolises to the area to dismantle the Persians' tower. The gold will finally be yours.

Bring your entire party to this spot—it's time to do some building. Begin by building a storage pit for your villagers to mine the gold. Next, build a siege workshop and an academy and enlarge your army. Once you've added some

Believe it or not, this little Iron Age suburb is what's going to enable you to win this mission. By building a large residential area, you enable yourself to train soldiers and build villagers without worrying about housing. By building a town center, you open the way to create more villagers, in case you lose some on the trail. This little town center can even provide you with food to last the whole mission.

helepolises, several phalanxes, and a catapult to your ranks, walk through the pass to the east.

Shortly after you enter the valley, you'll come to a wall blocking your way. You'd better turn your heavy catapults and helepolises around and start looking for another road. (Just joking: bash it into rubble.)

Right beyond the wall, you will find a second wall that is guarded by a ziggurat. Have your catapult destroy it, then demolish the wall. Have your helpolises ready—once the wall is gone, several swordsmen will pour out.

Continue moving east.

You will encounter several enemy soldiers and a couple of buildings in the east corner of the map. Have your helepolises level them all, then mine the gold behind their town center.

Be careful as you move in this area. There is a wall just north of the gold. The Persians who built that wall have catapults. Have one of your horse archer converts destroy the catapult. Remember, don't leave him in any one place too long or he'll get squished. After destroying the catapult, have helepolises destroy the horesemen behind the wall, then destroy the wall and move north.

After you pass through the wall, your trail will turn west along the edge of a lake. You'll find a city along the side of the lake, and it's here that the mission takes a sudden turn. This is no small town. And its ziggurats and firepower eclipse that of other locales you've encountered. This sleepy hollow is prepared to defend itself, and its temple of priests may convince some of your men to switch sides.

Clear out the temple and the ziggurats, then blast a hole in the wall and place your catapult inside the wall for safekeeping. You have more of this city ahead of you; there's another walled area and more ziggurats just beyond the one you destroyed but with one small difference: there's an artifact in the center. Once you've destroyed the people guarding the artifact, punch and collect your prize. This will initiate a 2,000-year clock. (The 2,000 years is in Age of Empires time—it's really a 20-minute clock.) If the clock expires before your men and the artifact reaches the top of the map, you lose.

Remember the extra villagers you created at the beginning of the mission? Remember all of the wood you gathered by leaving men behind with storage pits? This is where those moves pay off. The port you seek is actually an island across the lake to north of you. There are two ziggurats beside the lake. Have your catapult and your helepolises destroy them, then have your villagers build a dock.

Throughout this mission, stone walls will block your progress, but you should have the firepower to take care of them easily.

This Persian city is your last stop. Be careful as you destroy it; it's filled with hostile guards and ziggurats.

After razing the first city that you come to, you'll find a spot filled with animals to eat and wood to cut. It's a environmentalist's nightmare.

Last stop! Build a transport and take your artifact north to this island at the top of the map. You win as soon as you unload it.

You've reached the successful end of another great mission. Simply build a transport and take the artifact across the lake and you win.

Ways to Lose

The first and easiest way to lose this mission is to forfeit the ability to build a dock at the end. You do this by building anything other than a storage pit with your first 120 units of wood. Accidentally build a house and it's replay time.

You can also lose the ability to create a dock by running out of villagers before you build a town center. Once you have a town center, you can always start over, but until that moment you are completely vulnerable, so don't allow your villagers to get too close to any dangerous situations.

While this is not as challenging a mission as some others, it does require methodical handling. Do not let your soldiers look before they leap, lead them slowly, making sure that your

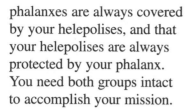

phalanxes are always covered by your helepolises, and that your helepolises are always protected by your phalanx. You need both groups intact to accomplish your mission.

Additional Hints

Build several houses once you have enough wood; that way you won't have to worry about creating houses to build soldiers later in the mission.

Remember that your villagers walk more quickly than your soldiers. If you move all of your men in a group, your villagers will get

Destroy these buildings and enter this pass and you begin a new leg of mission in which you fight active towns and cities and the pace of battles steps up a little.

ahead of your phalanxes and may stumble into a trap.

Leave a villager and a storage pit in the clearing where you killed the two lions. He can continue to cut trees for you through much of the mission.

Leave a villager by your first town center to tend farms. Have him build two farms so that he can go to the second farm when the first one dries up. That way you won't have to check back to see what he's doing.

Don't bother trying to convert enemy archers—they are too likely to kill your priest. Converting war elephants and swordsmen is much safer.

Keep your catapult in the very back of your line with your priest and your villagers and bring it out only when you have to destroy walls and towers.

Mission 8: Wonder

Talk about delusions of grandeur! You play this mission as Alexander. Accomplish your goals and you'll be known as Alexander the Great, lose and you'll be forgotten as just another Macedonian with visions of ruling the world.

AGE *of* EMPIRES

Greek
Heavy Catapult
— 60+1
0
0
27/150   13+2

Your catapults can hit the Lydians' wonder from outside their walls. Have them destroy it from outside, then send one of the catapults and the rest of your army back to your village to prepare for the next fight.

Your goal in this case is to destroy the Lydians' wonder of the world and stop the Phoenicians from building a wonder of their own. Of course, both the Lydians and the Phoenicians have good relations with the Persians, so this job may not be an easy one.

You begin the final Greek mission with a small-but-potent village that includes five heavy cavalrymen, five phalanxes, five composite bowmen, and five villagers. There are foraging bushes in your village, and you have 1,000 units of food, 500 units each of stone, wood, and gold.

It's time to get cracking, the Persians will attack when they find out that you're in their neck of the woods, and that's not the worst of it. The Lydians have completed their wonder of the world. You have to mount a grand enough army to break through their walls and destroy their wonder within 20 minutes while fortifying your city to withstand the Persians.

Not enough? Okay, the Phoenicians are setting new land-speed records as they construct their wonder of the world on the exact opposite corner of the map. You may not even reach the Lydians' wonder before the 2,000-year clock begins ticking on the Phoenicians, and you still have to defend against Persia.

So take a deep breath and start your mission. Assign two of your villagers to start cutting wood and two to start foraging as you send the third one to build a tower at the north end of your village along the inside of the trees.

Create new villagers while the others are out cutting, picking, and building. Send one villager to build a siege workshop and another to mine stone. Create more villagers to cut wood, and build two more towers along the north entrance to your village, then build three towers along the south entrance.

As you build towers and cut wood, you should also train scouts. As soon as you have two catapults and three scouts, assemble your army and head east toward Lydia. You will pass Persians on the way; do not get distracted, you don't have the time. Be sure to take two villagers to Lydia with the rest of your army.)

The first Persian catapults will arrive before you even finish putting together your army. Have your scouts rush the catapults and destroy them; they will be poorly guarded.

Do not stop building your army or your city.

The Phoenicians have defeated the Greek army but lost the war. Their last scout and swordsman will not be able to destroy the catapults before their wonder goes down in flames. (Check the 2,000-year clock. The mission was completed with less than two minutes to go!)

Construct a temple, train more scouts, and build two more catapults. You may need to begin your invasion of Phoenicia before your first army returns.

Do not charge straight for Lydia with your invasion force; instead head across the map in a slightly northeastern direction so that you end up just north of Lydia when you reach the end of the map. Now move slowly southward with your catapults leading the way until you see the first guard towers along the Lydians' northern wall.

Have your catapults inch forward just a little more, and you will see three archers just inside the wall. Have your catapults kill the archers, then destroy the towers. Once the towers are gone, inch forward and you will spot more archers and towers. Do the same thing—destroy the archers and then the towers. (The reason for killing the archers first is that they may try to attack you through breaches in the wall.)

Blast a hole in the wall, and have your catapults inch forward, killing archers as they go. They will be able to fire on the Lydians' wonder before entering the wall. Have them destroy it, then send one of your catapults and all

You won't even have time to start building your army before the first Persian attacks begin. They'll start out with catapults, but swordsmen and composite bowmen will not be far behind.

of your army, except your villager, back to your city to prepare to invade Phoenicia. (By this time the Phoenicians will have finished their wonder and the same 2,000-year clock will be ticking for them.)

Have your remaining catapult inch through the city and kill the remaining archers and towers. Then have your villager enter. As your catapult leaves, have your villager build a storage pit on the eastern side of the city, by the Lydian's gold deposit. Then have him begin mining gold.

Send your catapult all the way to Phoenicia, and assemble a large army. The Phoenicians have elephants and many more towers than the Lydians, and their 2,000-year stop clock has begun to wind down.

Approach the Phoenicians the same way you approached the Lydians, from north of their city. You should have at least five catapults and 25 foot or horse soldiers for this siege. The Phoenicians will not go down meekly.

Have your catapults destroy the towers along the north wall, and the first three towers along the east wall. Try not to break holes in the wall as Phoenician swordsmen and scouts will pour out in an effort to attack your catapults.

Once you've punched out all of the towers, assemble your soldiers along the north wall. (Make sure they're out of the range of the Phoenician composite bowmen, who will be angrily trying to defend their walls.) Line your catapults behind your men and level the north wall completely.

As soon as the wall is down, have your soldiers charge straight for the wonder. Only a few will make it, but they will distract the Phoenicians from your real offensive. Group your catapults and send them to attack the wonder.

The Phoenicians will dispense with your other soldiers and attack your catapults before the wonder falls; but it does not take much catapult fire to destroy a wonder, and five catapults firing at once will damage it quickly.

When the wonder falls, you go down in Age of Empires history as one of the "Greats."

The Phoenician army will pour out of the breaches in the wall. Pull your catapults back and let your army absorb the brunt of the attack.

Ways to Lose

This is no leisurely mission; you have to rush to the East then rush to the West while making sure you still have a village in the center. Play this mission too methodically, take too long performing a surgical strike against either the Lydians or the Phoenicians, and you end the mission with a loss. Those wonders simply must come down before the clocks run out.

You can also lose this mission by becoming too aggressive. Both the Phoenicians and the Lydians begin the war with towers, so there is nothing to be gained by marching your men to Phoenicia the moment the scenario begins in the hope of breaking into an undeveloped city and catching its army off guard.

Additional Hints

Send villagers when you attack Phoenicia and Lydia. The villagers at Lydia can remain and mine gold—you'll need it to fund more catapults. You'll need it even more should you decide to make a priest.

Go into your Diplomacy menu and mark everybody neutral. You don't want your catapults to get distracted trying to hit Persian villagers when they should be bombarding towers and walls.

Once you have a strong fighting force outside of Phoenicia, forget about Persia. You won't win this scenario by having a town to return to. The only way to win is to destroy both wonders, and you must be prepared to sacrifice every one of your people to do it.

Continue manufacturing catapults throughout the mission. The only time you should stop is after your invasion force has entered Phoenicia's walls. You'll need to focus all of your concentration at that point.

Have a villager build a tower within ballista-range of the Phoenician's wonder when your men and catapults go in for the kill. If the Phoenicians manage to destroy your army, the tower may be able to finish the job before time runs out.

Avoid going to battle with the Persians if at all possible. This mission is not about revenge, and it's not even about survival. You simply want to stop two nations from immortalizing themselves with wonders. If you have to die in the process, hey, you may be immortalizd.

Do not waste gold on cavalrymen and swordsmen in this mission. You can distract the enemy with scouts and clubmen, but only catapults have the range and firepower to destroy a well-guarded wonder.

Chapter Seven

THE BABYLONIAN SCENARIOS

Now that you have helped Egypt survive, it's time to try your hand in the less protective world of Babylon. The Egyptian missions provided you with enough time to consider various alternatives and with so much gold, food, and wood that you could develop huge armies and navies. Those days are gone, and it's about time.

You don't get to waste time trying various options in the Babylonian missions. Let your enemies get the upper hand on you in these missions, and you will see the proverbial handwriting writing on the wall. (Of course, seeing your empire crumble every now and again is a real character builder.)

Okay, it's not going to be all that bad. Well, some of it will be that bad. Just remember the lessons you learned playing the Egyptian missions. Babylonian and Egyptian houses and farms cost the same amount of wood and hold the same amount of people, upgraded farms give the same improved production, both nations have identical military capabilities—there are really only a few small differences (the biggest being that the Babylonians have cooler towers).

The Babylonians used to build huge towers known as ziggurats. Though real ziggurats were mostly used as places of worship, the ones in Microsoft's Age of Empires have a more practical purpose—shooting nasty arrows at approaching armies. It doesn't cost any more stone to build a fully upgraded ziggurat than it costs to build Egyptian or Greek towers, so if you find yourself guarding territory with a little extra stone in your bank, by all means build a ziggurat.

Mission 1: Holy Man

This scenario should have been titled "The Dark Missionary." Your job is to establish a city along the Tigris River by converting the people already living there. This is not like an Egypt mission, in which your entire objective might have been something as simple as learning how to build a house. In Holy Man,

First catch of the day! Elamite soldiers will come looking for you as you establish your village. Have your clubmen slow the visitors down while your priest converts them. You'll be amazed how large an army you can build by converting Elamite invaders.

you control one person, a priest, in a hostile world of stronger, more dangerous, creatures—namely, soldiers and lions. (Don't bother trying to convert the lions, though; they've been known to bite the hand that feeds them.)

You begin this mission with a priest, no village, 200 units of wood, and that's it. Your job to convert as many of the local inhabitants as you can—and you'll have to kill anyone that won't join your following. Sadly, you will probably find yourself killing many and "saving" few. Ah, the life of the cloth....

As the mission opens, you find your priest standing beside a river in the southern corner of the map. A lion is hiding in the blacked-out area just ahead of you, so stay close to the river as you head north. Hang a right when you come to the land bridge leading east across the water. The Akkadians on the east are far less formidable than the Elamites living to the west.

Look for villagers as you enter the eastern plain. When you see one, have your priest move in and begin chanting. The Akkadians will not take kindly to having their villagers converted, so expect a message saying that the Akkadians have changed their stance to enemies as soon as your priest starts chanting.

Once you've converted a villager, start looking for a suitable spot to build a town center. You'll find a grove of trees and some foraging bushes just east of the land bridge. Have your villager build your town center near the bushes, then have him start foraging. You need four more villagers, two to cut wood and two to forage. Once you have that crew in place, have a woodcutter build a barracks so you can build your army.

You can win this mission quickly if you are aggressive, as long as you do not allow the Akkadians and the Elamites to tap into their resources. You'll find yourself in a prolonged battle of attrition if you wait too long before attacking your neighbors.

If you get to the foraging area quickly enough, you will see an Akkadian construction site beside the bushes. The Akkadians are building a granary, and while the granary poses no threat, the construction workers should interest you. Why not convert them and add them

Once you have enough of an army, take the war across the land bridge and into the Elamite village. You may pass some new recruits along the way, assuming your priest is able to chant to them.

to your fold! With any luck, you may get five or six healthy workers while cutting the Akkadians off from their food supply.

The next step is building a barracks and houses so that you can prepare your village to defend itself. The Elamites will come, and soon, so you need a standing army.

Before you can create your army, you'll need to build some houses. Since most of your villagers are converts, you haven't had to worry about making houses. But the rule is that you need one house for every four people in your village, or you will not be able to create new ones. Build several houses and several clubmen as quickly as possible. Don't worry about advancing into the Tool Age until you have an army.

As you work on your village, you may see an Elamite villager straggle through. You can convert him if you wish, but the Elamites will become hostile if you do. (They weren't particularly benevolent in the first place, and your job is to convert them or kill them, so don't worry too much about the consequences.)

Once you convert an Elamite, it won't be long before the first Elamite axemen straggle into your village. Axemen are tougher than clubmen, so have

The first order of business in this mission is converting a villager. Your priest's first convert should be an Akkadian builder. As soon as you get him, have him build a town center. Note the stakes in the left of this screen; the Akkadians are erecting a granary near your village. If your priest converts the builder before he finishes, the Akkadians will send more builders for your priest to convert. Assign a villager to damage the construction site and the Akkadians will send every villager they have to complete it. Do this right and you can convert them all.

several clubmen attack each axeman while your priest scrambles to convert him. Once you convert axemen, have your priest heal them and they will become your loyal soldiers.

Keep your eye on your wood supply throughout this period. When you have enough wood, build a granary and a storage pit. Building these structures helps your villagers forage, farm, and cut wood faster, and one of your goals should be to acquire 600 units of food—enough to advance to the Tool Age and upgrade your soldiers to axemen.

If you play your cards right, those accommodating Elamites will continue to send axemen and archers to you one at a time. Have your priest stay well behind the rest of your army so that the invading warriors attack other soldiers while your priest chants. Do this right, and you should convert between 10 and 15 soldiers, enough of an army to invade the Elamites' lands.

As your village evolves to the Tool Age, select your storage pit and upgrade armor and hand-to-hand skills. You should also check to be sure you've upgraded your soldiers from clubs to axes, then make a formation with your soldiers and your priest. It's time to visit the Elamites.

You can avoid a protractive battle by invading the Elamite village quickly. They will probably have already entered the Bronze Age, but they are unlikely to have much of a standing army. You will undoubtedly encounter some resistance and a couple of towers, but on the most part, the Elamite army will have switched faiths and joined your Babylonian army.

Do not bother converting villagers—you need muscle not skills. Save your priest's energy for axemen and archers. Have your axemen attack any Elamite soldiers who approach them, then have them swarm the first tower. Once it is destroyed, lead them to your priest so that he can heal their wounds, then send them after the next tower.

Make sure to keep your priest far away from the fighting where he will be safe. You should be able to convert several more Elamite soldiers and use them during the final part of this mission-razing your enemies' villages.

Your axemen should only attack buildings that are out of the range of enemy guard towers. When it's time to raze the tower, have your men swarm it. If all of your men are healthy, you will not lose anyone on a single tower, and you can send them to your priest to be healed between razings.

You must destroy every last building. That includes docks. You will probably find that that the Elamites have built a dock at the north end of the river. You will also find two or three scout ships floating nearby and ready to defend it. Since you're not suffering from a shortage of wood, you can either build a fleet or have your axemen destroy the dock and convert the boats with your priest.

Ways to Lose

The surest way to fail this mission is to lose your priest. He's a fragile man, doesn't move fast, and doesn't carry weapons. If he stumbles into a lion, he dies. If he comes up on a group of soldiers, he may convert one but the others will kill him.

Once you convert some villagers, don't waste time overbuilding your village or you will find yourself falling behind. The Elamites have a head start

Once you've cleared out the land, its time to rid the sea of enemy ships. By now you should have so much wood that you can build an armada. Four or five ships will be more than enough to clear out the enemy and destroy their docks.

on you; they already have a town center, villagers, and soldiers. Since there's plenty of gold and stone on their land, there is nothing preventing them from building a vast city. Just build your army, largely with their men, and go out to conquer.

Additional Hints

Finish the Akkadians quickly; you don't want to be sandwiched between two hostile armies. The Akkadians probably won't have any soldiers when you first enter their land, but there's some chance that they will since they will already have a barracks, and you can stop them from building soldiers by cutting off their food supply—converting and/or killing their villagers.

Do not even bother mining gold. Advance to the Tool Age and you'll be too late taking the fight to the Elamites.

There is a good supply of stone slightly northeast of your village, along the edge of the map. Once you've got a steady flow of wood and food, have one of your villagers build a storage pit beside the deposit and mine it. Having a stone supply may come in handy.

Take a villager with you when you invade the Elamites. You may need him to erect a barracks so that you have quick access to more soldiers if the battle goes against you. Your villager can also build towers.

Keep your priest away from the fighting. Remember, it doesn't take much damage to kill a priest. You want him safely tucked behind a barricade of axemen who can slow enemy soldiers while your priest converts them.

Since you are attacking with a modest force, remember to check your men's health. Send them to the priest when they are damaged. Healing axemen is cheaper and faster than building new ones.

Do not worry about docks or boats until after you control both sides of the river. There's no reason to build fishing boats; the bushes around your village should provide you with enough food to last most of the mission. If the berries run out, build a market and start farming.

Mission 2: Tigris Valley

Neighboring nations have stolen two tablets containing the famous Code of Hammurabi. Boy, do they have the right idea: the Code of Hammurabi is one of the earliest samples of writing in all of human history. Talk about investment potential for future generations!

Perhaps Hammurabi should be flattered that the Elamites wanted to read his legal code, but he doesn't see it that way. Impressed by your priest's handling of the Akkadians and Elamites, Hammurabi asks you to get his code back.

You begin this mission with a small Stone Age village consisting of three villagers, four houses, a town center, and a dock. You also have 500 units each of wood, food, gold, and stone.

There are no foraging bushes near your village, so assign all of your men to cut wood and build lots of fishing boats. There are several fishing holes and a whale right in front of your dock, so create a big enough fishing fleet to keep the food coming.

With several villagers cutting wood and a large fleet of fishing boats, you'll be able to build a barracks, a storage pit, and several houses. You will also be able to advance to the Tool Age quickly. You'll need to make the jump to Tool Age

The first stolen tablet is on a tiny island, on a cliff overlooking the sea. The tablets are guarded by some relatively weak clubmen. Send axemen and villagers. Your axemen can kill the Elamites, and your villagers can build a storage pit and mine enough gold to get you well into the Bronze Age.

AGE
of
EMPIRES

Unlike the first set of tablets, the second set is on a well-fortified island with chariots and catapults and hoplites and towers. Making a suicide run for the tablets will only end in a massacre. You'll need to make a more organized campaign.

technology so that you can invade your neighbors.

Once you've advanced to the Tool Age, begin building scout ships. It won't take long before your neighbors cruise by to visit, so get your fighting fleet built as quickly as possible.

When your neighbors invade, they won't just come with scout ships. They'll have galleys, and it won't take them long to send transports, too. Having enemy soldiers walking around your Tool Age village is fairly destructive, so try to trap and destroy the transports with your scout ships.

This is when having a good navy starts to come in handy. Both the Akkadians and the Elamites have Bronze Age harbors, and they are going to continue to harass you until you close their docks down permanently. Build two Tool Age buildings so that you can move your town into the Bronze Age, upgrade your ships to galleys, and send your fleet over to the first dock. Be sure you have four or five galleys, or you may be overwhelmed.

The Elamites have a dock on the southern edge of an island located on the southeast edge of the map. If you attack them early enough, you'll find a Bronze Age dock that is poorly defended. They may have a galley or two around it, but they're mostly ripe for the picking.

Chances are, your fleet will barely get home before you start seeing Akkadian ships. The Akkadian dock is located on the eastern shore of an island in the southwest corner of the map. Be warned: you will be met by catapults and towers as you arrive. This dock is worth the trouble, however—destroy it and the Akkadians will remain stranded for the rest of the mission.

Since you will no longer have to worry about invasions after dealing with the Akkadians, you'll finally be able to focus your efforts on invading the Elamites and reclaiming your tablets. Their first base of operations is on a small island just west of your shore.

Load five soldiers on a transport and send it out. Keep your soldiers in a tight group; several enemy clubmen are hiding in the woods on the island. While your men will easily chew through them as a group, you will take unnecessary casualties if your men split up and engage in individual skirmishes.

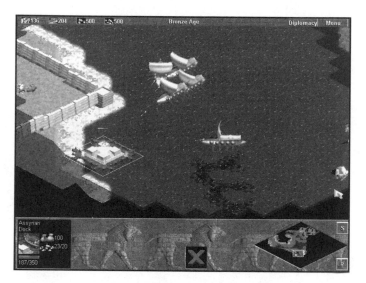

Destroy your enemies' docks early to make this a land battle. That way you can get all of your food from fishing and you won't have to be sorry about invasions.

Once your men clear the enemy off the island, gather the code and your soldiers, then load them on the transport. You've just accomplished the easier half of your mission.

You may have noticed a large deposit of gold on the island. Send three villagers back to the island to build a storage pit and mine the gold, and you'll have enough materials to advance to the Iron Age.

Now comes the hard part—liberating the second stolen tablet. It's on the island that held the first dock you destroyed, and the inhabitants of that island are very anxious for a chance to show you their gratitude.

When you launch your invasion, make sure to aim at the northwest corner of this island. The Elamites have built a wall around their island, but there are two gaps along the northeastern shore.

That doesn't mean your landing will be easy. The Elamites have built several towers, and they have a most productive crew cranking out catapults and cavalrymen. The trick here is to secure a large part of the island with your ships, then wear your enemies down.

AGE
of
EMPIRES

You can destroy an entire herd of catapults with one or two ships. In this case, two ships destroyed seven catapults, and the only damage they took came from a nearby tower. The rubble covering this shore cost the Elamites a lot of wood and gold.

Assemble a large armada (at least eight) of galleys. Destroy the towers guarding the entire northern edge of the island, then repair your ships. The Elamites will send catapults to chase your navy away, but you can destroy the catapults as quickly as they build them. Once you destroy the towers and catapults, go to work on any building or people within range of your ships.

Send a strong force of chariots, axemen, scouts, and more axemen in three or four transports to launch your invasion. You should also send a priest. Surround the transports with your galleys to provide cover because hoplites, cavalrymen, scouts, and chariots will immediately descend on your forces. Your ships should be able to thin those forces out, however, so that your men can establish a beachhead.

You should include some villagers in your invasion party. They can build towers while your soldiers engage the Elamites. Don't be surprised if your entire landing force is eventually killed. The goal here is to cripple the Elamites by destroying their barracks, stables, government workshops, and, if you are really lucky, their siege workshop.

Create more soldiers and chariots while your first crew clears the island and establishes a foothold. In an arena like this, where the fighting is fast and in close quarters, you probably don't want to invest in archers. More durable fighters such as swordsmen and hoplites stand a better chance of survival.

Your prize, the stolen tablets, is in the center of the island. To get it, you'll have to gain control of the ground around it. There are several ways to do this. The fastest way is to mount an enormous attack by sending five or six transports filled with swordsmen and cavalry. You'll have a hard fight on your

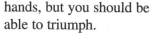

hands, but you should be able to triumph.

If you have laundry, telephone calls to return, or maybe an oven that needs cleaning, there's a sure way to finish this job without micro-management. Build a series of ziggurats in an arc around the stolen tablet. It may take them a few minutes to clean out the bad guys, but they will eventually kill anything within range. (Actually, you probably shouldn't go off to clean the oven. You may need to have your builder repair one or two of your towers.)

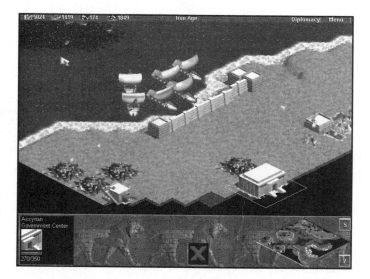

As you prepare for your final invasion, use your ships to clear out towers, stables, and any other unlucky structures that happen to be in range.

Ways to Lose

The Akkadians are your worst nightmare in this mission. They have more men and technology than the Elamites, and they seem particularly angry about something. (Interestingly, they are the only civilization in this mission that did not steal tablets from Hammurabi.) You start this mission in the Stone Age, but they start in the Tool Age and move to Bronze in a hurry.

If you don't upgrade to the Tool Age and start cranking out scout ships as quickly as possible, you'll get toasted. You won't have as powerful a navy as the Akkadians, but with a little strategy, you will withstand them.

The biggest threat, however, is not from the Akkadians' galleys, but from their transports. These disgusting little roaches may be helpless on the open sea, but let them land on you island and it's curtains for certain!

Both the Akkadians and the Elamites will begin their incursions with galleys, but their transports will follow. Try to clog the their routes as you build your navy. When you're strong enough, take the battle to their ports. Cut off their docks, or your enemies will continually harass you and a mission that

With ziggurats destroying everything in sight, you will be able to stroll up to the tablets, represented by an ark, and walk away with them.

should end reasonably quickly will become endless.

Finally, be prepared for Elamite catapults. Leave your ships unattended and close to enemy shores, and you'll only see splinters when you return. By the same token, you don't want to leave your landing parties all bunched up when you begin your invasion. One good shot from a heavy catapult can take out several men if they're huddled together.

If you see a catapult, convert it or charge at it.

Additional Hints

Don't get sucked into a long battle with the Akkadians: they don't have the stolen goods, so you won't have to invade them. Just shut down their dock so they can't send ships to harass you and forget about them. The Akkadians and Elamites may try to build new docks as soon as you demolish their first ones. Scour their island for new docks and watch out for towers.

One ship, even a scout ship, can destroy an entire battalion of catapults. When you see catapults aiming for your ships, move all but one or two of your ships to safety. Have your remaining ships shoot at the catapult and move to a new spot. It doesn't matter if you move your ships forward or backward or to the side, just keep firing and moving. It may take several shots to destroy a catapult, but they will die with a satisfying crunch.

Use the same strategy to destroy entire formations of catapults. Flocks of artificially intelligent catapults tend to group their fire at the same target. Continue moving and shooting, and they'll all miss your ship. It may take a few

minutes, but you will be able to dismantle dozens of catapults with one boat. (Actually, this process would be harder with three or more boats. Large fleets tend to get tangled and move more slowly.)

Use this same strategy when you convert catapults with priests—have your priest shuffle back and forth as he chants.

Don't bother building archers; they're not well suited for this kind of mission. Build towers instead.

Use your gold wisely; you won't get much of it— and don't waste it on technologies you won't use.

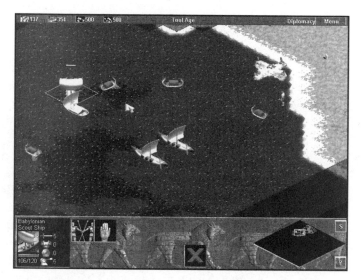

Learn how to trap transports so they cannot move. This makes them easy targets and insures that their passengers will not invade you. To set the trap, have one ship block the transport's path while two other ships close in behind it. The sluggish, unarmed transport will be unable to move to safety.

Place a villager on the small wooded island just north of the Elamites' island before attacking their towers. Your ships are bound to take damage while attacking their towers. With a villager on that island, your ships will not have far to go for repairs.

Have your ships clear all of the coastal towers and building on the Elamites' island. You won't be able to hit their siege workshop, but you will be able to destroy stables, archery ranges, and possibly soldiers and chariots.

Land your priest on the eastern edge of the island, specifically on the lip that extends past the wall. There, hidden behind the wall, your priest will be able to convert enemy catapults and turn them against their makers. If the catapults or archers start moving toward him while he's rejuvenating, quickly load him into his transport and take him off shore.

Mission 3: Lost

If there's a lesson to be learned from Babylonian history, it's, "Never underestimate your enemies." In this mission, the Hittites have sacked mighty Babylon and now plan to build a great city of their own. You and only a handful of men must defeat them. The obvious question here though: If they just destroyed a huge city like Babylon, how in the world will you beat them with a handful of men?

Frankly, this is one of the smartest missions in the entire game. You begin it with a ragtag army—six archers and a priest—that's trapped on a tiny island with few resources and no way to harvest! The first order is to find your way off of the island.

This mission has a tricky little beginning requiring a high degree of skill and luck, so don't feel miffed if it takes you a few tries to get off the island. Start your escape by grouping all of your archers so that they will all aim at the same target. That way you won't have some loose cannon shooting people that you need alive and converted.

Walk your entire population to the north end of the island, then save your progress. Silly as it sounds, you may get sick of grouping your men and marching them across the island. Save your progress at this point, and you may save yourself from some frustration.

There's a sandbar at the north end of the island. Send one set of archers to the top left corner of the sandbar, and the other group to the top right end. Have your priest go up the middle. Once you get there, you will see a priest and two archers. Have your archers kill the enemy archers while you

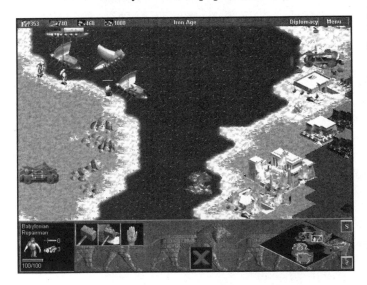

Heavy catapults can easily fire all the way across the channel separating the islands. Watch out for catapults and make special efforts to convert them.

convert the priest. It's the kind of operation that causes you to start and restart a mission many times. (Bear in mind that this is not the only way or the easiest way to do this. Check the additional hints that follow later in this chapter.)

Convert the priest...as if! Convert him too early and his archers will kill him. Wait until his archers are dead and he simply steps out of range. You have to time this perfectly. Convert him as he converts one of your archers. Succeeding at this will take only dozens of attempts, if you're lucky. It could take an entire irritating night if you're not lucky.

The easiest way to convert your way off the first island is to kill all Greek archers except one, convert their priest, then have him turn and convert the last archer. It's a long shot, both literally and figuratively, but it can be done.

The problem is that the priest and his archers tend to walk out of range once your priest starts preaching to them, and once they're out of range, you have no way to bring them back. One method of converting the enemy that has proven successful a fraction of the time is to kill two enemy archers then wait. The Greek priest will heal his last comrade just out of range of your bows.

If the enemy priest is healthy, he will be able to absorb two or three arrows. Have your priest convert him. Select the enemy priest during the conversion process. As soon as he is converted, have him begin chanting at the last enemy archer. If luck is on your side, you will convert that archer before he kills your new priest.

Now for the good news—there is a Greek heavy transport on the north end of the island. Let your newly converted priest rejuvenate from converting the archer, then have him convert the transport. Time for a deep sigh of relief: you ride has finally arrived.

Load your newly converted priest and archer on the boat. Unload them beside your first priest so you can heal your new priest's wounds (he should be

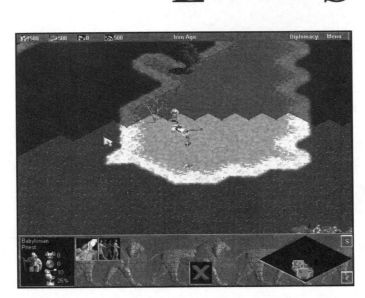

It takes several tries to convert your way off the island. More often than not, the Greeks will kill their priest once he's converted, or they will all walk away from your priest and leave him chanting to an empty congregation.

very near death). Next, load everybody back on the transport and head east.

The Hittites have built a tremendous city on an island in the eastern corner of the map. They have every conceivable weapon except one—priests. There are no temples or priests on the island.

Fortunately, you have two fully upgraded, industrial strength, long-range chanting, fast-rejuvenating, all-converting priests. (These guys can convert anything except town centers.)

So here's where you need to put your priests to work. You need a villager, and the Hittite city is filled them. It's also filled with towers that will try to sink your transport, priests and all.

There's an island just west of the Hittites that has gold and trees and elephants—all the things you won't be able to use until you have a villager. Unload your archers and one of your priests on that island. Keep an eye on what happens there—the Hittites have a dock nearby and they may send boats.

When the Hittites send galleys to attack your new settlement, use your priests to convert them. You'll be amazed at what a huge navy the Hittites will give you, one ship at a time.

Back to your villager-conversion mission. Look for a clear spot on the Hittites' island and unload your priest. Do not send the transport away. Once you convert a villager, you'll need to beat a hasty retreat. (You will also have to scramble if a heavy catapult shows up. One shot from that dinosaur and your priest will discover the truth about his religion.)

Fortunately, there are a lot of villagers on this island. Watch for one who has a chance of escaping once he's converted, then have your priest start

chanting. Load your priest and his new follower on your transport and return to your island, where you will establish a town center and several houses. Remember, you're starting this mission with enough archers and priests to fill two houses. You won't be able to build more villagers until you take care of their housing requirements.

All of the boats in this picture are converts. The Hittites do not have priests in this mission, so they cannot convert your ships to their way of thinking. (Note that there are two destroyed docks; the Hittites tried to construct a second dock the moment the first one collapsed.)

It's time to build a thriving but carefully planned city. Build a dock and ships, as you'll need control of the channel between your island and that of the Hittites. Mine all of the stone and gold on your island: you're going to want towers and you never know if you'll also need to train catapults and priests.

The next step involves a forceful naval action. Destroy the Hittites' dock with your galleys. Concentrate all of your firepower on the dock and any catapults that come to defend it. The Hittites' dock is so close to your island that you should be able to convert any new galleys that appear with your priests.

Once the dock is gone, clear away the guard towers along the western edge of the island with your ships. This will not be a smooth operation; several catapults will appear as you move in. Finally, demolish any archery rangers, barracks, stables, or academies that are within range of your ship. You will probably have the opportunity to slaughter a few enemy soldiers while you're at it.

Now that you've made a clearing, it's time to launch a small invasion. Send a priest and a villager. Have the priest watch for catapults and soldiers while the villager erects a ziggurat close enough to shore to be in your ships' firing zone.

With no towers in the immediate vicinity, the western edge of the island is a safer bet than the eastern end. You may have to risk losing a priest to convert a villager, but it's an important trade. You cannot hope to beat this scenario without a villager.

Once the ziggurat appears, go into the Diplomacy menu and make sure that all of the nations on the menu are listed as enemies. Your ziggurats will now begin firing at enemy buildings and people automatically.

A wave of Hittites will probably storm your ziggurat, but don't worry. They won't damage it much. Have a villager and priest stand by. Your villager can repair the ziggurat while your priest converts a couple of the attackers.

Once your ziggurat and your ships finish killing the attackers, have your villager build a second ziggurat, and then a third. These towers should be spaced tightly enough to defend each other. Have your ziggurats destroy enemy towers and buildings.

Have your towers attack people, too. The only thing they should not attack is the Hittites' siege workshop, which is located in the center of the island. Have your priest approach that workshop and convert it under the cover of your towers.

Use your new siege workshop to create two heavy catapults while your towers pound enemy buildings. Use those catapults to clear out the final towers and buildings. The mission ends when you convert or destroy the last building.

Ways to Lose

There are a dozen ways to lose this mission, and they all occur in the opening moments. Kill the Greek priest on the nearby island and you lose. Convert him and allow the unconverted Greek archers to kill him and you lose. Allow the

priest or his archers to walk out of range and you lose. Getting those first conversions just right will take practice.

The next most vulnerable spot in this mission is the time your men spend on your transport. Let that boat get cornered by enemy ships or shot down by towers while it's carrying your priests, and the mission ends in failure. So long as you keep your priests alive and convert a villager, you are likely to succeed in this mission. The real challenges all take place in the first few moments.

Additional Hints

If you get tired of watching that priest die as you try to convert him, here's an alternative—kill him and all but one of the archers. That's right; kill the priest and convert an archer instead. Have that archer walk around the transport and chase it south by firing arrows at it, then have your priest convert it.

Don't build a government center or a market; your entire village is already upgraded. Government centers and markets are only important if you want to make upgrades.

Keep your priests near each other as much as possible. These are not durable men. Shots that injure other units kill priests, so keep them close together to heal each other.

Watch out for heavy catapults, unless they're yours.

Mission 4: I Shall Return

(So, Douglas MacArthur was Babylonian?) Don't even bother defending Babylon against this Elamite invasion, just get out and head north while you still can. The best you can do is hope to escape with a good supply of villagers and to help you rebuild your forces. In order to save Babylon, you're going to have to raze Babylon.

This mission begins on a frustrating note. The opening screen displays your dock and a transport, the only units in your entire nation that are not getting creamed by Elamite ballistas and soldiers. Quickly shift the view to your city, select every person on the screen, and have them flee to your transport.

You have two options early in this mission. The first is to build a scout ship while men and villagers run to your transport. This will deplete your wood supply and you won't be able to build a town center right away. You will have enough wood to build a storage pit and you'll have a ship to defend your shores—and you can build a dock, fish, and collect wood without a town center.

The priest's congregation is growing. All of these units were captured (cavalry, catapult, axemen, and villagers) with relative ease by sending a lone priest to the Elamites on sporadic crusades.

The last remnants of the Elamite possession lie in flames as a Babylonian catapult shells them. Welcome home!

(This is especially valuable if you start the game at a harder skill level.)

The second option, and probably the smartest though not the safest, is to run to the transport and build a town center. Having a town center allows you to build more men and speed up the work. You'll lose everything if the Elamites discover your island, but that's only a small gamble.

Either way you go, the idea is to build up enough of an army to take the war back to the Elamites. But the longer you take, the more entrenched they become.

The first thing you need to do is secure your island, which contains lions in its corners. Stay in the clearing in the middle of the island until you have the manpower to kill them. Next, harvest wood. Don't look for berry bushes; you will build a dock and fishing boats for your food. And don't worry about building a standing army. The first order of business is to keep the enemy off the island, and that means towers and ships. (Fortunately for you, there

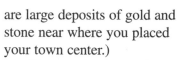

are large deposits of gold and stone near where you placed your town center.)

You may be tempted to put together a couple of scout ships and try an early invasion at this point. Don't. The Elamites already have galleys and heavy catapults. You'll just waste your time and ships.

Instead, focus on developing a rapidly progressing society. Build a market so that you can improve your food and wood production. Start farming to create a steady food supply. Build a navy to defend your shore, and build towers to

Behold the mighty juggernaught, slow but with great range, this juggernaught doesn't just nibble around the edges of the island; it can shell.

help your navy. This is not like the Holy Man mission; you will not avoid a long battle by rushing headlong at your enemy.

As in others, this mission has a certain quiet period during which you can build your forces and determine what strengths you wish to develop. The Elamites may try to invade you during this period, but you will be able to deflect any invasion if you have a strong navy and available repairmen.

Use this time to advance through the ages. Build a government center and purchase the engineering so that you can switch from catapult triremes to juggernaughts. This is a particularly expensive upgrade, especially at the end of the mission, but it will more than pay for itself. If you upgrade to juggernaughts, you won't need to upgrade from stone throwers to catapults, and strengthening your priests will be less expensive. One other matter: upgrading to juggernaughts costs 2,000 units of food and 900 units of wood, but the ships themselves cost no more to construct than normal catapult triremes. A bargain!

Once you've built some juggernaughts, its time to soften up the Elamite defenses. Send a lone trireme along the north edge of their island to look for

Lions hide within the fog of war on this island. Listen for the telltale roaring sound so that your villagers don't stumble into them. When you have the right ships, hunt the lions on the north side of the island. When you have a hunting party and archer or catapult, destroy the lion on the plateau to the east.

catapults. juggernaughts are great at demolition, but they're not good at fast-paced battles. Triremes, on the other hand, have the speed to dodge catapults and the firepower to destroy them. If catapults come out to attack your trireme, dodge their fire and take them out. Do not engage towers or archers; that's what juggernaughts do best.

After you clear the area of catapults, send your juggernaughts along the north shore of the island and have them destroy everything within their range. You'll be amazed: juggernaughts can shoot nearly halfway across the island. You'll be able to destroy houses, farms, stables, government centers, archery ranges, storage pits, granaries, and untold numbers of Elamites. It makes for a bloody slaughter, but it brings the mission to a quicker close.

The next step is to scourge the southern edge of the island. This job requires triremes as much as juggernaughts because it could involve a naval battle. The first job is to destroy the Elamites' dock. Send four or five triremes around the eastern side of the island. Be prepared for attack; there should be some Elamite triremes waiting for you.

The good news here is that you will not only outnumber them, but you will also have more firepower per ship. The bad news is that there will be archers and catapults awaiting your arrival. Try to keep your ships as close to the southern edge of the map as possible as you engage the Elamites. This will keep you out of their archers' range. You may still have to dodge catapult fire, but their balls will take so long to get to you that you'll be able to destroy any enemy ships that engage you.

Keep your trireme fleet at four to five ships. If one of them is damaged during the battle, send it to be repaired and replace it quickly. Once you've annihilated the Elamite fleet, check for catapults and ballistas. If you find some, attack them with a trireme.

Leave you trireme fleet in place as you bring in a juggernaught. Juggernaughts have a very wide range of vision, you will be able to see and bombard soldiers, chariots, and cavalrymen long before they know you are there. Use this to your advantage as you approach the dock. Kill or injure every Elamite, be he civilian or soldier. If this sounds ghoulish, remember that you don't win this mission until every trace of the Elamites is wiped from the island.

Use your juggernaught to blast the dock into oblivion, then begin destroying all buildings. Start with the siege workshop, destroy it so that the Elamites have no means of obtaining more catapults. Go all the way around the island and blast every building that

Don't bother trying to go back for the gold in Old Babylon. It's guarded by the frustratingly powerful combination of a catapult and a galley.

The Elamites will send transports to your island. Clog the waterways around their island, and the transports will make exceptionally easy targets. Here's a major Elamite invasion gone down the drink.

You begin this mission with axemen and archers; the Elamites start out with scouts, swordsmen, catapults, and ballistas. Don't even think about standing up to them, just turn and beat an emotionally draining retreat to your transport.

comes within range of your juggernaught's catapult, then place juggernaughts on either side of the island so that they can blast any inhabitants wandering into view.

The last step of this mission is a simple mop-up. There should be a half-dozen cavalrymen and scouts hiding in the center of the island, out of range of your juggernaughts. Have your triremes line part of the island, then land two transports filled with soldiers. (Remember the cavalrymen and catapults you converted—this is their turn to play.)

Use your cavalry to lure enemies out of the center of the island so that your triremes can hit them. If they won't come, blast them in their hiding places with your catapults. You will find a government center and two or three towers in the center of the island—blast them with your catapults as well.

Ways to Lose

This is a fairly straightforward mission with very few hidden pitfalls. Do not dawdle on your way to the transport in the very beginning of this mission; there's no way to win that battle so you'd better get out with as many men as possible.

If you want a taste of utter futility, try to rush your return invasion. The Elamites will have galleys while you're still in scout ships. They'll have triremes when you make it to galleys. Want to try something really clumsy? Just try defeating a trireme with galleys while a heavy catapult socks your ships from shore.

The last and greatest pitfall, however, is the threat of invasion. The Elamites will send fully loaded transports your way, and they won't be filled with tourists. Just be sure that you have enough ships to detect and sink any transports that come your way. Letting a heavy transport through could be fatal.

Near the end of the mission, you will use triremes to clear out ballistas and catapults, thus clearing the way for your juggernaught to destroy everything else.

Additional Hints

Don't even bother creating soldiers unless you want to fight a long land battle. This is a fight that can be fought almost entirely at sea.

Use your scout ships to kill the two lions on the north end of the island. You'll be able to get them earlier and protect your men.

During down time, send a priest from your island to the quieter parts of Old Babylon. You'll be able to convert and kidnap cavalrymen and maybe a heavy catapult.

Clog the waterways around the Elamites' island. They built their port on the southern edge, and the only way for their ships to move toward attacking you is to pass through two very narrow waterways. Build a blockade at the mouths of these waterways and you effectively neutralize the Elamite navy.

Make sure that you have the Elamites listed as enemies in your Diplomatic menu. That way your ships will begin shooting at them automatically.

Invest in engineering, catapult trireme, and juggernaught upgrades. You won't believe the difference two juggernaughts can make in the last leg of this mission.

Try to be economical with wood, gold, and food. You'll need to have 2,000 units of food very late in the scenario to build a juggernaught.

Mission 5: The Great Hunt

And now for something completely different! It's time to take an offensive stance. Instead of wilting before an awesome Elamite invasion, upgrading your forces, then wreaking revenge, this time you lead an invasion that might have been dreamed up by Rube Goldberg.

Here's the deal. King Nebuchadnezzer has placed you at the head of a pitiful little army that's supposed to invade an Elamite stronghold in search of a statue (handily represented by an ark). You begin your invasion with nine axemen—not a bad force if you're hijacking a chicken farm, but not nearly enough to mount a major invasion.

Your job is to lead this sadly homogenous party through the winding hills in search of a statue of Marduk. The first problem you'll run into is lions. The hills are a regular "Lion Country Safari," but unfortunately your men are locked out of their proverbial car.

Group your axemen and lead them south along the trail—move cautiously a little at a time. There's no way to avoid the lions, so take the offensive. When you see one, tell your men to attack it, but be aware some of them are going to die.

After you've killed the first four lions, you'll encounter a new trap. You will find a little oasis (an exception to the laws of nature) in which a lion and two elephants are living happily side-by-side. These animals may mutually tolerant, but the have no love for Babylonians. Ungroup your men after the fourth lion has been slain, and have them run through this area as fast as they can. The elephants may charge after you, but they're slow and will give up.

Actually, it doesn't matter if you lose as many as eight axemen, as long as one makes it far enough to find the archers waiting for you. No sooner will you get these welcomed reinforcements than you will run into a troop of enemy archers. Kill them.

Next comes an evil fork in the road. The road is split by a growth of trees. It doesn't matter which way you go; there are archers on either side. If you send your archers first and go along the right side of the trees, you'll lose all but one of your archers, but you should be able to avoid the archers on the left.

Once you get past the trees, you will encounter two friendly scouts who will join your party. Guard these scouts; they're your best bet for surviving the terrible gauntlet awaiting you.

The next group of obstacles will be four more archers followed by no less than eight towers. Forget about your axemen and archers: they may make it past lions, elephants, and archers, but they're too slow for guard towers. Get your scouts past this gauntlet and know that you've done well.

Make it past the towers and you'll be met by six cavalrymen who want to join your cause. You may see a pattern brewing. You get axemen who are tough but slow, and all you have to do is slip them past wild

The first half of this mission involves battling through one ambush after another. This becomes particularly grueling on the second set of cliffs.

animals. Next you get archers, faster and able to kill animals, and the scenario throws teams of archers at you. Then you get scouts who are tougher than axemen and faster than archers, but you're up against towers. Now that you've got cavalrymen who are very fast and very durable, you'll be facing elephants and ballistas. Just head north along the trail as quickly as possible.

You'll run into two ballistas first. Swarm them and hack them to splinters. After that, you have to make it past two sets of elephant archers. Don't stop to fight them—you can't beat them (and you actually want them to follow you).

Now you must thread your men through two sets of two towers followed by a pair of stone throwers (small catapults). Run past the towers and attack one of the stone throwers at close range. Make sure that your men do not harm the second catapult. Be quick—there are other dangers awaiting if you stay in one place for too long.

Make it past all of this and you get your first prize—you will run into a pair of imprisoned priests. They can heal your men if you spring them from prison by bashing a hole in the wall that surrounds them. They'll be a huge help throughout your mission, but you can't do it alone. You're going to need help destroying the wall.

Small threats, such as this party of Elamite archers, try to whittle your forces down as you begin the mission. The first leg of The Great Hunt can be characterized as having a break-through-and-conquer mentality.

As luck would have it, help is on the way. Remember that stone thrower you did not attack? It's following you. Charge at it and run away to draw its attention, then have the imprisoned priests convert it. Do this quickly; this thrower sees no moral dilemma shooting fish in a barrel or priests in a prison. Once it's converted, however, it can smash the wall and free your priests.

Now that your priests are free, have them heal your men, then send your stone thrower to destroy the towers in front of the prison. You're going to have to take all of your men back in that direction, so you want to clear the road as much as possible.

You may have noticed two stone throwers on the island that shot at your cavalrymen as they rode through the gauntlet. They will make a great addition to your invasion party if you convert them. Just remember, they'll shoot at your priest as he chants to them, so have him call down to them from the cliff and move to safety when they shoot at him.

One of the neat little facts about catapults and stone throwers is that they do not shoot at objects right next to them. As soon as your priest converts one of the stone throwers, see if you can move right up against the other.

There's a transport boat waiting for your party in the river below the cliffs. (You may have noticed an arrow formed by a grove of berry bushes; it's pointing at your transport.) Once you convert your catapults, you can send the transport to pick them up, but you've got more members to add to the party before your cavalrymen and priest can catch a ride.

After you demolish the prison with your catapults, send them to destroy the four towers you passed right before reaching the prison. This is not just a

cleansing act of wanton revenge; it will clear the way for some very special missionary work.

Remember those elephant archers you passed on the way to the prison? Elephants are awfully tough, they may come in handy later on. Lure them to your priest with your cavalrymen and convert them, but make sure to bring them one at a time. There's no telling what damage an angry elephant can do.

Elephant archers are not known for their intelligence, artificial or otherwise, so don't be surprised if you

Working your way through the wetlands involves a lot of island hopping. There are several enemy ballistas and stone throwers scattered on small islands. Your job is to convert these units or destroy them.

have to ride right up to it, bash it with your sword, then wait for it to catch up to lead it to your priest. Just have your priest ready for when it arrives.

You can repeat this process several times—but use elephants instead of cavalrymen (they can handle the abuse). You passed four archers on the way to the prison, and with the dangers lying ahead, you'll need all the help you can get.

There's a thin shore running along the cliffs on the far side of the lake. Have your transport drop your priest there. Do not take any units with him; he'll need the space to move around. His job will be to move south along that shore and convert any enemies on the far side of the cliff.

The Elamites have catapults, stone throwers, and ballistas on the other side of the cliff. These units may just kill each other off if your priest converts them, but it's better than having them shoot at your men later in the mission, and you should be able to save and enlist one or two of these high-powered units for later use. (When you covert the northernmost unit, a catapult, a ballista, and a stone thrower will immediately destroy it.) The other units along the cliff will be safe; unfortunately they are just lowly stone throwers.

Right click to attack this unit.

Egyptian Cavalry
150/150

Swarm the ballistas and they will become overwhelmed and stop shooting at you.

Now we begin the tougher legs of this mission. You have to cross over the lake to the next row of cliffs. If you destroyed the towers with your catapults, you can simply walk back along the trail to the end of the lake. The problem isn't getting to the cliffs; it's fighting your way across them. There are towers, ballistas, heavy catapults, and lots of priests just ahead. Expect casualties, but keep your priest healthy and you can also earn some very good rewards.

There are eight towers guarding the entrance to the cliffs. Arrange your elephants in a protective line in front of your stone throwers and just out of the range of the towers, then destroy the towers with your stone throwers. The towers cast a foreboding entrance to a forbidding stretch of mountainous desert.

There's an ambush waiting for you at the top of the cliffs. You'll run into six ballistas and a heavy catapult, more than enough firepower to disintegrate a row of elephants in a matter of moments, so be careful and remember: you can afford to lose any of your men except your priest.

Believe it or not, you can put your four elephants and three stone throwers on auto-pilot and defeat these bushwhackers. You'll probably lose two of your elephants and most of your stone throwers, but having your men fight this one on their own will enable you to sick your priest on that catapult, and you'll need the catapult's enormous range for the challenges still ahead.

This cliff has a dogleg bend. Just beyond that bend you will be met by five catapults. Defeat them and you will have destroyed the second Elamite army. (Don't celebrate just yet, however; you still have three more to go.) If you have converted a catapult, you'll be able to pick off some of the attacking catapults at a distance; otherwise, have your army attack them up close, and

have your priest attempt to convert them from a safe distance after they've engaged your elephants and cavalrymen. Again, you cannot afford to lose your priest.

The last real terror on this mountain is probably the most insidious. Not long after the row of catapults, you will come to a plateau crawling with priests and archers. (Even if they can't convert you, they still want to make sure you get the point.)

This is one of the reasons you needed at least one priest; those ravenous

You'll find two priests trapped inside a protective wall as you make your way through this mission. Lure a catapult toward them and have them convert it. Without a priest, you don't have a prayer of winning.

ministers at the bottom of the slope will convert your men. You have to convert them back and heal them while killing off the priests. (This would be an exceptionally easy task if you were able to convert a catapult, but it's very challenging if all you have left are elephants and stone throwers.)

If you have a catapult, blast the priests and archers from the edge of your range. They're slow moving and relatively weak—you should be able to get all of them.

If you don't have a catapult, place your elephants in front of your stone throwers so that the priests go after the pachyderms first. Place your priests beside your stone thrower. Have him convert your elephants back, then heal the stone thrower. You can survive this battle with casualties, but you'll have to act fast.

Just beyond the archers, you will run into a trio of composite bowmen. Have your elephants approach them without firing back. They will concentrate their arrows on your elephants, and you should be able to convert two and possibly three of them. Just make sure that your converts do not start shooting the unconverted bowmen.

AGE of EMPIRES

Your first foe in this game is nature. These early hills are filled with patriotic lions and elephants that wish to serve their nation by eating your men.

Well, the relay race is finally over. The next step is shuttling across some marshes to pick up those catapults you converted, then mounting an attack on a mountain teeming with priests and ballistas. After the events you suffered to get to that mountain, it should sound like a walk through the park.

Go down the slope to the waterside, where you will find a transport boat waiting. Before doing anything else, send the transport to pick up the stone throwers you converted along the side of the cliff. It's time for another little skirmish.

There's a land bridge leading from your shore to a small island. On that island you'll find stone throwers, cavalrymen, and archers. Lure them over with one of your elephant archers, convert as many of them as you can and kill the rest. If you can lure them in small groups, you will not suffer any losses and you should be able to convert most of them.

The next challenge is island hopping. There are ballistas and catapults on many of the islands in this marsh, so you'll have to clear a path for your transport.

The statue of Marduk is on a hill in the north corner of the map. To get to it safely, you're going to have to blast any ballistas or catapults in the western side of the marsh. There's an enemy stone thrower on a small island just north of the island you just cleared. Send two stone throwers to the north shore of the island and have them battle that catapult.

It's time to begin island hopping. Send your transport to take the stone throwers you just used to the island they just bombarded. Unloading them on that island will clear away the fog of war surrounding that area. From that island take your stone throwers slightly northwest and unload them on the southern tip of that island.

There are two ballistas on the next island. Send a stone thrower, an elephant, and a priest to attack them. Have your thrower destroy one ballista, then send in your elephant archer with your priest nearby. While the elephant archer takes some hits, your priest can convert the second ballista.

Be careful as you pick up your ballista; there's a stone thrower on the island to the northeast and a ballista on the island to the northwest. Convert one of these weapons and the other one will destroy it. Either way, it's one less weapon to

Just when it looks like things couldn't get worse, they do. There's a second row of towers behind these, followed by a row of ballistas, a row of catapults, and eventually a row of priests.

deal with later, and you can turn around and convert the survivor with the elephant-offering trick.

Your stone throwers will have one advantage over the other weapons in the wetlands—you have a priest to heal them between battles. Make sure you do it. You'll find a little surprise waiting for you off an island just north of the two ballistas—a friendly transport. Sadly it's empty rather than filled with catapults, but it will help you get all of you men to the final battle.

There are stone throwers on islands just east and west of the spot in which you found the transport. Perform the old priest-and-elephant trick on the one to the east. (You're going to have to go through a few more steps with the other one because there are no large islands within conversion range.)

Unload your priest on the southern shore of the small island beside the stone thrower's island. Since there is no room for an elephant on that island, use your transport to distract it, then have your priest move in.

One word of caution: elephants can sustain 599 damage points and be healed by your priest. Your transport sinks after 150 damage points, and you do not have a villager to repair it. Be especially careful with that boat.

AGE of EMPIRES

Reach the statue, which looks suspiciously like the Code of Hammurabi, and the Egyptians' artifacts, and you win.

Once you convert that stone thrower, perform your elephant-and-priest traveling show for the remaining units around the marsh. You won't get to keep the ballistas on the five tiny square islands to the east. Their neighbors will kill them off as soon as they switch sides. There's a stone thrower on the island beside the Elamite mountain. Add it to your forces.

By the time you get through, you'll have more projectile weapons than the enemy, and you should have a decent enough army to invade the Elamites' island. The final stumbling block is a lone ballista guarding the only part of the island on which you can land. Don't bother converting this fool: destroy him, assemble your troops, and start shooting at targets along the edge of that island with your catapults. Your invasion is at hand.

The cliffs around the Elamites' island form a maniacal spiral with the statue of Marduk at the top and hordes of catapults, ballistas, and soldiers blocking the way. You enter this spiral on the west side by going up a slope that touches the edge of the map. Your forces will have to land on a sandbar, and yes, it is a trap. The moment you entered it, you set off a time clock. You now have 20 minutes to fight up that mountain and capture your prize.

No sooner do you land your men than catapults emerge to thump them. Place some of your stone throwers on the sandbar along the west edge of the island and you will slow them down, but you're going to take casualties in this fight. It's that simple.

Fight your way up and clear a path for a stone thrower; it's time to clear the tower that stands in your way. Place your elephants beside your stone thrower—they'll do a decent job of protecting it. Now work your way forward.

The end of this mission is a straightforward fight with you trying to clear cliffs using your archers, ballistas, and catapults. Once you get this far, the ballistas you captured become very important. They fire more rapidly than stone throwers, and they do not kill their fellow soldiers with friendly fire. If you have sufficient forces, keep your catapults along the west rise of the mountain and let your ballistas finish the job.

Ways to Lose

There are so many great opportunities to fail at this mission, it's hard to know where to begin. Chronologically speaking, the most obvious way to fail is to get killed by the lions and elephants. If your axemen form a tight ball or are too spread out, only a few of them will fight back against the lions and several of them will be injured. Try to get them to march in one or two rows so that their formation will collapse around the attacking lions and several men will strike them at once.

Above all else, do not let your axemen stand around and try to hash it out with the two elephants. Fortunately, the elephants in this game do forget. They are so slow that they stop chasing your men after a few seconds and go back to their peaceful grazing.

It's very easy to fail this mission by going backward. Do not send your archers back to kill the elephants, do not send your scouts back to kill the archers, and do not send you cavalry back to attack the towers.

You are unlikely to survive this mission is you run out of priests before the final invasion. You need to keep them safe, but you can't shelter them from seeing action. Another sure way to fail this scenario is to try to take the mountain with insufficient forces.

One of the ingredients that makes this mission so special is the change in pacing. You have to sprint through the first part. You don't even have time to look back for your lost men as you lead your scouts through the row of towers. The goal is to run as fast as you can.

Once you get your priests, however, the mission suddenly becomes a strategy-and-tactics exercise. Your men can't run over that second set of cliffs or they'll be pulverized by catapults, tenderized by archers, and converted by priests.

The last obvious period of vulnerability occurs when you are shuttling your forces to the Elamites' island. Make sure you have scoured those wetlands for

stone throwers and ballistas. If you lose one of your transports, it will take forever to move your army. If you lose both of your transports, you forfeit the mission because you can no longer reach the statue.

Additional Hints

If you inch your way along the trail, you may be able to get the lions to attack you one at a time. You'll have a better shot at overwhelming them and losing less men if you can get the lions to attack you in an orderly fashion.

When your cavalrymen run into the ballistas on the mountain trail, have them swarm the second ballista. Because they're confined to such a tight space, both units will stop firing when your men crowd them.

Don't be surprised if you are unable to keep both priests alive. Once the stone thrower knows they're there, it will go after them.

Make sure your priests are as far from the wall as possible when you punch a hole in the prison with your stone thrower. It sounds like a silly warning, but you will kill your priests if they're too close to the wall.

Make sure to have your priests heal your men after every encounter. With so many enemies lurking nearby, you want your men as healthy as possible.

Keep your transport right beside your priest when you send him to convert the catapults on the far side of the cliff. The shoreline is narrow and he won't have room to dodge their attacks, so have him jump into the transport instead.

When you pick up your stone throwers, be sure to keep your transport as close to the cliffs as possible. These waters are filled with enemy ballistas and catapults.

Have all of your forces up near the Elamites' island before launching your invasion. The moment you fire a shot or convert an Elamite unit, a 2,000-year clock starts, and you have 20 minutes to steal the statue or lose.

Mission 6: The Caravan

Having just survived a very sophisticated and lengthy mission, you're probably ready for a short head-to-head battle, and here it is. Your job is to protect the statue of Marduk that you stole from the Elamites and bring it to a Babylonian temple. This is one of those missions you can complete in half an hour.

You begin with a view of a Babylonian temple, located on the northwest edge of the map. That is your destination. Your five composite bowmen and the statue are in the south corner of the map.

Group your men so that they will all shoot at the same target. Your best chance at killing your enemies in this mission is to kill at a distance, one at a time.

Move your men north with small steps. Do not lunge ahead. If you listen carefully, you'll hear nearby lions and you'll run into elephants in no time. Remember, these elephants are slow and stupid. Keep your distance and slip past them by going along the far side of the trees (there's no benefit in killing the elephants).

About a third of the way up the map, the shape of the forest will lead your men east or west. Look for a break in the trees and head north through the meadows. There are enemies scattered throughout this mission. Taking the scenic route means nothing but trouble.

You will next come to a river. Backtrack in a southeastern direction until you come upon a group of lions. Have you archers shoot each of them, and

The edges of the map In this mission are fraught with danger. In this case, a group of archers run into a wall that slows them, then two war elephants that kill them. No survivors.

Safely high on a ledge, a party of archers slowly destroy the Elamites' academy.

AGE
of
EMPIRES

All things being equal, archers don't stand a chance against hoplites. This cliff makes things very uneven and the archers have the advantage.

remember to focus on keeping your distance and shooting the animals one at a time.

You'll find a narrow land bridge that crosses the river just beyond the lions. Cross the river. You cannot go back north along the river; a rock ledge blocks the way. Head east past the Elamite flag, then head north and up the slope to the top of the cliffs. Expect to be spotted; your enemies are near. You should now be standing in front of an Elamite town center. Don't bother attacking it.

On the other hand, this ledge provides a wonderful vantage point from which you can shoot all those slow-but-dangerous hoplites without retaliation. Kill them. You may even want to destroy their academy from this safe spot; that way you won't have to worry about replacement hoplites looking for revenge.

Once you've killed the hoplites, there's no reason to skirt around their part of the woods. Have your party walk down the eastern slope of the hill, then head north past the Elamite academy and toward your temple. Check the palm trees along the lake before passing them. There may be wounded hoplites hiding inside the grove.

As you head north, you'll come to a wall. Walk as close to it as possible—there are war elephants in these parts, and you want to slip past them if possible. You'll come to a spot marked by a small grove of trees on your left. Turn left when you come to the top of that grove. You can now walk directly toward the frontier temple. Deliver the statue of Marduk, and you win.

Ways to Lose

Simply put, you can't lose this mission as long as you have control of the artifact. Keep your men around it. The only time you don't want them around the artifact is if you're forced to sacrifice your men so the artifact can make a run for it. (The artifact is so slow that it had better be a short run.)

Additional Hints

You have to avoid elephants all the way through this mission—both domesticated and wild varieties.

Stay in the center of the map as much as possible—you won't stand a chance against the armies stationed along the edges.

Avoid elephants and soldiers on elephants; it takes too many arrows to kill them.

The artifact has no loyalty. It obeys whomever is closest to it, even villagers. Keep an eye on it or you may lose it.

Slow as it is, the artifact can move on its own. If you find yourself cornered by war elephants, sacrifice a

Tho artifact is so slow that even an elephant can take it in a foot race. In this example, the only way to save the artifact was to sacrifice an archer. He shoots the war elephant to distract it while the artifact rolls on toward the temple.

Deliver the statue of Marduk all the way to the temple door and you win.

bowman. Have him shoot the war elephant to lead him away from the artifact, then continue guiding the artifact and any remaining soldiers to the temple.

Mission 7: Lord of the Euphrates

Babylon is stuck between a rock and a hard place... again. You must admit, with the Assyrians to the west and the Chaldeans to the north, the price of real estate in your village is probably dropping.

You begin this mission with six villagers, 200 units each of wood, food, gold, and stone, a quaint Bronze Age town composed of barracks, a granary, a storage pit, and houses. Something you don't have, however, is time. The Chaldeans have more men than you do, and they are preparing an invasion. Your first job is to make axemen and prepare to defend yourself.

As your barracks cranks out axemen, start looking for food. There is a small grove of berry bushes near your granary; send five of your villagers to forage food from them and you'll have a steady supply coming in for a while. This will enable you to build a strong enough force to repel the Chaldean attack.

Next, create two villagers to cut wood and a third one to mine stone.

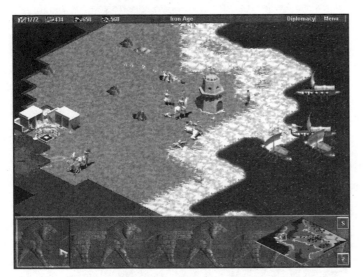

When an invasion starts to fall flat, this ziggurat can be worth its weight in gold. It can withstand heavy bombardment, and it attracts enemies to their deaths.

The resources around your village will dry up quickly, so be prepared to hunt for more.

You'll see your first Chaldean within the first three minutes of your mission. He'll be a lone hunter; don't worry about him. He'll be followed by axemen a few minutes later.

Different players use different strategies in these situations. Some players favor archers and cavalry to fight off invasions. They use the archers to destroy foot soldiers, such as axemen, and the cavalry to attack

siege weapons. This is a sound strategy.

In this mission, given your resources, you need to train axemen quickly, but be aware that you have enough resources to build a temple and train a priest. Having a priest will help your men last longer, and he may be able to find a few recruits for your army.

While you work on your army, monitor the coastline just north of your village; an enterprising Chaldean builder will attempt to erect a tower along your coast. Send men to destroy his work as soon as the stakes appear. Destroying partially completed towers is painless—an ounce of very important prevention.

As you gain strength, build more villagers. Use this time to build a dock and galleys. If you take control of the bay that sits between you and the Chaldeans, you will be able to stop their incursions and prevent them from fortifying their land with coastal towers. You'll also be able to stop the Assyrians from sending transports with chariots and catapults.

Ignore the Chaldeans and they will bring the fight to you. In this case, an Assyrian galley defends a tower built by the Chaldeans.

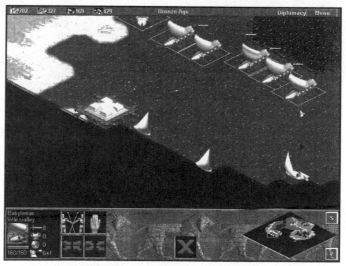

The Assyrian dock is in the center of their island, just off the equatorial line of this map. Destroy this—and the one they try to construct immediately after their first dock falls—and you leave the Assyrians landlocked.

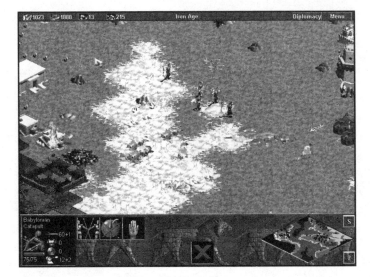

The Assyrians have a belt of important buildings across the middle of their island, and a serious group of dangerous buildings along the southwestern edge of the map. Make the mistake of thinking you have crippled them after you chew through the first line of buildings, and you'll be in for a painful surprise later on.

You need only five ships to take control of the ocean in this mission. Once you have a sufficient fleet, scour the coast along the west edge of the map and destroy the Assyrians' dock and ships. Don't leave the scene too quickly, though, as they will try to build a second dock almost immediately.

Once you have 10 to 15 axemen and a priest, you're ready to march into the Chaldeans' territory. Use your priest judiciously in this invasion. Remember, he needs time to rejuvenate between conversions. If you squander his faith converting villagers and axemen, he may not be ready when the next Chaldean cavalryman rides into range.

Take a peasant with you on this invasion to build a tower in the center of the Chaldeans' city. The tower will serve like a lightning rod—enemy soldiers will often attack it before attacking weaker targets. With a villager there to repair it, your tower will attract and kill a great many Chaldeans.

Your Chaldean siege should end quickly if you mounted it early enough. By annihilating the Chaldeans, you take control of the entire continent; you inherit two large forests and a couple of stone and gold deposits scattered around the map. Use these materials to prepare for your invasion of Assyria.

Invading Assyrian territory is not going to be as easy an operation as the Chaldean invasion. The Assyrians have had more time to entrench. They have also converted more resources into fighting units. You should expect to encounter hordes of chariots and several catapults.

Before beginning your invasion, upgrade your ships and missile weapons so they are better suited for attacking the towers guarding the Assyrians shores. You can land your invasion in the center or top half of their island, but there is no shore for landing on the southern end, and that's where they have the bulk of their power.

As soon as you land, destroy the stables and archery ranges located in the center of the island. The Assyrians have duplicate sites, but you will diminish their ability to train archers and scouts quickly.

Create a thick picket line of composite bowmen to bisect the island laterally, then place catapults (not stone throwers) safely behind your line of archers. It should take between 15 and 20 bowmen to seal the line, with three catapults to destroy any stone throwers the Assyrians send to challenge it. (Have at least one priest just behind the line to heal wounded archers and convert enemy chariots.)

Both the Chaldeans and the Assyrians want to control the bay that lies between you and the Chaldeans. The navy controlling that area regulates who travels between your villages. In this screen, both a Chaldean and an Assyrian scout ship try to stop the Babylonians from building a dock.

As you begin your invasion, you may be tempted to attack storage pits, granaries, government centers, and markets. Don't. Have your soldiers kill the villagers to cut off their food and supplies while your catapults destroy buildings that pose an immediate threat (stables, academies, barracks, and siege workshops).

Send villagers as part of your invasion force so that they can build an archery range. This will provide instant reinforcements for your army. If you find your picket line fading, have the villagers construct two ziggurats just behind the line. These incredibly powerful towers will draw fire away from your archers while killing dozens of enemy soldiers.

You will run into the strongest resistance along the southwestern corner of the island. Have your picket line collapse to form a perimeter around that part of the island and focus all of your catapult fire on the Assyrian archery range, siege workshop, and stables. Have your archers and priests take care of the

Because of their proximity and large population, the Chaldeans are a very real threat. Put together an army of axemen and knock them out of the scenario as quickly as possible. With more men and stable resources, they will overwhelm you if you give them enough time.

stone throwers and chariots you meet.

Once you crush the Assyrians in this quarter of the island, you will have broken the back of their military structure. The rest of the mission will be about taking out minor pockets of resistance and destroying useless buildings.

Ways to Lose

Though you begin this mission with Bronze Age technology and a nice location, your lack of men and facilities will open the door for serious problems. The Chaldeans are simply too close to ignore, and they are eating up resources you'll need in your fight against the mighty Assyrians. If you wait too long to attack the Chaldeans, you may not be able to defeat them.

By the same token, the Assyrians are not to be underestimated. Focus all of your attention on the Chaldeans, and the Assyrians will sack your village in your absence. Take away the Assyrians' sea legs as soon as possible.

Additional Hints

There is a gold deposit east of your village; create villagers and mine it early or the Chaldeans will commandeer it for themselves.

Control the ocean between your village and the Assyrians. You not only ensure that they won't interfere in your battle with the Chaldeans, but you also create a good source of food. There are lots of fishing areas in the waters to the south.

The Chaldeans' cavalrymen, their best fighters, are being trained in a stable in the northeast corner of the map. Destroy that building as quickly as possible. The easiest way to do this may be to raze it with your galleys or scout ships.

Be sure to hunt down and destroy Assyrian transports or they may continue to send catapults and soldiers to harass you even after you demolish their dock.

Once you have control of the seas, make a fishing fleet. Upgrade it so that your boats can obtain food more quickly. You'll soon have enough food to wage a huge invasion.

Upgrade your villagers' siege ability so they can attack towers on the Assyrians' island.

Mission 8: Nineveh

Hang on to your helmet strap, Nineveh is the toughest and the most aggravating scenario in Age of Empires (it's also my personal favorite in the game). It not only pits you against larger well-entrenched armies, but also holds a stopwatch near your ear and says, "Finish this mission in time or else."

You may be thinking, *Big deal, the mission is timed. So what?*

Here's the big deal: you start this mission on a small island in the southern corner of the map with a great Bronze Age-city complete with a siege workshop, a government center, an academy, a granary, and a temple. You even receive a full-blown navy with scout ships and transports. Sounds generous, right? Not exactly.

Sure, you get every conceivable building, except one—a town center. That would not be a problem except that you don't get people either. You're allotted 2,500 units of wood, 2,000 units of food, 2,000 units of gold, and 400 units of stone—practically enough material to build a wonder. Unfortunately, you don't have any villagers to erect a wonder or even a town center.

In the meantime, your enemies, the Assyrians, are building a wonder, and your job is to stop them. Fortunately, it takes a long time to build a wonder—you even get a 2,000-year period (that's 2,000 computer years, better known as 20 minutes in these circles.)

So what's the problem? You have more than enough money to build an army, and you've got the facilities to build an army. Just assemble your men and disassemble the Assyrians, right? Not hardly. Their island is pitted with fully upgraded towers. You won't be able to land on the island with a Bronze Age-fleet; the towers are too tough for your galleys; and you cannot upgrade to

*The Assyrian wonder of the world. Once they build it, you
have 20 minutes to break through their lines and destroy it.*

Iron Age ships like triremes and juggernaughts without advancing to the Iron Age—you'll need a town center.

Here's what you need to know to get started. The Assyrians are about to send triremes and galleys to destroy the guard tower on your eastern shore. Create at least two catapults and four priests as quickly as possible. Since the Assyrians have Iron Age ships and you do not, the best deal is to convert their ships. If you can't convert them, blow them into foam as quickly as possible. Take too long and the Assyrian's catapult triremes will probably kill your priests while sinking your ships and destroying your towers.

While your catapults and priests take care of the Assyrian navy, you should put another priest on a transport and send him after a villager. There's an unfriendly Babylonian city on an island just north of yours. Like Nineveh, the Assyrian city, this island has already entered the Iron Age and has more than enough towers, heavy catapults, chariots, and archers to repulse an invasion.

The bottom edge of the island, however, has a narrow shore running along a large and dense forest. Have your transport boat run along the southwest edge of the map and unload your priest on the bottom corner of the island—go any further in, and your priest will be greeted with catapult fire and arrows.

There is a villager on this island who frequently walks along the shore by the woods. Do not try to convert him while is too far away. You'll get him, but so will your enemies. The idea is to convert him and keep him alive.

Have your priest begin chanting as the villager approaches. Left-click on the villager so that you can control him the moment he's converted. You need to load him on your transport and get him back to your island before his ex-comrades kill him. If possible, send the transport over to pick up your priest as

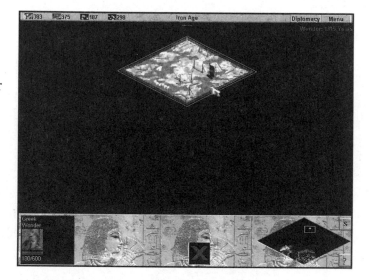

well. He's not as valuable as that villager, but you will need lots of priests for this mission.

Bring the villager to your island. Have a priest heal him if he was wounded, then have him build a town center in the middle of your island. Once the center is built, you can assign your villager to cut wood or mine stone and gold. You can also send him to repair your ships and towers. The important thing is to create several villagers and to advance your village to the Iron Age.

The Assyrian navy will continue to harass you while

This pile of scrap is what the mission is all about. The stopwatch started the moment the Assyrians began building this structure, and your victory depends on your ability to destroy this wonder within 20 minutes of its completion.

you erect your town center and build your villager work force. Try to convert Assyrian triremes and catapult triremes, but have your ships and catapults sink Assyrian galleys. Your priests need to rejuvenate after each conversion, and you may miss converting a more valuable ship.

By the way, even though you start out with a good supply of food and materials, you'll need more before this mission is over. Make three small fishing boats while you wait for your villagers to get going; there are two small fishing holes along your island, and a spot with whales just a little to the north.

In order to cut through Nineveh, you'll need a lot of soldiers, which means you're going to need a lot of food. Upgrade your farms to the max. You should also use your Iron Age government center to upgrade your ballistics, projectile weapons, and engineering (meaning catapult triremes). It takes a lot of gold to make these upgrades, so use your gold wisely.

While you're making upgrades, remember to give your priests some firepower as well. Give them fanaticism and afterlife so they convert more effectively; upgrade them with polytheism so they walk faster, monotheism so they can convert towers, and mysticism so they don't die so easily. Your entire

| 3350 | 2850 | 251 | 1193 | | Iron Age | | Diplomacy | Menu |

Egyptian Juggernaught
35
0
0
185/200   10+2
S
?

Your neighbors to the north and east have lined their islands with powerful towers. You can destroy these towers with juggernaughts, but the most you can hope for with any other kind of ship is to survive sailing through this corridor.

mission hinges on the success of your priests, navy, and catapults with protective support from other units.

Now that you have your island in order, it's time to find additional materials to continue your arms build-up. There's a largely uninhabited island in the east corner of the map. Your enemies have built towers on this island, so you're going to have to start building triremes and catapult triremes before taking the island. (You'll have to upgrade to juggernaughts before beginning your final assault.)

Once your ships clear the towers away, send several villagers and priests to the island on a transport. Build a town center on the island—that way you can create more villagers instead of sending for them, then have your villagers begin cutting trees and mining stone and gold.

Once you've upgraded your docks as far as they can go, make three juggernaughts and begin clearing the towers from the edges of the Assyrian island (the island along the northeast edge of the map). Do not worry about the antagonistic Babylonians to the west because they do not have ships to leave their island. As long as your men stay clear of their ziggurats, the Babylonians cannot hurt you.

Watch out for priests when you send your juggernaughts to destroy the Assyrian towers. Their island has more priests than the Vatican, and you may find yourself under attack from your own juggernaughts if you do not blast enemy priests as soon as you see them. Keep an eye out for catapults and heavy catapults as well.

If you've upgraded your priests with afterlife, they will have a very wide field of range. Have a priest stand on the little outcropping at the north end of the eastern island. You should be able to see a thin strip of the Assyrian island from that vantage point. When elephants or other soldiers walk within range, have your priest convert them. They'll be killed upon conversion, but it's better than losing your men.

Once you've destroyed the towers on the outside of the island and had your ships shoot any men that came in range, it's time to begin your invasion. Send triremes and catapult triremes to the southern shore of the Assyrian island to provide cover for your transports. Put

An Egyptian scout learns an important lesson that you should know—don't take this invasion lightly. With priests, towers, elephants, hoplites, and archers, you don't want to lunge ahead blindly once your invasion begins.

together a landing team with at least four catapults, three priests, two villagers, and several cavalrymen or hoplites.

There's a road that runs between two walls on the southern end of the island. Drop your men in front of that road.

Your first job is to destroy the towers that guard the road. They're out of your ships' range, so you'll have to do it with your catapults. Arrange your soldiers in a protective formation around your catapults, and begin shelling the towers. Enemy elephants and horses will come to attack your catapults. Be sure to convert at least one elephant—it will be very handy later.

If you look closely, you'll see Assyrian ballistas along the walls between the towers you are attacking. Have your catapults destroy the ballistas as well. Assyrian priests will come to try and convert your catapults; if your priests have monotheism, they'll be able to convert those priests. Either way, take care of enemy priests quickly as they pose the biggest danger to your invasion.

Once you make it past the tower, you'll come to a crossroads with more towers and several large buildings. While your fighting forces dig in for a battle at this site, have your peasants build a siege workshop and a stable. That way

Fourteen towers guard this entrance into Ninevah, and this is the easier entrance. You should see what the Assyrians have on the other side of town.

you can have a steady supply of reinforcements without having to send ships to other islands. (The stable is good because, weak as they are, horsemen can get to your forces and protect your catapults quickly.)

This part of the battle is not going to be easy. The Assyrians will throw several priests at you, and they're bound to convert some of your men and weapons. Group your men so that they can kill any converts. This is especially important with catapults.

Have your catapults attack the towers and buildings in this part of the town. The Assyrians will continue creating heavy catapults and archers until you destroy their buildings. Also, be prepared to interrupt your siege to destroy any priests that come out. You don't want your invasion cut short because of a converted catapult. Finally, save your progress after every successful skirmish. One thing you do not want is to start this mission all over again.

You should receive a message that the Assyrians have completed their wonder when you enter their town. That doesn't mean you've lost; it simply means you have 20 minutes before you lose...or win if you get to the wonder in time to destroy it.

The crux of the matter here is that you have to shatter the Assyrian line of resistance, and that requires a lot of shelling—they have too many men to fight up close. Have your catapults attack Assyrian priests and archers. Use your priests to convert Assyrian elephants and hoplites. Above all else, try to take out the towers that guard the wonder. You should be able to see it along the top of your screen.

If you do not have enough time to destroy the towers, have your elephants attack them, then have your catapults attack the wonder while the towers

are distracted. Remember, the Assyrians win if their wonder survives for 20 minutes. Time is of the essence. You may have your priests convert the towers while they're shooting your elephants.

Ways to Lose

There are so many ways to lose this mission that it's hard to believe you can possibly win. Failing to convert a villager is a sure way to lose. You simply cannot beat this mission with a Bronze Age army.

You can also lose by playing too methodically. Don't waste your time attacking the yellow-colored Babylonian army to the north. It's nearly as tough as the Assyrian army is, and the wonder will be several millennia old by the time you finish.

You should be careful not to waste valuable opportunities in this level. Converting Assyrian catapult triremes, for instance, will provide you with a very powerful fleet. Converting enemy soldiers is another rare opportunity. Performing conversions will force the Assyrians to attack their own men.

Do not underestimate your enemies on this level. Send in too few men, and you'll lose everything you've invested. You need several priests, several catapults, and a host of soldiers to act as a barrier for them.

Additional Hints

Keep a repairman by your ships during the early naval battles. The enemy's triremes and catapult ships will inflict heavy casualties on your scout ships and galleys; if you don't have somebody standing by, you'll lose them.

Use your gold wisely. You need lots of gold to make juggernaughts, catapults, and priests, and you need several of each of these to pull off this mission.

Move into action quickly. Have your temple and siege workshop build priests and catapults while you're capturing your first villager. Try to divide your attention between several tasks. You'll want to keep your food and wood coming in right up to the time that you begin your invasion.

Upgrade your farms. You won't get much food from fishing in this mission, and you don't want to have to keep looking back at your farms.

If you were able to convert an elephant at the beginning of your invasion, you can now use it to convert an enemy tower. Destroy three of the four towers

along the road to the center of the island, then have your elephant attack the last tower. Elephants can absorb a lot of abuse; if your priest has healed its wounds, you won't have to worry about it dying too quickly.

While the tower is shooting at your elephant, have one of your priests convert it. Having a tower on your side will clear out the fog of war and give you a clear view of most of the island. The tower will also attack any enemies that may be hiding near by.

Chapter Eight

The Yamato Scenarios

In the Yamato missions, we leave the familiar settings of the Mediterranean for ancient Japan. This is not the relatively recent Japan of samurais and shoguns; this is the practically prehistoric Japan. There aren't many books about early Japan in most libraries and barely any mention of this era in most encyclopedias. It's as if Japan flared into existence in 1185 A.D. with the beginning of the Kamakura period.

Collectively, the Yamato missions are the most difficult in the game. Starting with Mission 1: The Assassins, you are expected to take the lessons you learned in the other campaigns and adapt them to more demanding situations; so prepare to pull some bigger rabbits out of your hat.

Mission 1: The Assassins

To appreciate the historic accuracy of this scenario, you have to consider its story line in context. Part of what helped the Yamato Clan emerge as the unifying government of Japan was an intricate web of alliances. The leader of the clan made pacts with so many other clans that he rose in prestige above his peers, who eventually became unequal, often subservient, partners with the Yamato.

In this scenario, the leaders of the Izumo Clan hope to attack some of the Yamato Clan's allies. Larger and with more allies, the Yamato Clan could probably defeat the Izumo in battle, but that would offend some nations the Yamato do not wish to offend. The only answer is to punish the Izumo privately by assassinating their leader.

In this particular scenario, you lead a team consisting of a bowman, three swordsmen, and a cavalryman as they work their way through enemy territory to kill the Izumo leader. You have no resources and no way to obtain any. This mission is strictly about surviving until you find and kill your target.

You'll run into your first lion as you move south along the edge of the map. Kill it and any other lions that come close to your path.

Don't bother killing lions far from your path. They cannot see you and they won't bother your party.

You begin in the northern corner of the map. Since the Izumo have towers and a powerful army lurking around the center of the map, work your way around the edges. Have your cavalryman go first. March him nearly to the brim of the fog, then move your swordsmen forward. Finish by moving your archer.

The first half of this mission is about killing lions. Apparently lions were not an endangered species in ancient Izumo territory; they seem as common as jackrabbits. Your archer will be able to see the lions before they can see him, so have him clear the way for the rest of your men. It should take three to four arrows to kill each lion.

You'll encounter your first lion as you make your way south along the northeast edge of the map. It will be standing in your path eating a freshly killed deer. Have your archer kill it.

The next lion you pass will be to the left, just inside your archer's line of sight. It will not attack your men as long as they stay along the edge of the map. Kill it if you like, but there's no point.

The third lion is only a few paces further, just beyond a small row of trees. This one is too close to your path—your archer will have to kill it, as well as the next one, which is only a few feet away.

Ignore the next lion—it's far enough from your path for you to slip past without being attacked. You should be especially careful to slip past the lion and the elephant near the next grove of trees—the lion is not particularly dangerous, but that elephant could put a serious crimp in your assassination plans.

You will find the Izumo leader, represented by a swordsman, in front of his palace. He has 120 hit points, so it will take more than one of your men to kill him.

As you pass the lion-and-elephant exhibit, you'll see another lion separated from them by some trees. Kill him. You're going to have to turn left and go along the trees at the bottom of the screen, taking you too close to that kitty for comfort.

There are several chilling touches to this level. The first is the ambient sound. You will hear lions growling moments before they come into view. You may also hear them attacking someone. When you hear this, more often than not they are attacking Izumo villagers. Sometimes, however, they are attacking someone else.

There is a priest waiting for you just below the trees. He can heal any wounded members of your party, but he is rooted to his spot and cannot join your party. (If you do not get to the priest quickly, you may only find his remains. Lions will discover and attack him.)

With your archer in the lead, make your way toward the southern corner of the map after visiting the priest. Be careful—there are still three more lions between you and your destination, including a sneaky one hiding by the trees just west of the priest. You'll find a river running vertically through the center

AGE
of
EMPIRES

All five of your men are on this screen, but one of them is hiding behind a tree. If you cannot find all of your men when the mission opens, drag your cursor across the screen to find stragglers.

of the map. Cross it using the sandbar in the south corner.

Lions become less of a threat once you cross the river. Now the Izumo become the problem. Continue following the edge of the map. You will encounter villagers on the way up as you pass a small village. You'll find a second immobile priest halfway up the southwestern edge of the map, just outside the walls of the Izumo city.

Interestingly, luck may impact your game at this point. This will not happen in every game, but sometimes an Izumo villager will pass by while you are with the priest. If this happens, have the priest convert him.

A word about the villagers in this mission: they may not be strong and they may not be bright, but they are fast—in fact, faster than your cavalryman and faster than any of the Izumo's warriors. If your priest can convert a villager, you can use him to lead the entire Izumo army on a wild goose chase.

If you aren't lucky enough to have a villager stumble into your grasp, you're going to have a tougher task. The Izumo leader has far more hit points than any of your men, and so do his soldiers.

Have your men walk east along the wall surrounding the city until they come to its entrance, then divide them into two groups. Send two of your swordsmen on a blind march through the city toward the northwest edge of the map. They will die. Your goal in sending them is to draw off enemy troops and catapults while your other swordsman, your archer, and your cavalryman slip through the center of the city toward its northeast side.

This is the point where you have to thread the needle blindfolded. You cannot continue along the wall once you enter the city; there are towers along

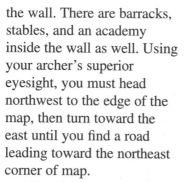

the wall. There are barracks, stables, and an academy inside the wall as well. Using your archer's superior eyesight, you must head northwest to the edge of the map, then turn toward the east until you find a road leading toward the northeast corner of map.

Your intended victim is the broad-swordsman waiting for you at the end of the road. Have all of your men attack him at once—he's far tougher than any of your men, so you must attack him with a group.

Ways to Lose

Considering what your Yamato assassins are up against, this mission should have been titled "Survivors." Not only do they have to slip by hordes of lions and an army of soldiers with superior fighting skills, but they've also been sent to kill someone who can break their necks.

You will probably get past the lions should you decide to march through the middle of the screen, but you'll still lose. The Izumo

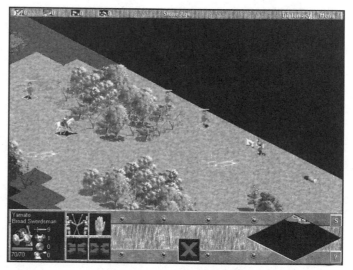

Watch your men carefully as you shepherd them across this territory. They sometimes follow their own paths, even when you've told them to go elsewhere.

There are four priests hidden throughout this level. They're unable to move or assist you in your quest, but they can heal your soldiers' wounds.

AGE of EMPIRES

With the exception of the two catapults guarding the government center, your archer will be able to see every animal and person in this mission before they can see him.

have towers along the northern river portion of the river. Your archer has better eyesight and skills than lions, but not towers, and without your archer, your other soldiers don't have a prayer.

Finally, avoid the soldiers around the Izumo palace. You'll need two and possibly three men to kill the Izumo leader. Lose too many men on the way to him and you might as well go home.

Additional Hints

If you do not see all three of your swordsmen as the mission opens, sweep the area while pressing the left button on your mouse. One of your men may be hiding behind a tree.

Make sure you keep your swordsmen and cavalryman well within your archer's field of vision as you move across the map. Move your men to the edge of his vision, and they may fall prey to lions.

If you are able to convert a villager, use him to destroy the Izumo village. Have him lead the catapults to buildings, then have him run around the buildings. They are far too slow to hit him, and their loads will damage the structures.

Monitor your soldiers' movements when you march them in a group. Looking for a shortcut or a way to avoid bumping into each other, they will sometimes walk around trees and obstacles and stumble into lions or enemy soldiers.

There are two additional priests around the Izumo palace. One is near the northwest corner of the palace, and the other is near the Izumo leader behind some trees. (This information is totally worthless and those priests will be of no use to you, but you purchased this strategy guide so you deserve to know.)

Mission 2: Island Hopping

Even without their leader, the Izumo know how to get on the Yamato Clan's nerves. They have stolen five treasures (artifacts) from the Yamato, and scattered them throughout their islands. Your Yamato leaders are outraged at this offense, and they want you to scour the Izumos' islands and recover the stolen treasure.

You begin this mission with three composite bowmen, two galleys, two phalanxes, a catapult, a ballista, a light transport, and a heavy transport. The Izumo greatly outnumber your men, but your ballista and catapult represent much greater firepower.

You should approach this mission with two immediate objectives, both involving taking control of a moderately sized island southwest of your island. There are actually two islands off your southwest shore. One is tiny and inhabited by a composite bowman and two enemy

Do not underestimate the alligator guarding the third treasure. If it gets close to your catapult, it will bite it.

One of the Izumo composite bowmen guarding the second treasure may leave his post to take a shot at your transports. Have your catapult take him out.

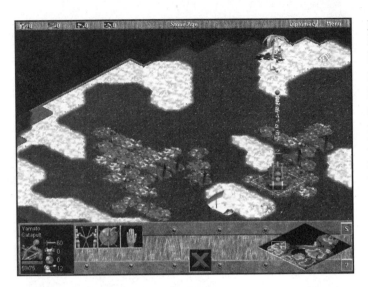

Your catapult will be able to clear out most of the Izumo archers guarding the fourth and fifth treasures by skulking around the "E"-shaped island and blasting them with long-range shots.

priests. Do not attempt to land on that island or you'll lose your men. A little farther south, there is a larger island, inhabited by lions and elephants. One of the missing treasures is there. If you can land on that island and take control of the treasure at the outset of the mission, you'll avert catastrophe.

An Izumo galley will pass the island very early on as it makes its way to your island along the northeastern edge of the map. As it passes the island, it will come in close contact with the only treasure not controlled by the Izumo, thus gaining control of all the artifacts and setting off a 2,000-year clock. If you can land your men along the north face of that island and gain control of the treasure before that ship sails by, you won't have to worry about the clock. You will not need to worry about killing the lions—as long as your beat the Izumo galley, you'll be able to command the treasure to go to your transport. Collect your treasure and return it to your island for safety.

Now load your catapult and an archer on your light transport. It's time to take control of the seas.

This job involves a little island hopping. You begin this journey by going on a safari. Return to the island where you got the treasure and kill the elephant and lion on its southeastern shore. Now use your catapult to kill the archer and priests on the smaller island—you're doing this to ensure that they do not convert or kill your ships; there are no treasures on their island.

Now head south to the large island near the corner of the map. (To avoid running into Izumo galleys, make sure you sail to the next island along the recently cleared eastern shore.) The only inhabitants on this island are three innocent Izumo villagers busily cutting wood. Crush them—that wood is being

converted into the Izumo galleys intended for attacking your island.

The Izumo will not be napping while you capture the treasure; they will be sending galleys to annihilate your men at your home base. Move your heavy transport along the southern cliffs of your island and group your ballista, archers, and galleys, and your men will be able to fight off the first Izumo galleys on their own.

This situation cannot go on forever, however. Once the priests and archers are gone, load your men on the heavy transport and move it along with your galleys to the north part of the

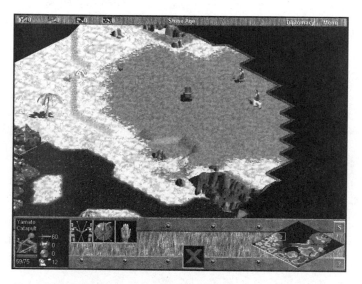

The fifth treasure is on a large island. Two clubmen are beside the treasure, but three archers and six phalanxes are close at hand. Destroy the clubmen with your catapult and send a composite bowman to collect the treasure, and you can escape without much bloodshed—assuming you don't want bloodshed.

woodcutters' island. Next, unload your ballista and archers on the small island and move your galleys into their firing range as you send your transport to the southern edge of the island. The final Izumo galleys are bound to find your men; this configuration will enable your men to fight them off while suffering only minimal casualties.

Land your catapult on the island in the southern corner of the map. Ignore the houses along the island. Send your catapult to the west shore of the island and destroy the Izumo dock. This will guarantee the safety of your catapult and your ballista. From this point on, you can deploy them on smaller islands to soften or destroy enemy armies and prepare the way for your archers and phalanxes.

There is a treasure guarded by two composite bowmen on the island just north of the island on which the Izumo had their dock. You'll be able to catch those bowmen off guard if you land your catapult on the southernmost or northernmost edges of the island and pick them off. Once they are dead, send

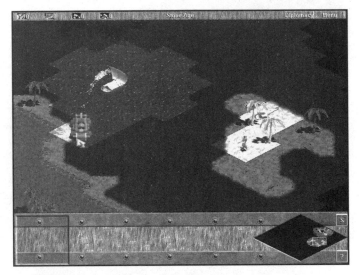

Even though the catapult eventually killed him, this Izumo priest was able to convert the Yamato's only catapult, effectively thwarting the Yamato invasion.

The Izumo have a dock and an island full of wood. They will send galleys to harass you as soon as they locate your whereabouts. They'll eventually overwhelm you unless you can shut down their naval might.

your composite bowman to collect the treasure.

The treasure is on an island along the southwestern edge of the map, almost within sight of the Izumo dock. It's guarded by three archers and a nasty little alligator. If you land in the southeast corner of this island, you should be able to pick off the archers and collect the treasure without any problem. Do not underestimate that alligator, however. It can do a lot of damage to a catapult, so have your composite bowmen kill it as soon as you land.

Three additional archers can be found guarding the tiny islands scattered around the western corner of the map. Move your catapult to the sandbar and kill the archer on the island to the north, then transport your catapult to that island to kill an archer on another northern island.

Next, transport your catapult to the "E"-shaped island. As you move along this island, you'll see an archer on a small island to the west guarding the fourth

treasure, which is on an island near the northwest edge of the map. Kill the archer and have your transport collect the treasure.

The fifth treasure is on a large island just north of the "E"-shaped island. You'll be able to see it from the top of the island. Have your catapult cross the sandbar connecting to that island and kill the two clubmen guarding the treasure.

And now for the little surprise. There is a sixth treasure on an isolated island near the northern corner of the map. Collecting this treasure is a bit tougher because the island is so small that there is no way to sneak up on the three composite bowmen guarding the treasure. To win this island, you'll need to launch a two-pronged attack.

Load all of your men and weapons on the heavy transport, then send everything you have to that final island. Begin your assault on this final island by sending your remaining galleys to attack the archers. While they sink your galleys, make your landing. Your

The Izumo dock is on an island along the southwestern edge of the map. Send your catapult to destroy the dock before embarking on your mission to capture the treasures.

Begin your mission by killing the animals along the eastern shore of this island. This will clear the way for you to attack the priests on the next island.

Land your catapult on the extreme southern tip of this island and the composite bowmen guarding the second treasure will not be alerted to your invasion.

The third treasure is alone on a small island. Don't be fooled, however. The Izumo archers have instant access to the treasure by crossing sandbars

phalanxes and weapons should make short work out of the archers. Once the island is clear, collect your prize and celebrate. You've accomplished another mission.

Ways to Lose

There are three major threats in this mission, and you should eliminate all of them in the opening minutes of the scenario. The 2,000-year clock poses a problem because 20 minutes is not enough time to hunt for six treasures and reel them in. The way to avoid this problem, as stated earlier, is to gain control of the closest treasure before that Izumo ship passes by.

The next threat comes from the Izumo priests. Given the chance, they will convert your transports and catapult. Don't throw archers or your ballista at them; you need your catapult's range to take them out without being converted.

The last and most serious danger is the Izumo navy. You can only go island hopping if you have ships, and given the chance, they will overwhelm your galleys and transports. Kill the Izumo woodcutters quickly, then take the battle to their dock before they have the chance to sink your fleet. This mission becomes much easier the moment you control the waters around these islands.

Additional Hints

Leave your catapult to help defend your shores against the first Izumo attacks as you collect the first treasure. Your navy will need the assistance.

Make sure to move treasures deep within your island when returning them. If they're too close to shore, they may convert over to the Izumo.

Since the Izumo do not have a town center, they'll be unable to create more villagers once you kill their three woodcutters. With no villagers, they cannot build a new dock. Destroy their dock and kill their villagers, and you'll control the waters in this mission.

Even though only one of the archers guarding the third treasure poses any threat to collecting that treasure, they will fire at your ships throughout the mission. It's worth the effort to clear them out of the way, especially as you go to collect the fourth treasure.

You will never have to deal with the six phalanxes and three archers guarding the eastern cliffs of the island with the fifth treasure. Just kill the clubmen and slip on and off of the island quickly.

If you want additional points to achieve a high score on this mission, wipe out the Izumo. Land your catapult and ballista on the island in the center of the screen and have them destroy the Izumo army on the island to the west. Destroy their houses and their storage pit, and you will achieve a winning score.

Mission 3: Capture

You are about to embark on one of the most unique missions in Age of Empires.

Your job in this mission is to capture an Izumo artifact. This is not going to be easy—the artifact is safely hidden within the thick walls of a fortress that has been buttressed with several fully upgraded guard towers. To make matters worse, the fortress is on an island with only one entrance—a land bridge in the center of an Izumo stronghold.

Get to the yellow Izumos' gold supply quickly enough and the only resistance you'll encounter will be a group of axemen. Have your ships kill them and hold the area until you can send an invasion force to control the land and a work force to build a storage pit and mine the resources. You should include a catapult in that invasion. The Izumo have erected a tower at the edge of the map just out of your ships' range.

With the island fortress in the center and the land forming a ring around it, the map for this scenario looks a bit like a clock. For this reason, the most accurate way to describe enemy sites and mineral deposits will be to describe them as if they were placed on a clock. An item placed at 12:00 will be located in the northern corner; items described as located at 6:00 will be in the southern corner; and items at 10:00 or 11:00 will be along the northwest edge.

You begin this mission with four villagers, six axemen, and a Bronze Age village located at 9:00 on the map. You start out with 400 units each of wood, food, and stone, and 200 units of gold.

To win this battle, however, you'll need to advance to the Iron Age, and to do this, you will need gold. Unfortunately, all of the largest gold deposits are guarded by Izumo towers. They are located at 11:00, 1:00, 3:00, and 7:00 on the map. To get that gold, you'll have to make your move quickly and fight for it before the Izumo harvest it.

There is one 300-unit deposit of gold along the northwest edge of the map, at 10 o'clock, not far from your village. One of your first objectives should be to mine that deposit as you fortify your village against Izumo invasions.

Begin the mission by assigning three of your villagers to cut wood while your fourth villager picks berries from the bushes near your granary. Build four more villagers. Assign two to pick berries and two to go north with four axemen to build a tower and a storage pit beside the gold deposit (where they will mine it).

Use this time to develop your village and to expand your territory. Build a dock and upgrade your ships from scouts to galleys, then build three fleets. Send one fleet to the southern corner of the map to kill the Izumo villagers as they harvest gold and stone from the rich deposits near their village. Keep another fleet in your port to defend your village. Send the third fleet to help defend your men as they harvest the small gold deposit along in the northwest, then send the fleet farther north to kill the Izumo as they approach the gold supplies located at 11:00.

Do not send your villagers after those supplies, however, since they are guarded by a tower, as are the deposits at 7:00. At this point in the mission, you will have to accept the notion that stopping the Izumo from reaching gold deposits is almost as good as mining the deposits yourself. As long as the Izumo cannot mine the gold, you have the potential of owning it.

Have your catapult triremes or juggernaughts clear the entrance for your men to enter the island. This may be a slow process—the Izumo have constructed very sturdy walls and towers to block the way.

Once you've broken the back of their resistance to your gold mining, have your ships take the battle to the yellow Izumo city located at 6:00 on the map.

You can destroy the Izumo towers that guard the island fortress with triremes, but that process takes a long time and your triremes will be easy targets for Izumo ballistas.

The Izumo will not take your expansion lightly. The yellow Izumo will march north toward your village, sending axemen, cavalry, and archers. The brown Izumo will send chariots and ships along the top of the map to attack your men as they mine gold.

Use your fleets as your primary defense against these invasions. Your ships will be able to destroy enemy cavalry and foot soldiers without taking any damage, and you can repair them easily after they duel with enemy archers and catapults. Make sure to beef up your fleets so that you have four or five ships at all three strategic locations.

Build a tower by your dock in your village and a second tower by the shore at your mining outpost. With only 400 units of stone, you won't be able to build and repair these towers indefinitely, but you will inherit excellent stone deposits as you take more territory from the Izumo.

Your secondary defense should come from your towers and your axemen. Your towers will begin firing arrows at any enemies that slip by your fleets. This will draw them to your towers where your axemen can finish them off.

As you develop your village, build a siege workshop and a government center. Having these buildings will qualify you to enter the Iron Age once you have 800 units of gold, but more importantly, they will enable you to build powerful catapults.

Your catapult's first mission should be to open the way to the southeast. The Izumo have a tower just south of your village. Send five axemen and three villagers with your catapult and destroy that tower. Next, move down the map toward the gold deposits at 7:00.

Move your ships close to shore to kill soldiers who come to defend their territory, then move your invasion force within catapult range of the Izumo towers. Destroy the Izumo towers and storage pit and build a storage pit of your own, then send your catapult back to town.

The yellow Izumo will send several villagers to try to reclaim the area by erecting towers and other buildings. Kill them and destroy their buildings. They will send soldiers, too. Your ships should have no trouble defending your claim as the Izumo will exhaust their population trying to reclaim it. Once the Izumo stop challenging your territory, you'll encounter little resistance when you march into their city, claim their stone deposits, and destroy their buildings.

Do not rush into your attack on the brown Izumo harbor. Work your way slowly down the northeast coast destroying buildings and soldiers. This way you will not encounter major resistance as you destroy their dock.

The battle may not go quite so smoothly along the northern half of the map. The brown Izumo have a dock, a siege workshop, and enough gold to manufacture several catapults. They will continue to harass your ships with archers and catapults and to challenge your fleets with ships of their own.

Once you've emptied the small gold deposit just north of your mission, send your ships, catapult, and foot soldiers to clear the way for the next deposit, which is located at 11:00 on the map. This deposit is guarded by two towers. Have your catapult destroy the towers while your ships and men guard against Izumo soldiers arriving to protect their territory. Then have your villagers build a storage pit and begin harvesting the gold.

While your combined Bronze Age fleet could destroy the Izumo dock, the casualties would be astronomical. Wait until you have enough gold to advance to the Iron Age, then upgrade your galleys to triremes. You may even want to upgrade your dock to build catapult triremes so that you can include that

Guarded by four heavy towers and three ballistas, the entrance to the Izumos' island stronghold is well fortified. Do not march in blindly. Destroy the towers, the ballistas, and the first wall, then use the second wall as protection while your priests or catapults deal with the deadly phalanxes.

additional firepower when you attack.

Once you've upgraded your navy, it will be time to close the brown Izumos' dock and begin destroying their town. Their harbor is located in a tight corner at 3:00 on the map. If your fleet marches straight into the harbor, they'll be surrounded by chariot archers, catapults, and more.

For safety's sake, have your ships move slowly down the northeastern shore destroying all enemies that challenge them and all buildings that come within range. The Izumo will throw all of their resources into attacking your fleet, but they will be unequipped to stop you. Just be careful to destroy catapults as soon as they appear. An unchecked catapult can destroy an entire fleet of ships.

Like the yellow Izumo, the brown Izumo will exhaust their resources trying to fight off your invasion. Once your ships have destroyed their dock and most of their city, your ground forces will encounter only minimal resistance when you send them in to finish the job.

The final phase of this mission involves attacking the red Izumo stronghold in the center of the map. This stronghold is built on an island with sheer cliffs on all sides. The only entrance to the island is a tiny pass that's blocked by a wall and guarded by four heavy towers.

Begin your assault on this island by destroying the two towers guarding its rear. You can make this assault with a catapult trireme or a juggernaut. Either way, you'll find that these towers can absorb lots of damage before collapsing.

You will also discover that the island is guarded by three ballistas. There is no need to look for these ballistas; attack the towers and the ballistas will find

you. Because these ballistas are very capable of sinking your ships, concentrate your fire on them as they arrive, then send your ships back for repairs as needed until you've destroyed the ballistas and all four of the towers guarding the island.

Once the ballistas and towers are gone, the only enemies remaining on the island will be four Izumo phalanxes. If you've upgraded to juggernauts, you'll be able to kill these foot soldiers wherever they go. If you have catapults, they may be able to hide from you in the center of the island.

The yellow Izumo will not give up on these precious gold and rock deposits easily. Have your ships annihilate their men while your catapult destroys their guard towers and market. If a huge wave of Izumo pours in, load your catapult and villagers on a transport for safety while your ships resecure the area.

Either way, the next step of your invasion is to raze the first wall blocking the entrance of the island. March a priest and a catapult past the destroyed wall. You can convert the phalanxes with your priest, then let them kill each other or try to shoot them with your catapult. The only way they'll be able to move out of your priest's and catapult's range will be to move in range of your ships.

Once the phalanxes are dead, have your ships destroy the second protective wall at the front of the island. Once it is gone, march in and claim the artifact and the mission is over.

Ways to Lose

Play this mission gingerly, and the Izumo will triumph. You have to be prepared to expand and take enemy land so that you can offset the imbalance of natural resources. You will need 800 units of gold to move into the Iron Age and more

gold to build catapult triremes. Again, the only way to get that gold is to take it, and take it quickly, before the Izumo mine it for themselves.

The second danger in this mission is not preparing for invasions. When you break into the Izumo harbor, assuming you break in early enough, you'll discover they have several transport ships as well as galleys. These transports were not built to take tourists sightseeing along the picturesque coastline.

Make sure that your ships are deployed where they can stop any transports from landing and kill any troops that march into your village. Have sufficient ground strength to finish the Izumo that slip past your ships. They will destroy your village if you give them the chance, so be sure to defend your property carefully.

Additional Hints

Use your granary to upgrade your towers as quickly as possible; you will need towers to secure outposts throughout this mission.

Do not bother building farms in this mission. The waters in this map are filled with great fishing sites. Just be careful to protect your fishing boats.

There are large groves of berry bushes near the gold deposits at 7:00 and 1:00 on the map. If you need more food quickly after conquering the yellow and brown Izumo, build granaries in these areas and have your villagers forage for food.

Watch out for catapults. The Izumo will send several to sink your fleets. When you hear a warning trumpet, check your small map and see where the action is. If it involves your fleets, chances are the Izumo have sent a catapult.

Have either your ships or your catapult kill the elephant at the top of the screen. Left on its own, it will crush your villagers if you do not kill it.

In the first part of the mission, the only civilizations that matter are the yellow and brown Izumo, located at 3:00 and 6:00 on the map, respectively. They have better resources than your village and will expand quickly to find more resources. Let them get too big and you'll be unable to regain control of this mission. (The red Izumo are trapped on their island and will not try to invade you.)

Do not let your fishing boats or galleys go near the center of the lake or the Izumos' heavy towers will sink them.

Mission 4: Mountain Temple

Having their leader murdered was a huge embarrassment to the Izumo. You humiliated them when you recaptured the treasures, and they were humiliated when you broke into their stronghold and stole their artifact. Now you can disgrace them even further by destroying their temple and building one of your own in its place. In Japanese society, disgrace of this magnitude can be fatal.

You begin this mission with a Stone Age village consisting of a town center, two towers, and three villagers. You have 200 units each of wood, gold, and stone, and 400 units of food, plus two berry bushes that represent 600 additional food units. Your village is located on a ridge on one side of a small island. The Kibi, a clan allied with the Izumo, have a village on the other side of the island.

Assign one of your villagers to forage while your other villagers build barracks. Once they have finished the barracks, assign your builders to erect three houses, then forage. You need to build an army of clubmen and march east to destroy the Kibi before they harvest the gold and wood in their village. You need it more than they do.

From the outset of this mission, there will be two axemen and three clubmen defending the Kibi village. It will not take them long to develop this army; they will add 15 more clubmen if you let them. Begin leading the Kibis' soldiers into your towers as early as possible, then invade them when you have enough clubmen.

You will need at least ten clubmen to wage a successful invasion. The Kibi will build their army quickly, but continue making more since you may need them.

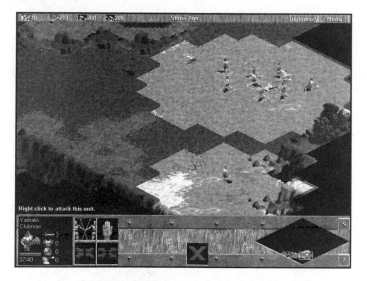

The brown Kibi will send axemen to reinforce the yellow Kibi's army. Two axemen can kill a fistful of clubmen, so don't try to fight them head-on. Lead them toward your towers and let the archers in your towers do the job for you.

Clearing the brown Kibi island will require a stone thrower, a priest, and a lot of patience. The island is crawling with composite bowmen, and the best way to deal with this threat is to blast the bowmen from a distance.

A stone thrower clears two Izumo bowmen, clearing the way for a group of scouts to storm the mountain and flush out the Izumos' priests.

The Kibi will have stationed several clubmen along the beach on the northern edge of the island. Try to slip your army past the southern ridges so that you can overwhelm the clubmen in the village and begin destroying their barracks as the clubmen from the beach straggle in.

Once you have destroyed their army and their barracks, destroy any villagers left in the village and send your villagers over. It will not be long before enemy galleys will begin patrolling the shores and attempting to kill your men and destroy your buildings, so try to keep away from the edges of the island as you move east. Your objectives will be to forage for 500 units of food so that you can enter the Tool Age, then to build a dock and two scout ships to clear your shores.

Don't expect the Kibi to sit by idly while you do this. They will send invaders, mostly archers, to your shores, so have your men ready to meet their transports and destroy them as they land. They will also continue

sending galleys to patrol your shores.

The only way to keep the Kibi off your island is to build a dock and chase them away. To do this, you must find a secure area that the Kibi are unlikely to discover until after your dock is completed. There is a small stretch of beach on the western end of your island. Send soldiers along your ridges to lure the Kibi ships east, then send a villager to build a dock. Build three scout ships, and prepare for a sea battle.

The objective of this mission is to march a stone thrower up the Izumos' holy mountain to destroy their towers and temple and replace them with a temple of your own.

You do not want to build ships and engage the Kibi navy until you have three ships and enough wood to repair your ships during the battle. Their galleys will be more powerful than your scout ships, so make sure you have a villager and at least 100 units of wood ready as you send your ships out to fight. Once you take these precautions, you'll be able to clear the Kibi from your waters. Taking control of the seas and destroying the Kibi dock will require more preparation.

The first thing you need to do is advance to the Iron Age, an act that requires 1,000 units of food and 800 units of gold. You can find the gold you need on an island just west of your home base. Build a transport and send three villagers to the island. Have them run toward the island quickly; there are three alligators along the beach. They may come in handy for food later, but at this point they simply pose a low-grade threat to your villagers' safety.

Have your villagers build a storage pit on the island; there is a gold deposit on the back side. Have two villagers mine it while your third villager cuts wood. As soon as you have enough gold, advance to the Iron Age and upgrade your ships from galleys to triremes.

The Kibi dock is in a corner of land between the Izumos' mountainous territory and the Kibis' island. An Izumo tower overlooks the dock, and another

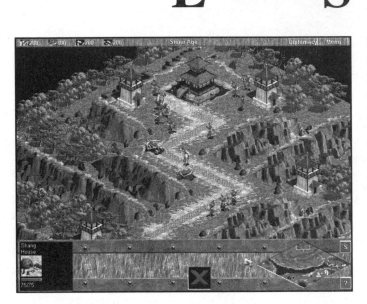

To win this mission, you'll have to get past this strong and well-positioned army. Don't expect this to be a fast scenario. You will have to move through most of it methodically.

tower looms near enough to strike your ships when you move in for the attack. In order to destroy the dock, you will need to attack from the south and fight your way across the Kibis' island. Destroying the Kibi dock is not merely a question of attacking their shores; it's a matter of razing their entire town.

You will not need a lot of men for this attack, just a stone thrower, a priest, and a lot of patience. Rather than staging a full invasion, you should simply destroy everything with your stone thrower. The problem is that the Kibi will have an army of compound bowmen who do not want to see their island destroyed. What you have to do is unload your stone thrower along the island and destroy towers, buildings, and people until you work your way across the island.

Start by destroying the towers along the eastern edge of the island. You can demolish the first one from the beach of your island, then transport your stone thrower across the channel and start destroying the other towers. If your stone thrower takes damage, send it back to your island and have a priest repair it. Never let your stone thrower stray far from your transport. That way you will be able to load your stone thrower quickly and send it to safety if Kibi archers close in on you.

Destroying the Kibi after this fashion is downright dull, but it gets the job done with a minimum of casualties. You have limited resources in this scenario, so you'll have to perform each task methodically.

After you annihilate the Kibi, your next task is to soften the Izumo defenses so that you can break into their territory and mount an attack on their sacred (and well-guarded) hill. Begin the softening process by using your triremes to destroy the towers guarding the Izumo shoreline. Fire at everything you see—

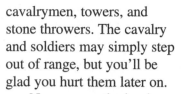

cavalrymen, towers, and stone throwers. The cavalry and soldiers may simply step out of range, but you'll be glad you hurt them later on.

Now comes the hard decision. With very little gold and no chance of finding any more, you must decide whether you want to build several stone throwers and attack the Izumo mountain with stone throwers and scouts or strengthen your priest and try to convert your way in. Either way, you're in for a fight.

The final assault will send you up a winding path

With galleys in front of it, a Kibi tower behind it, and an Izumo tower overlooking it, attacking this dock will be no small job. Don't just throw ships at it, or you'll waste time and resources.

past five stone throwers, three ballistas, four priests, 12 composite bowmen, and four heavy towers. Don't expect to charge in and win. No matter how many scouts and archers you train, your priests and stone throwers will ultimately decide whether you win or lose.

Upgrading your priest's range is probably the better choice since it will enable you to convert a stone thrower or two during your assault. It will also enable you to convert some very expensive cavalrymen who are guarding the cliffs. With these men on your side, you stand a better chance of accomplishing your ultimate mission.

Once you've knocked down the towers guarding the coast of the Izumo island, you can send your priest to convert their men. Have your transport unload him along the beach toward the west side of the island. You'll see two cavalrymen. With their path to the beach blocked by boulders, they will not be able to attack your priest as he chants to them.

Convert the first cavalryman, then have your transport pick him up. The second one will attempt to reach your priest. Load the priest into your transport; the boulders at the front of the beach usually block the cavalrymen, but they

Build stables at the base of the Izumos' island so that you have access to more men as you need them. As large and strong as this force appears, it is not powerful enough to take the hill and destroy the temple.

sometimes find their way around it. When you think your priest's faith is recharged, unload him at the far edge of the beach and have him convert the second cavalryman, then have your priest heal both soldiers before you transport them to safety.

With his added range, your priest will be able to convert some of the archers lining the first part of the mountain pass leading to the Izumo temple. Convert as many as you can. Their fellow archers will kill them, but that still thins the Izumo ranks.

A stone thrower will attempt to kill your priest. Dodge its barrage of stones and convert it. Though the Izumo cavalry will eventually destroy it, your stone thrower should be able to clear all of the archers along the first stretch of the path.

Use your priest wisely and you should be able to acquire seven or eight cavalrymen before you even begin your final invasion. That will strengthen your landing force considerably. (Remember, cavalrymen are catapult-killers.)

Now you need to get serious about this invasion. There is a spot not too far from the western edge of the Izumo coastline where the path between the cliffs and the coastline is very narrow. Your triremes should be able to shoot anything moving through that area. Move the entire fleet to that spot. Now transport your entire population to the island.

Have your villagers build stables on the island. From this moment on, the only type of units you should build are scouts, and you should build as many of them as possible. Next, move one of your catapults along the edge of the cliffs to kill the archers and towers along the first terrace on the sacred mountain. Retreat to the safety of your triremes at the first sign of retaliation. Your ships

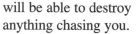

will be able to destroy anything chasing you.

Next, put your extremely expensive priest to work converting the row of stone throwers along the next ledge of the trail. The Izumo will destroy each stone thrower as you convert it, but you would probably rather have them shoot each other than your army.

Once you upgrade to triremes, you'll find It much easier to deal with the Kibi navy. If they continue to send transports, send your triremes to clog their waterways until you can safely attack their dock.

The first two stone throwers are along the wall on the third tier of the trail. Have your priest inch up until one is in sight, then have him convert it. As soon as it is converted, have it turn and fire at the stone thrower beside it. Chances are they will destroy each other, but you may get lucky and kill a couple of Izumo composite bowmen before your stone thrower is destroyed.

Next, have your priest move down along the bottom of the first cliff and convert the remaining cavalryman. (If you run into an archer before you reach the cavalryman, convert the archer and send him to your stocking area while your priest recharges his faith.) Send him to join your forces at the western edge of the island, then have a stone thrower come and annihilate the remaining archers, completely clearing out the first ridge of the sacred mountain.

The Izumos' two final stone throwers are just above the area where you slaughtered the archers. Send your stone thrower up to that area and destroy the first one that attacks you. (Remember to move your stone thrower back and forth after every shot so that it doesn't get hit.) The second stone thrower will also join the battle, but do not destroy it. With the other three stone throwers destroyed, this last one will be able to do a lot of damage if you convert it. Send your priest in and make it yours. (Again, remember to move as you chant or that stone thrower can make juice out of your priest with its first shot.)

AGE
of
EMPIRES

Once you have triremes, you'll be able to attack the towers guarding the Izumo island. Do not approach these towers with galleys or you'll lose your ships.

Move your stone thrower east the moment it's converted, then take it north and use it to destroy the first tower that comes in sight. The Izumo will send a ballista, three composite bowmen, and a priest to kill it, but the converted throwers should be able to take the tower and a few bowmen before going down.

Once the stone thrower is dead, allow your priest to recharge, then send him to convert the ballista. Once you've gotten the ballista, turn it on the Izumo priest before he reconverts it. With a little luck, the ballista will get the priest and two bowmen before dying. Use your priest to convert the final bowman; you never know what may turn the tide of the rather treacherous battle that looms ahead.

Having destroyed the archers lining the first terrace and the stone throwers overlooking it, you're ready to march your forces toward the Izumo temple. Bear in mind that the Izumo still have three towers, three priests, and a lot of composite bowmen waiting for you, so this will not be easy.

The first target that will come in range will be a tower. Have your scouts form a ring around your stone thrower to protect it, then move in and destroy the tower. If bowmen come down to attack, send your scouts after them and move your stone thrower to safety. Remember, you cannot afford to build more stone throwers.

The next target will be two composite bowmen stationed two thirds of the way up the final hill. Have your stone thrower kill them, then move it to safety and bring the rest of your forces up.

There's an old proverb among martial artists that says that you should never take a weapon to a fight unless you know how to take it away from your opponent. The idea behind the proverb is that if your opponent gets hold of your weapon, you'll need to know how to defend yourself against it.

This adage is quite appropriate for this part of this scenario. The Izumo have three priests waiting for you to attack. Whatever you send at them, you can bet they will try to convert it; so make your next attack a weak one so that the Izumo use their faith on disposable targets—scouts and axemen. (Cavalrymen take too many hits to kill and you don't want to risk a stone thrower.)

Send five or six scouts up the hill to destroy the Izumos' remaining ballistas.

If your priest can convert the first Izumo stone thrower before others arrive, you will be able to do untold damage with it. In this example, it annihilated six archers before succumbing to a second stone thrower on a higher ledge.

Chances are that between the ballistas, the bowmen, the priests, and the towers, your five scouts will not achieve their goal, but they will cause the priests to use up their faith temporarily.

There's no room for elegance in a moment like this; send all of your cavalry, axemen, and remaining scouts up the hill to kill the priests, the ballistas, and as many bowmen as possible. The towers will kill several of your men during this strike, but not before they get the priests and ballistas. And with those threats out of the way, your stone throwers can march up the hill, kill the remaining bowmen, and destroy the Izumo towers and temple.

Once you've finished this demolition job, send some villagers up the hill to build a temple over the spot in which the Izumo temple once stood. You have accomplished your mission when the new temple is built.

Ways to Lose

Give them the chance and the Kibi will end this mission for you in a hurry. If you wait too long to attack the first Kibi town, they will develop a large enough

army to overwhelm your forces. They will also use up the resources you need to continue the mission.

The brown Kibi, on the eastern island, pose an equally dangerous threat. They will send galleys to patrol your waters and transports with composite bowmen to invade your island. These are dangerous threats. Even if the galleys do not get your men, they can shoot buildings and cause you to expend resources you'll need later.

You will face the standard perils as you ascend the Izumo mountain, but there may be one additional threat you've overlooked. Do not run out of wood at the end of this mission. Ridiculous as it sounds, you'll need enough wood to erect a temple over the ruins of the Izumo temple or you'll have to start again.

Additional Hints

The Izumo have no villagers or barracks. Their army is in place the moment this scenario begins, so there is no value in rushing to attack before you have sufficient forces.

Build your first houses and barracks as far inland as possible so that enemy ships cannot destroy them from offshore.

Use your storage pit to upgrade your soldiers and armor as soon as you enter the Tool Age.

Use your market to upgrade your woodcutting and farming throughout the scenario.

The Kibi navy will attack your repairmen and try to kill them before attacking your ships, so have your repairmen walk to a safe spot between naval battles.

Do not try to convert the Kibi composite bowmen on the eastern island. There are too many of them and they will kill your priests before they are in range. Kill the bowmen with a catapult.

The cavalrymen and scouts in this game are downright stupid. Do not trust them to go places; once you assign them a destination watch, make sure they make it or they will get lost.

You will mine less than 2,000 units of gold in this mission. That means that priests and catapults are irreplaceable; keep them safe and healthy.

Build a government workshop and upgrade your catapults and missile weapons. Having powerful projectile weapons will serve you well during the final assault.

After you have converted all of the cavalry near the cliffs, send cavalrymen up to lure additional suckers into your priest's range.

Mission 5: Canyon of Death

You didn't think you could rest once you defeated the Kibi, did you? The Yamato want to unite Japan, and that means there are more clans to fight and more alliances to be made.

Your next battle will be with the Shikoku, a southern clan who has stolen an artifact from the Yamato. Your job is to lead a small army through treacherous grounds. Make it through this trap and you'll be given a large enough army to defeat the Shikoku and recover your treasure.

You begin this mission with six cavalrymen, four composite bowmen, four horse archers, and four short swordsmen. Your immediate opposition includes axemen, archers, composite bowmen, stone throwers, horse archers, towers, short swordsmen, and lions. Survive all of that and you'll face a small but potent force with composite bowmen, cavalrymen, stone throwers, and phalanxes.

As the mission opens, you'll hear a lion attacking off in the distance. Believe it or not, this is good news. The lion has just killed two Shikoku archers.

Your first task will be to clear a path for your men. The lion that killed the Shikoku archers is just west of your men. Just beyond the lion is a ridge overlooking three enemy archers. Two more archers and two axemen await your army beyond some trees to the north. None of these threats will destroy your force, but they will chip away at it. What you need most is to keep your army intact for as long as possible.

Send two composite bowmen to clear all of these threats. Keep tight control on both men and have them concentrate their fire on the same targets. This will ensure that the lion and axemen do not reach them, and that the archers will be killed before they get in range to fire back.

Once the lions and enemy soldiers are eradicated, move your men north to the base of the hill. From here you can either move north or west. If you head north, you'll have to fight your way past several bowmen, two towers, and a stone thrower. This approach is a bargain compared to what you'll meet if you head west. Have your archers clear the three lions just beyond the trees, then start moving toward the top of the map.

The Shikoku have built a wall to block your path. The only way to get to the transports is to destroy this tower then break through the wall.

You'll see a rock ledge as you get past the trees. Two lions are resting just to the west; do not let your archers kill them. You can use these lions to save some of your Yamato lives.

There are four Shikoku composite bowmen and a tower at the top of the cliff and a stone thrower and tower on the next ledge up. The first tower and bowmen will see your men coming, so you have no range advantage. This is the time to make a strategic sacrifice.

Send a cavalryman to attract the lions, then send him up the hill toward the Shikoku bowmen and have him attack their tower. The tower and bowmen will attack your cavalryman, but the lion will attack the bowmen. If you get really lucky, the stone thrower will descend from the next ledge and the lion will destroy it. (Your men will have to kill any archers who survived the lion. That goes for the stone thrower as well.)

The next task involves threading your men up the hill and trying to slip them past the first tower. There is a safe spot at the top of the hill against the edge of the map. Send a horse archer to that spot and have it kill the lion hiding beyond the trees at the top of the hill. Now send three swordsmen to that spot, then have the swordsmen raze the upper tower to clear the way for the rest of your army. As soon as they engage the tower, send your cavalry to assist them. (You will unavoidably take casualties at this point.)

Once you make it past the towers, you'll encounter a horse archer and three composite bowmen. Have your cavalry swarm and overwhelm them.

The next part of the mission is the toughest. You must lead your men down a long slope to the west until they reach the seashore. There they will be greeted by swordsmen, bowmen, two stone throwers, four towers, and a wall.

You need only one man to make it past these obstacles to complete your mission; that will not make this task any easier.

Three things that can make this part of the trek a bit less perilous. There are three lions hiding behind the trees. Have a horse archer lead these lions along the shore and they will kill the swordsmen and one of the stone throwers. There are no clever tricks after that; your cavalry and swordsmen will have to hack through the remaining Shikoku and break through the wall to get to the transports. (They may also have to put some wounded-but-useful lions out of their misery.)

Once you hack through the wall, quickly lead your men to the end of the peninsula. There you will find two heavy transports waiting for you. Your fortunes in this mission are about to take a serious turn for the better.

Have the transports move along the southwest edge of the map and you'll find a tiny island crawling with blue soldiers. Unload

Head north with your transports and you'll find this army waiting to serve you.

The final showdown in this scenario takes place on a Shikoku stronghold. The Shikoku outnumber your forces, but you have priests.

Some of your best weapons in this mission are the lions inhabiting these lands. Lead the lions to the enemy and they'll do all kinds of damage. This lion has killed a bowman and a stone thrower.

your remaining men and have the priests heal them, then load everybody on the transports.

Take your transports north to the Shikoku stronghold. Unload one of your stone throwers on the southern shore and have them destroy the Shikoku towers, then bring your entire army to the island.

The landing force you picked up on the last island is strong, but not strong enough to go toe-to-toe with the Shikoku. Use your transports to shuttle one of your stone throwers along the side of the island to harass the Shikoku and shoot at their stone throwers. When they send bowmen down to investigate, have your stone throwers kill them. This will enable you to thin their numbers.

Your harassment will also cause the Shikoku to move their stone throwers to the ledge of the cliff. By keeping your transport nearby as an escape hatch, you should be able to engage and destroy one or both of the Shikoku stone throwers. This will give you a decided edge during the final fight.

After you have destroyed the stone throwers, go after the Shikoku archers and horse archers. If you're able to kill them, the Shikoku will no longer be able to shoot arrows at your stone throwers. The only way they'll be able to attack them will be to send slow-moving phalanxes down the slope. (The bowmen and horse archers may wound your stone thrower; be sure to send it back to the priests before it takes too much damage.)

Once your stone throwers have eliminated the archers and bowmen, send your priests in the transport to convert the Shikoku cavalrymen. Cavalry are adept at destroying catapults, so converting their cavalry will improve your chances of protecting your stone throwers. (Remember to keep your transport

nearby should your priest need a quick escape.)

At this point, you'll be able to overwhelm the Shikoku with your forces or you can continue to whittle their numbers with your priests and stone throwers. Once you're ready to finish the scenario, send a stone thrower to destroy the tower at the top of the hill and cavalrymen to capture the artifact. Once the artifact is safely deposited on your island, the mission ends in your favor.

Use your transport to take priests and stone throwers to this small stretch of beach below the Shikoku stronghold. You will be able to thin their forces here.

Ways to Lose

You spend the first half of this mission hoping to survive so that you can spend the second half of this mission fighting an uphill battle.

Simple mistakes can cost you this entire mission. Head west instead of north, and you'll find yourself fighting much stronger forces. You may well beat them, but the fight will be harder and your men will be in much rougher shape as they sprint along the beach and attack the wall.

Do not kill the lions. The Shikoku are trained to kill your men as soon as they see them; they will not necessarily attack the lions, and the big cats may clear a lot of enemies out of your way. They are particularly good at clawing catapults.

Finally, do not waste your priests by sending them after large forces when you invade the Shikoku stronghold. Remember that your priests need to recharge after every conversion. Send them to convert two or three bowmen, and the unconverted bowmen will likely kill them as soon as they stop chanting.

AGE of EMPIRES

Two transports await the members of your invasion team that make it through the first phase of this mission. To get to these transports, you'll have to break through enemy lines and hack through a stone wall.

Additional Hints

Move very slowly and methodically through this mission. If your men bunch up and move along a wide path, they will attract additional lions and archers.

Have your men hug the water as they move along the shore. If you do not get too close to the trees at the end of the peninsula, you will not be attacked by the stone thrower and five bowmen who move along the edge of the cliff at the end of the beach.

Remember to save your progress often throughout this game. You should save your progress as you make your way to the transports, then save your progress again after you destroy the Shikoku stone throwers that are guarding the artifact.

Mission 6: Oppression

How many plates can you keep spinning at one time? An evil warlord wants tributes of gold. To satisfy his insatiable appetite, you must mine for gold, trade for gold, and build your army until you are strong enough to just say "No." In the meantime, you must fish for food, cut wood, build a city and an army, and pay tributes.

You begin this mission with four villagers and a Stone Age village. You have 400 units each of wood, food, gold, and stone. As a menacing reminder of just how primitive your forces are, your enemies have six phalanxes and a catapult stationed around your village.

Assign your first villagers to forage the berries by your granary and cut wood. Make more villagers, build a dock and fish for food. Build trading boats

and trade food for gold with the yellow town at the top of the screen. You will not finish any of this, however, before you receive a message stating that the Kyushu demand a tribute of 200 units of gold. Pay it.

Advance to the Tool Age as quickly as possible, then to the Bronze Age. The latter will enable you to upgrade the size of your ships. Your upgraded trading boats will bring in more gold, and your upgraded fishing boats will bring in more food. When you have 1,000 units of gold, you can stop trading and build your food supply.

As you build up your food, you might want to send two or three villagers to the small island along the northwest edge of the map. This island has a large gold deposit. Have them build a storage pit, mine the gold, and cut the wood on the island.

In the western corner of the map, you'll see a bay filled with fish. Send your fishing boats there when you've cleaned out the waters around your village, then seal your boats in and

The Kyushu make a small show of muscle by having their catapults and phalanxes march through your village as the scenario begins.

The Kyushu will send their fleet to commandeer all of the fish in this bay if you do not seal it off. Lead two of your fishing boats into the bay, then build a dock in the mouth of the bay to cut it off from other boats.

You need gold and this island has some. Have your scout ship kill the lions, then send three villagers to build a storage pit and mine the gold.

Kyushu phalanxes will parade through your village as the mission opens. Stone Age clubmen, your only warriors, cannot even hope to hurt phalanxes.

your neighbors' boats out by building a dock at the opening of the bay. You should also leave a villager there to cut the wood and mine the stone deposits around the bay.

As the scenario winds down, you may decide that you need more villagers. Good news! The yellow civilization on the north island has no army, so you don't have to worry about the military ramifications of that group changing its diplomatic stance. Just send over a priest and make as many converts as you like. Consider it a good source of cheap labor.

With your tributes paid, the Kyushu will leave you alone. This is your chance to go after all of the resources on the map as aggressively as possible. Mine the rock deposits and wood to the west. Fish and farm until you have thousands of units of food. Develop a large army of bowmen, and upgrade your ships to juggernauts.

The Kyushu (the fools!) trust you. Use this trust to your advantage. Build towers beside their walls; seal the north, south, and east entrances to their city. Station your juggernaughts beside their port. Place priests near the catapults they have sent to various outposts. By the time you finish preparing for this fight, it should be like shooting fish in a barrel.

As soon as all of your forces are in place, begin the battle by changing your diplomatic stance to that of an enemy and converting their catapults. The entire scenario map will instantly light up with conflicts as your towers attack their towers and men.

Lead your bowmen to their city wall and spray the Kyushu phalanxes and catapults with arrows. Have your juggernaughts demolish their dock and government center. This battle ends the moment you destroy the Kyushu government center.

The red Kyushu will send huge work teams to mine wood and stone from around your village. These teams pose no danger to your men, but they will eat away your resources, so send lots of villagers to mine the stone before the Kyushu carry it all away.

Ways to Lose

The biggest danger in this scenario is aggravating the Kyushu before you're ready to fight them. You need to pay them off because you won't have any forces that can stand up to their phalanxes and catapults until you enter the Iron Age.

Build your trading fleet quickly and make sure you always have enough gold to meet their demands.

As long as you pay your tributes and do not attempt to attack or convert any red Kyushu units, you will be able to co-habitate with your oppressors.

AGE *of* EMPIRES

Trusting as they are, the Kyushu will not complain when you build towers along their walls. They will even remain silent as you seal the entrances to their city.

Additional Hints

Do not build your dock next to the Kyushu guard tower or it will attack your dock as soon as you miss a tribute payment.

Several lions inhabit the northwest island with the gold deposits. Send a scout ship to kill the lions and clear the island.

You may need to destroy your own dock if the Kyushu send too many trading boats and start depleting your gold supply.

When you run out of wood and gold on the northwestern island, build a granary and farms.

There is a lake with several schools of fish in it near the west corner of the map. You can build a dock in the lake if you need food.

Play your cards right throughout this mission and you should have thousands of units of wood, gold, and food by the end of the mission. If you are aggressive about mining stone, you should have nearly 2,000 units as you prepare for the final showdown.

Upgrade your villagers so that they can destroy walls and towers. You should have a surplus of villagers as you enter the fight.

Build a siege workshop and upgrade your projectile weapons. This will give your towers a fighting chance against the Kyushu's sturdier but less powerful heavy towers.

Mission 7: A Friend in Need

Having gained control over most of Japan, the Yamato have turned their attention to Korea. They founded a colony in Korea and formed an alliance with the Paekche Kingdom, a non-aggressive civilization struggling to maintain

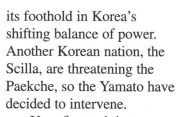

its foothold in Korea's shifting balance of power. Another Korean nation, the Scilla, are threatening the Paekche, so the Yamato have decided to intervene.

Your first task is to save the Paekche government center from destruction. The mission opens with the Scilla attacking their city, which is located along the northwest edge of the screen. Scilla cavalry have entered the city, and more importantly, two Scilla catapults are firing into the city from behind its western wall.

Most of your soldiers and workers are safely tucked away inside your village as the mission opens—you have six axemen in the Paechke village. Send them through the entrance to the city to attack the catapults. Have them charge one catapult and strike at it until the second catapult fires at them. As soon as it does, have your men turn and attack the second catapult; the shot from the second catapult will destroy the first one.

Scilla cavalrymen will descend on your axemen and kill them as they destroy the second catapult, but you

The mission begins with two Scilla catapults just a stone's throw from the Paechke government center. Send your axemen to destroy the catapults by coaxing them into shooting each other.

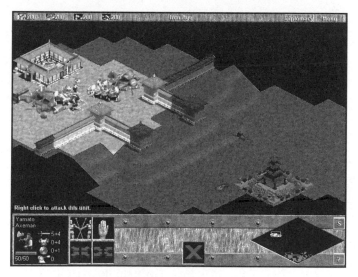

Once you destroy the catapults, Scilla cavalrymen will attack, and your axemen don't stand a chance. The Paechke will need more help defeating the Scilla; but for now, their government center is safe.

Make several priests in this level. You can use them to increase your army by converting Scilla cavalrymen and long swordsmen. Do not try to convert horse archers; they shoot back.

will have given the Paekche government center a reprieve. With the catapults destroyed, the Paechke will be able to mount a decent defense while you send your cavalry and short swordsmen to chase them away.

Once the Paechke government center is safe, it's time to focus your attention on building your city and army. You have an Iron Age village with eight short swordsmen, eight composite bowmen, four cavalrymen, and nine villagers. You have 200 units each of wood, food, gold, and stone, and there are forests around your village and berry bushes to the east, near your granary. There's also a small gold deposit near the south corner of the map and a stone deposit along the western edge of the map, just north of your village.

As you develop your army, create enough villagers to cut wood, forage food, and mine the various mineral deposits around your village.

You will find that your village is protected by natural barriers—a small row of trees extending from the northwest edge of the map and a long row of trees along your northeastern flank. These trees form a strong wall with two breaks—one north of your village and one along the southeastern edge of the map. Since Scilla Central is located in the eastern corner of the map, expect most of their attacks to come through that second break.

Build a wall to seal that entrance. Build towers along the wall and send composite bowmen to fend off attackers. Once you've built a siege workshop, you may want to send a couple of stone throwers to protect the wall. This area will be a weak link if you do not seal it off properly. The Scilla will attack it repeatedly, sending catapults and horse archers to destroy the wall if possible.

Once you have sealed that area, it will be time to take control of more territory. There is a large gold deposit (3,600 units) in the center of the map. Send a large squad of composite bowmen, a priest, a stone thrower, and four villagers to take control of that area.

Two towers guard the gold; have your stone thrower attack them. (The towers will have better range than your stone thrower, so you'll have to send your stone thrower to be healed halfway through each attack.) Once the towers are down, have your villagers erect three guard towers around the site and place your bowmen

The most vulnerable part of your village is located along the southeastern edge of the map. Trees form a natural barrier around most of your village, but there is a break in the trees in this area, and the Scilla will send many units to exploit it. Build a wall to close the gap between the trees and the edge of the map, then build towers to protect the wall. You might also send some composite bowmen to protect the towers.

beside your towers. Next, have your villagers build a storage pit and begin mining.

The Scilla will continually challenge your hold of the central gold deposit. They will start by sending horse archers. Wait until the horse archers begin shooting at your towers, then have your priest convert them. You'll be able to amass a fairly sizable army this way.

Once you've assembled a strong enough army around the gold in the center of the map, send villagers and cavalry to build an outpost beside the Paechke city. There is a large stone deposit just south of their city and a grove of bushes to the north.

Paechke towers and soldiers will offer your forces some protection, but you should expect the Scilla army to invade your outpost. Build additional towers and either an archery range or stables so that you can expand your forces.

If you have enough stone, you will discover that the easiest way to move east toward the Scilla city is by building towers, then converting the soldiers

The Scillas' towers have long-range bows that can hit your stone throwers during their attacks. Monitor your catapults as they attack the towers and have a priest ready to heal them. This catapult was killed while attacking a tower.

Work your way north along the top of the Scillas' plateau. Have your archers attack any enemy soldiers while your stone throwers clear away the buildings.

the Scilla sent to destroy them. You'll want at least three priests for this operation. Starting with the towers you built around the central gold deposits, build two towers at the very edge of your existing towers' range. The Scilla will send horse archers and long swordsmen to destroy them. Have your priests convert as many of the Scilla as possible, then have your archers kill the rest.

Your eastward trek will be blocked by sheer cliffs about three-fourths of the way across the map. The Scilla have built their city at the top of these bluffs; go too close and they'll shoot arrows at you. For a better look, send a horse archer to ride by the base of the cliff. This will help you locate the towers and buildings.

The Scilla have built a walled city on the top of a large plateau which they've also carpeted with towers. Have your stone throwers attack the towers along the edge of the plateau. The Scilla will send cavalry to attack your throwers, so send composite bowmen and

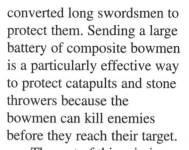

converted long swordsmen to protect them. Sending a large battery of composite bowmen is a particularly effective way to protect catapults and stone throwers because the bowmen can kill enemies before they reach their target.

The rest of this mission is a simple clean-up operation. Send your force up the southern slope of the plateau and have your bowmen form a line behind your stone throwers. (Don't worry, these lines never stay straight. As long as your bowmen do not get between your stone throwers and any attackers, you'll be fine.) Have a priest beside your

The Scilla city is on top of a plateau. Have your stone throwers clear the towers away from the ledge of the plateau, then have them hunt for pockets of soldiers congregated along the ledge. You may be able to thin out the Scillas' population before invading their city.

stone throwers throughout this operation so that you can heal your throwers as they take damage.

Have your stone throwers attack all towers and military buildings first. (Remember, the towers can shoot their arrows farther than your stone throwers can toss their loads, so you will need to have a priest heal your throwers as they attack each tower.) Leave the houses for your cavalry and swordsmen. Work your way across the plateau, killing every man, beast, and building that you pass. The mission ends when you have razed every building on the plateau.

Ways to Lose

You will lose this mission in a hurry if you do not stop the Scilla catapults from destroying the Paechke government center. This is not a difficult task on the easier levels; the Paechke will pretty much fend for themselves. On the more difficult levels, however, the Scilla are not so easily turned away.

One of the keys to beating this mission is finding and controlling these gold deposits located in the center of the map. Control this area and you will restrict the Scillas' gold and stone supplies to the large deposits located near their city walls. They will still have a lot of stone and gold, but you will have more than they do.

If left unchecked, the Scilla will destroy the Paechke city, government center and all.

The Scillas' catapults are their main weapon of destruction. Left alone, they will destroy dozens of Scilla soldiers as they shoot at the Paechke. More often than not, one of the Scilla catapults will destroy the other while shooting at Paechke soldiers; but the remaining catapult will be within range of the Paechkes' government center.

On the hardest level, the Scilla will try to bolster their invasion by sending additional forces. You will need to send most of your army to meet them while assigning your villagers to forage and cut wood. The Scilla may even visit your village while you rebuild, so have villagers concentrate on gathering food while you rebuild your cavalry. (You'll lose if you don't have an army when the Scilla roll into your village, too. They will annihilate your villagers, then destroy your buildings. Very methodical.)

If you succeed at controlling the center of the map and the gold deposits therein, you will avoid some very nasty

pitfalls. With tons of towers around their city, the Scilla are well prepared to fight off an archer and cavalry invasion. You will need stone throwers to destroy their towers and gold to make those stone throwers.

Additional Hints

Don't assume that your farms and villagers have been upgraded simply because you are starting with an Iron Age village. Build a market and upgrade your farms. Also, upgrade your villagers' siege ability and wood cutting.

It generally takes them a while, but the Scilla will get around to destroying the Paechke government center. You lose the moment that burning building crumbles.

Even though the priests in this mission have a limited range of abilities, they're extremely potent at converting enemies. Build a temple early in the mission and have fully upgraded priests available.

Once you have enough gold, use your storage pits to upgrade your soldiers' armor and fighting ability. The Scilla have powerful soldiers; you will need those upgrades to match them.

If you have the gold and resources, don't be afraid to upgrade your horsemen to cataphracts or your horse archers to heavy horse archers. These fast and powerful units can pay for themselves when the fighting gets heavy.

Controlling the gold supply in the center of the map is similar to controlling the center of a chessboard. This will allow you to cut the Scilla off from everything but the gold and stone within their city walls. (They have 2,400 units of gold within their walls; more than enough to build an army of catapults.)

If you move east by building towers to attract the Scilla, have villagers handy to repair the towers after every attack. Scilla long swordsmen can damage or destroy a tower very quickly.

AGE *of* EMPIRES

If the ancients had napalm, this would be the time to use it. The Shang are converging their forces along the river to prepare an invasion. If you have a juggernaut, you'll be able to scatter and kill them.

Mission 8: Tang Invasion

(Author's note—the game refers to this dynasty as both the Tang and the Shang. The title of the mission is "Tang Invasion," and the instructions refer to the Tang, but the unit descriptions refer to them more correctly as the Shang.)

You survived the Shikoku, the Kyushu, and the Scilla. Take a deep breath and clear your head; you are about to face the Yamatos' fiercest enemy, the Tang Dynasty, from China. To beat this scenario, you will have to build a huge army to defeat a very large army that has a decided home-court advantage.

You begin this mission with a Bronze Age village, three short swordsmen, four archers, nine villagers, and one scout. (Three of the villagers are hidden by the fog of war.) You have 100 units each of wood, food, and stone.

The map for this mission is divided into three horizontal strips. Your village is located on the southern strip. While there is a lot of timber and wildlife on your land, your territory has very little gold and stone. Both deposits are located on a butte near the southern corner of the map.

The middle portion of the map is uninhabited and has multiple deposits of gold and stone. Most of these mineral deposits are located on buttes and are guarded by Shang towers.

The Shang inhabit the northern third of the map. They have a large village with large foraging areas. There are two gold deposits near their village that hold a combined 42,000 units of gold. The Shang also have large stone deposits. In short, don't try to starve them out.

The Shang will gather their considerable forces into one spot along the river as the mission opens. It's an immense army with chariot archers, chariots, stone throwers, scouts, cavalry and more. On the easier levels, they will gather along the north shore of their river and stop, sending only a lone stone thrower to harass your village. On the more difficult levels, they will send villagers to inspect your lands, followed by cavalrymen, scouts, and swordsmen.

There are four buttes that form a row along the center of the map. You'll find rich deposits of gold and stone on these buttes. Slip teams of villagers and stone throwers onto these buttes and build towers to guard them.

You can launch an early offensive to claim the center region on the easier levels, but on the more difficult settings, you will need to build walls along the land bridges along the river and build your army before you attempt to take more land.

Unfortunately, the 100 units of stone you're allotted as you begin this mission is not nearly enough to wall off the three land bridges leading to your area. If you send a villager to look for the stone deposits near the southern corner of the map, he will discover a storage pit with three villagers standing beside it. Send the villagers to mine stone. When they finish with the stone, have them mine gold.

Build your first wall at the mouth of the land bridge in the middle of the map. When that one is closed, send most of your soldiers to block the bridge on the western side of the map while your archers and villagers seal the bridge in the east. Once that is sealed, send your villagers to seal the western bridge. This will not keep the Shang out forever, but it will buy you enough time to develop an army.

There are two weapons that can give you an edge to help control your shores at this point. The safest choice is to build a dock and have galleys patrol

It's the last mission in the final campaign of the game. You have lots of resources, so why not go out with a bang? Build a wonder on one of the buttes. (Check your gold supply. You don't want to bankrupt your war effort showing off with a wonder.)

the waters. Galleys arc smart weapons. They will stalk villagers and foot soldiers, and you can use them to destroy Shang stone throwers as they attempt to breach your walls.

Unfortunately, galleys are susceptible to attacks from stone throwers and archers, and they sometimes get so close to shore that cavalrymen can ride up and attack them. On the other hand, you'll want juggernaughts before this mission ends, and upgrading to galleys is the first step to building juggernauts.

If you don't want to waste wood building a dock and ships in a river, you can train priests. You'll need to increase their range by purchasing the Afterlife upgrade from their temple. Once upgraded, your priests will be able to convert enemy units all the way across the river.

Converting enemies is good because it weakens the Shang while it strengthens the Yamato. Convert a Shang stone thrower and you'll be able to start clearing the towers from the buttes in the center of the map, clearing the way for you to mine the gold. If you convert a Shang villager, you can have him build a storage pit and mine enough gold to move on to the Iron Age. (Once you're in the Iron Age, you can have him build a town center and start an entire village.)

As powerful as priests are, they have an inherent weakness: they are costly and fragile. They're great at converting foot soldiers and cavalry, and they can be used effectively against stone throwers, but they're too slow to convert archers and bowmen.

The galleys are probably the better choice, largely because you need to save 800 units of gold to move to the Iron Age, and you only need wood to

make a galley. Either way, your job is to beat the Shang away from your shores, then the villagers and stone throwers across the river. (If you build a dock, you can send them in transports; otherwise, you'll need to blast holes in the walls you built to block the land bridges.)

The Shang will try to invade your village from the first moments of this mission. This early invasion includes an archer, two short swordsmen, two scouts, and a cavalryman.

There are four large buttes in the center strip of the map. The westernmost butte has 1,500 units of gold and stone guarded by one Shang tower. The entrance to this butte faces the Shang side of the river, and there is a land bridge to the Shang homeland that ends near that entrance. Sneaking onto the butte may be difficult, and holding it will be nearly impossible.

The entrance to the next butte faces the Yamato side of the map and there are no towers on it; unfortunately, the only thing on this butte is a herd of gazelles. Though it will have strategic value later, the butte is not worth taking at this point in the mission.

Just like the first butte, the third butte has 1,500 units of gold, a tower, and a land bridge. There is an excellent chance that you could slip men on to it, but it won't be easy to defend.

The easternmost butte has 1,500 units of gold and stone and faces the Yamato side of the map. There are no land bridges that spill directly on to it, and you could defend it with one or two towers and a stone thrower.

Slip two villagers and a stone thrower across the river. Have the stone thrower destroy the tower on the eastern butte, then have your men build a storage pit and towers on the butte. You'll only need two towers along the northern ledge initially, but you may want to build more as the Shang begin their invasions.

The Shang will send waves of invaders to try to retake the center strip. You'll be able to foil these invasions with a combined force of heavy horse archers and towers.

Once you've taken the eastern butte, slip three villagers and a stone thrower on to the western butte. This one will be a bit trickier to take. The Shang use the western land bridge frequently and they've built a tower on their side of that bridge.

Send your stone thrower around the east side of the butte. You won't be able to shoot at the tower guarding the gold until your stone thrower begins moving up the sloped entrance to the butte. Send your villagers on to the butte as soon as your stone thrower destroys the tower.

Because the Shang are so close and the resources on this butte are so valuable, you should take special precautions to insure that the gold and stone do not fall into Shang hands. Have your villagers seal the entrance to the butte with a stone wall, then have one of them build five towers along the northeastern ledge while the other erects a storage pit and begins mining the gold and stone.

Once you have control of the first and fourth buttes, you should begin sending reinforcements. Have your men take control of the second butte, even though there is no stone or gold on it. By building a row of towers along its western ledge, you'll create a gauntlet that will prevent the Shang from slipping past you.

After your men have begun mining the other buttes, send villagers and a stone thrower to take the final butte. Seal this one with a wall, and build several towers on it. The Shang will be especially keen about trying to recapture this piece of real estate.

Build lots of towers and move your other units into position; the Shang will send waves of invaders to try to recapture the center of the map. With all of the

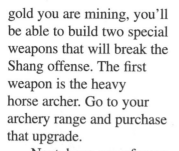

gold you are mining, you'll be able to build two special weapons that will break the Shang offense. The first weapon is the heavy horse archer. Go to your archery range and purchase that upgrade.

Next, have one of your villagers construct a dock at the widest point in the river that separates the Shang homeland from the second strip of land. (The widest part of the river is just a little north of the middle land bridge.) Once the dock is built, upgrade your ships to juggernauts.

The Shang will send stone throwers to try and clear your walls away. If you have priests, you should be able to convert these units and add them to your force.

Build two or three juggernaughts and a trireme. These units will allow you to destroy most of the Shang buildings, including more than half of their towers. The Shang will send stone throwers to attack your juggernauts, but they won't have enough range to defend themselves against your ships.

Once you've forced the Shang into the top of the map, send a party of ten heavy horse archers to finish them off. You accomplish your mission and finish the campaigns when you've killed the Shang and razed their buildings.

Ways to Lose

Do not let the Shang get a foothold in your land. They enter this battle with a larger and more powerful army than you, and if they slip into your land, you won't get them out again.

Your goal in this mission should be to move into the second strip of land and take control of the buttes as quickly as possible. The more gold and stone you control, the easier you'll find your task.

Building a wonder is not only satisfying—it also boosts your score at the end of the mission.

Additional Hints

There is a storage pit with three villagers hidden near the southern corner of the map. Send a villager to find them. Assign your newly discovered villagers to mine stone while your original villager cuts down trees.

Use the trees around the center land bridge as part of your wall. The Shang will not fire at them, so the trees will become the strongest and least costly part of your defense.

Upgrade your walls and towers; you're going to need them.

Even with towers and walls, the Shang will continue to try to attack you. Use priests to convert their stone throwers and foot soldiers.

There are no fish in the streams; don't bother building fishing boats.

Build a government center during your Bronze Age so that you can access its upgrades the moment you move into the Iron Age. Purchase engineering so that you can build juggernaughts and upgrade your projectile weapons.

Build an archery range and a siege workshop as soon as you make it to the middle of the map. From this point on in this mission, your new units will come out of those buildings.

Remember to move all of your combat units to the middle strip of the map to protect your dock and mining efforts.

Chapter Nine

AGE OF EMPIRES TEAM SECRETS

Rick Goodman, an Ensemble Studios game designer, was kind enough to share a few of the game's secret codes:

Pepperoni Pizza:	1,000 units of food
Coinage:	1,000 units of gold
Woodstock:	1,000 units of wood
Quarry:	1000 units of stone
Steroids:	Enables your villagers to construct buildings quickly
DieDieDie:	Destroys all enemy buildings and units
Hari Kari:	Destroys all of your buildings and units
Home Run:	Gives you an instant victory in a scenario
Resign:	Resigns your game

Now I ask you, what kind of a person lets you instantly destroy your enemies by typing *DieDieDie*? No one at Ensemble would tell me who came up with these codes, but one person hinted that the culprit's name rhymes with Hick Hoodman.

Age of Empires was largely a collaborative effort that involved Rick Goodman, Tony Goodman (Ensemble's president) and Bruce Shelley. Shelley, a veteran game designer whose past credits include such important titles as *Civilization* and *Railroad Tycoon*, had been talking with Rick and Tony Goodman about doing a game for years. Ensemble already existed as a computer consulting firm when Shelley and the Goodmans started making plans; so they created Ensemble Studios as a separate division of the company.

"We founded our company two and one-half years ago and we played around with several ideas that in retrospect we're very glad we never went very far with," says Shelley. "We wanted to do a blockbuster game."

"I believe games should have big topics to have a chance of being a big hit. We all noticed that real-time games were doing well. They're great for

multiplayer gaming, and a real-time game would give us the chance to use some of the stuff I'd learned making *Civilization*. I'm not really sure who proposed Age of Empires first, but Tony Goodman was the visionary who put it together."

"Tony, Rick, and I ended up having two or three meetings a week by telephone, and that somehow came to be the idea that we thought had the best chance of being a big hit. So Rick became lead designer and project manager."

From that simple beginning, Bruce and Rick developed a design document to describe their game. They also put together a team to help build it. Back in the old days of *Choplifter* and *Mystery House*, creating computer games required no more than a dedicated programmer with an exciting idea. Games like Age of Empires, however, require large teams of creative workers with specialized skills. One of the first people Rick and Bruce brought on to their team was a young sound engineer named Chris Rippy.

"Chris was already a full-time Ensemble employee working downstairs doing sound effects for our business applications. We identified him as the guy who would do our sound effects and sound, so you could say he was there from the start," says Shelley.

Rippy, a dedicated owner of a Sony PlayStation video-game console, had a natural talent for games. Once he was on the team, he began studying real-time games and forming ideas for missions rather than just working on the sound.

Before long, Rippy was doing more than sound engineering. He began working with Shelley designing the levels themselves.

Other members of the team also made enormous and innovative contributions to Age of Empires. Dave Pottinger was brought in to create the artificial intelligence (AI) for the game.

"We met Dave at the Game Developers Conference," explains Shelley. "He's been with us for a year and a half, and he's really a key guy. From the time that we first started discussing the game, we knew that we wanted artificial intelligence that wouldn't cheat. We decided it would have to discover and build and go forward just like human players had to do, and Dave built an elaborate hierarchy of AI brains that makes that possible."

There are other heroes. According to Chris Rippy, lead programmer Angelo Laudon has brought expertise and dedication to the team. As Rippy points out, many of the features that make Age of Empires so strong were created by people whose titles did not reflect everything they added to the game. For

example, Rippy lists artist Thonny Namuonglo, who designed two of the game's finest scenarios—The Great Hunt and I'll Be Back.

The final fortuitous addition to the Age of Empires team was Microsoft. Impressed by an early iteration of the game, Microsoft agreed to publish it and assigned Tim Znamenacek as the manager to oversee the project.

Microsoft's entertainment team has paid careful attention to Age of Empires to ensure its appeal to a wide range of gamers. The idea of adding Yamato, Choson, and Shang armies arose from a Microsoft suggestion that Asian nations be added.

You don't have to look long at Age of Empires to notice room for a few more armies. Ask Bruce Shelley or Rick Goodman about the Romans, Genghis Kahn, and perhaps the Incan or Aztec empires, and they simply smile. They won't comment on upcoming projects at this time, but perhaps they will have new empires to conquer in their future.

Appendix One

MAKING YOUR OWN WORLDS

According to Chris Rippy, the Scenario Builder included with Microsoft's Age of Empires is the same one used to create the scenarios in the game. He should know; Rippy designed most of the missions in the game.

Once you've played through all of the pre-packaged missions in Age of Empires, you may want to try your hand at creating scenarios of your own. You'll be amazed at how easy it is to make an attractive and challenging level with these tools.

To access this tool, click on the Scenario Builder button in the main menu, then click on the Create Scenario button in the Scenario Builder Menu. Your monitor will show you a large map with nothing but grass, and you'll see menus along the top and bottom of your screen.

If you're in an ambitious mood, you can start building your map from scratch, or, if you'd rather tweak a ready-made map, click on the Random Map button on the bottom of the screen, then click on the Generate Map button. (Since map tweaking is one of the steps in creating a map from scratch, we'll cover it later in this discussion.)

The first step in creating a scenario is deciding what kind of mission you want to make. If you want epic naval battles, for instance, set your scenario in the ocean rather than the desert. By the same token, you probably won't have exciting chariot battles if your map is set to island terrain.

Rippy, as mission designer, says, "I usually start with a clean green map and start drawing in where I think the water should be, and I usually use those as strategic spots as placing grounds. I'll decide that I want a battle to take place in a certain spot, so this is where I want to throw some people."

For simplicity's sake, let's assume you want to make an inland mission. Click the terrain button along the top of your screen. Menus for setting your brush type and size will appear on the bottom of your screen along with a list of terrains. To form cliffs and hills, click on the elevations option in the brush types menu and experiment with the different elevations. (Don't worry about

creating a realistic-looking landscape. If you don't like what you make, you can always start again.)

Elevation 1 indents the ground. Use this if you want to create slopes and small valleys. Elevation 2 creates flat ground. Use this to erase holes or hills you're not happy with. Elevation 3 creates single-terraced hills. Sacred buildings such as ruins and temples look great on Elevation 3 hills.

Elevation 4 creates double-terraced hills, Elevation 5 creates triple-terraced hills, and you can probably guess what Elevations 6 and 7 create. To create these hills, choose a location on your blank map, select the elevation of the hills you wish to lay down, move the hills to the desired location on the map and left click your mouse to place them.

Placing cliffs is even easier. Click on the Cliff button in the Brush Type menu. To place cliffs, press the left button on your map. If you don't like how they look, you can erase them with the right button.

(If you want to restart your scenario, click on the Map button at the top of the screen, click on the Blank Map button on the bottom of the screen, and erase your map by clicking on the Generate Map button.)

Now that you've got the cliffs and hills in place, you may want to add streams, lakes, and maybe even an ocean. Click on the Map button in the Brush Type menu at the bottom of your screen and you'll bring up a new menu titled Terrain.

You may want to place deserts around your cliffs and then a river running through your desert; the options in this menu will let you place terrain tiles throughout your map. You may, for instance, try clicking on desert terrain and small brush. Bring your cursor to the map and place desert tiles one at a time by left clicking your mouse, or lay a row of desert tiles by holding the left button down and dragging your mouse.

Try experimenting with the different terrains. You may want to build a forest-covered island in the middle of your lake, or place a stream running along the top of your cliff. No one is checking your map for accuracy, so put that pine-forest island in the stream in the middle of your desert, on the top of your mountain.

Now that you have the basic map, it's time to decide how many nations will be competing and which nations they will be. Click on the Player button at the top of the screen.

There's nothing tricky about setting up the game. Click on each of the 13 menus along the bottom of the screen and select the options that fit. It's very straightforward. If you want your nations to concentrate on fighting from the start, give them lots of food and resources and start them in the Bronze or Iron Age. If you want a freewheeling battle, create several players. If you want to right to fighting, create just two nations.

OK, so now you've got a Garden of Eden with no Cains and Abels to fight in it. Where should you put your nations and how will you set your battlefields?

"I usually put down player one and then the enemy so I know where they're going to be, then I start dropping in all the resources near where I want the battles to take place," says Rippy.

Rippy makes an interesting point. If there is one place where your men are likely to fight your opponents' men, it's near gold mines or quarrics.

Look at your map and decide where you want to place your civilizations. It's usually a good idea to put a lot of space between your

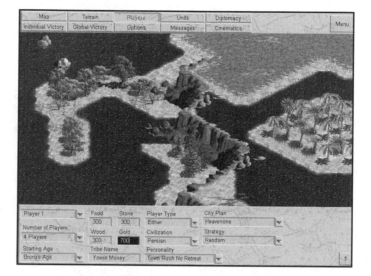

Once you've created the land formations and placed the water and vegetation around it, click on the Player button to set the terms of the game.

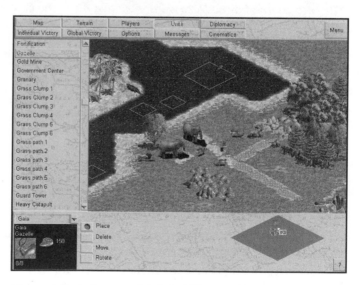

You can find plants, animals, and natural resources in the Gaia menu in the Units section of the Scenario Builder.

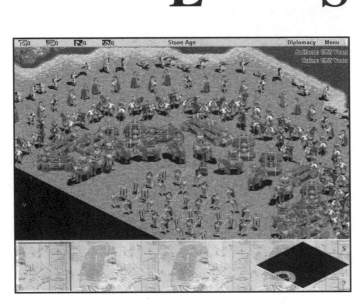

In this scenario, Player 2 has two villagers, a Stone Age civilization, and all the resources in the world. Player 2's objective is to steal Player 1's artifacts and capture his ruins. They are guarded by 50 Nuke warriors (a unit not in the final version of Age of Empires), 40 long swordsmen, 60 heavy horse archers, 18 heavy catapults, 18 elephant archers, and 40 centurions. (Not included in this picture is a ring of 60 lions.)

nations, but you can place them close beside each other if you wish. You can even create a nomadic nation with nothing more than a villager and enough wood to build a town center.

You should begin by building your Player 1 civilization. Choose men and buildings from the scrolling menu along the left side of your screen, and place them wherever you wish. (Remember, if you've decided to create a mission that begins in the Stone Age, you'll create an anachronism by placing centurions and juggernaughts in the middle of your village. Not that anachronisms aren't great fun, it's just that a single centurion can skewer a tremendous number of clubmen, and that may take some of the mystery out of your mission.

The next step is to place resources around the map. If you want a scenario in which your civilizations spend time developing lots of technology, place plenty of gold and stone around the map. If you'd like to see a battle of attrition in which clubmen bash it out like college frat-boys in an apocalyptic pillow fight, limit the resources to wood and very little food. (Interestingly, Stone Age civilizations have no use for stone.)

To place stone, gold, trees, gazelles, elephants, lions, wild horses, alligators, and berry bushes around your map, stay in the Units directory, but select Gaia from the menu at the bottom of the screen. They're all there—the fish, the animals, the trees, the pathways, all of the ingredients that made the missions in Age of Empires so attractive and wonderful.

Having these ingredients does not guarantee that your recipe will be a success. "Balance usually comes from watching people play," says Rippy. "I've gotten it right on the first try a couple of times, but that's pretty rare. I usually have to go back and make a couple of changes."

Of course, some scenarios are fun precisely because they are out of balance.

Appendix Two

··▶

MULTIPLAYER STRATEGIES

The multiplayer Microsoft's Age of Empires game has a completely different flavor than the single-player version. Multiplayer matches are often punctuated with extravagant strategies. Single-player specialists tend to play conservatively; you seldom see juggernaughts and cataphracts in single-player games. Many head-to-head and free-for-all specialists love to throw the really big weapons into the mix.

As you're probably aware, when it comes to gaming, some players specialize in competing against computers and others live to play online against human opponents. During development, Ensemble recognized the importance of having a multiplayer specialist working on their multiplayer scenarios.

"Ian Fischer is the key person doing our multiplayer scenarios," says Chris Rippy. "I think the real key to doing multiplayer scenarios is balance. You want to make sure that everyone has a fair shot, and you can do that in a number of different ways."

"Making sure everyone has the same amount of resources to start with isn't as important as making sure they have the same access to everything. One of the cooler multiplayer scenarios pits six players against one. It seems unbelievably out of balance when you first look at it; but we've given that lone player a central island and tons of resources. He's got a pretty good starting point, so if he's good, he's got a fair shot against all the human players coming after."

If balancing access to materials is essential to creating a good multiplayer scenario, finding ways to isolate opponents and cut off their supplies is a great strategy for winning.

AGE of EMPIRES

Shang villagers cost 35 units of food, making them the least expensive units in Age of Empires.

Two Exotic Strategies

Most of the mechanics of winning multiplayer Age of Empires are fairly straightforward, but some players have invented special late-game strategies to cancel out all of the expensive fighting units that online gamers tend to use.

Deadly Shang Tide

Each nation in Age of Empires has one or two unique strengths. The Shangs' strengths are doubly strong walls and extra-cheap villagers. (Most villagers cost 50 units of food, but you can create Shang villagers for 35.)

Cheap villagers and strong walls are great strengths for nations taking a defensive posture. You can use those strong walls to keep enemies at bay while your villagers mine stone and gold, construct buildings, and farm. The Shang make wonderful teammates for nations such as the Assyrians, who have very aggressive attributes.

Once you reach the Iron Age, villagers become a stronger offensive force. Purchase siegecraft from your market, and your villagers will become masters at breaking down walls and destroying towers. Next, make your villagers dangerous with the Jihad upgrade, which is available through your temple.

Jihad will not turn your villagers into centurions, but it will give them a bit more bite. Their attack rating will raise from three points to ten, which makes their attack more powerful than that of an axeman or a standard bowman.

The final step is to build multiple town centers and turn your town into a Shang Horde factory. Train at least three priests, then create as many villagers

as you can until you reach your population limit. This deadly swarm will be able to overcome nearly any obstacle.

The best way to use this fighting force is to have your priests convert centurions, cataphracts, heavy cavalrymen, and other non-bow and arrow using units as your peasants swarm them. A healthy centurion will kill five or six of your upgraded villagers before dying, but if you send your priest to convert him during the attack, you can preserve villagers and add a very powerful unit to your army.

The Spiral of Death

The Spiral of Death is a method of depleting your enemies resources and army while building your own. This strategy is particularly effective if you have a Babylonian society, and it only works if you have a lot of stone.

The Spiral of Death was inspired by a crowd-control

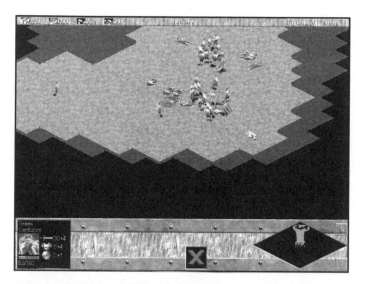

You'll lose villagers when they swarm centurions and heavy cavalrymen, but you can continually build more. With 6,560 units of food, this player can build nearly 200 additional villagers.

Four centurions are greeted by dozens of upgraded villagers and three priests as they march into a Shang town. Two are converted and two succumb to the rising tide of Shang power.

device utilized by banks and airport ticket counters, and it was epitomized by Disneyland. Have you ever been to a crowded airport or visited Disneyland? Remember those spots in which lines of people are herded back and forth through chained areas? What if there were archer towers lining the last row of those chained areas? That's the idea behind the Spiral of Death: you guide your enemies to their doom.

Build a city in a protected location, such as a corner of the map or along a forest, anyplace where at least two and possibly three sides of your city are invulnerable to attack. Next, build a row of at least five towers along the exposed edge of your city to protect it. (The reason this strategy works best for Babylonian societies is that they have the best towers.)

Now build a protective wall extending beyond all of your towers, and leave a gap on one end of the wall to allow your troops to leave the city should they need to. Once that wall is complete, build a wall in front of your first wall, leave just enough space between the walls for your troops to pass through single file, and make the gap in this wall on the opposite side from the gap in the last wall. Now build two more walls with space and gaps.

If you've built your walls correctly, you should have a corridor that ushers troops back and forth as they enter your city. It's very important to place fast units, such as cavalrymen and horse archers, at the city's entrance. You may need to send them out quickly.

When enemies try to enter your city, your towers will have several opportunities to fire arrows at them because the path you build will force them to walk back and forth. By building this path four rows deep, you not only force enemies to pass your towers four times to enter the city, but you also protect your towers from catapult attacks.

Your enemies will likely attempt to raze your Spiral of Death with their catapults, but that's where your cavalry comes in. When the enemy sends catapults to attack your walls, send your cavalry out to attack their catapults. Your cavalry will have no problem scooting through the spiral and neutralizing their attacks.

Teamwork

Ensemble's design team took great pains to make Age of Empires a great team sport as well as an individual event. Careful attention was paid to creating nations that would complement each other and scenarios that would be especially fun for team play.

"We really enhanced the team play by creating differences in our civilizations to make players want to cooperate with their teammates," says Dave Pottinger, the lead artificial intelligence designer of Age of Empires, and devoted online gaming fiend. "If you pick Egyptian and somebody else picks a good counter to your priests and your elephants, you're going to have to work a lot harder, but it also makes the game a lot more fun."

"The single biggest difference between our multiplayer game and others is that we require people to consider a lot of pre-game strategy about what civilization to pick and what strategy they're going to use as a team."

You may be wondering just how much difference Phoenicia's inexpensive elephants and Persia's quick-firing triremes can make. The answer is that these subtle advantages can mean the difference between victory and defeat. The key is learning each nation's strengths and finding ways to play to them.

"Say you're doing a three-on-three game, and all three people on one team pick the same civilization. If the other team has a little more understanding of how the game works and picks civilizations that complement each other, the second team is probably going to win," says Pottinger.

Index

Bibliography

Casson, Lionel, *Ancient Egypt* (Time Inc., New York: 1965).

Cottrell, Leonard, *Life Under the Pharaohs* (Holt Rinehart and Winston, New York: 1960).

Hopper, R.J., *The Early Greeks* (Harper and Row Publishers, New York: 1976).

Hutchinson, Warner *Ancient Egypt: Three Thousand Years of Splendor* (Grosset & Dunlop, New York: 1978).

Mellersh, H.E.L., *Sumer and Babylon* (Thomas Y. Crowell Company, New York: 1964).

Rauch, Jonathan, *The Outnation: A Search for the Soul of Japan* (Harvard Business School Press, Boston: 1992).

Roux, George, *Ancient Iraq* (The World Publishing Company, Cleveland: 1964).

Register Today!

Return this
Microsoft® Age of Empires™: Inside Moves
registration card for
a Microsoft Press® catalog

U.S. and Canada addresses only. Fill in information below and mail postage-free. Please mail only the bottom half of this page.

1-57231-529-6A   *MICROSOFT® AGE OF EMPIRES™:*   *Owner Registration Card*
   INSIDE MOVES

NAME

INSTITUTION OR COMPANY NAME

ADDRESS

CITY   STATE   ZIP

Microsoft®*Press*
Quality Computer Books

**For a free catalog of
Microsoft Press® products, call
1-800-MSPRESS**

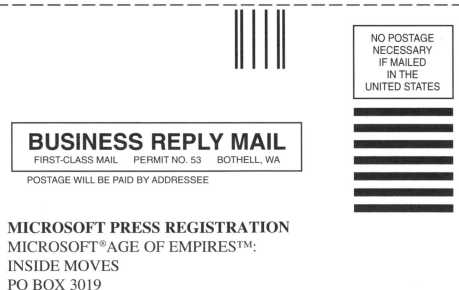

NO POSTAGE
NECESSARY
IF MAILED
IN THE
UNITED STATES

BUSINESS REPLY MAIL
FIRST-CLASS MAIL   PERMIT NO. 53   BOTHELL, WA

POSTAGE WILL BE PAID BY ADDRESSEE

MICROSOFT PRESS REGISTRATION
MICROSOFT®AGE OF EMPIRES™:
INSIDE MOVES
PO BOX 3019
BOTHELL   WA   98041-9946